Island Queens and Mission Wives

Island Queens
and Mission Wives

HOW GENDER AND EMPIRE

REMADE HAWAI'I'S PACIFIC WORLD

Jennifer Thigpen

THE UNIVERSITY OF NORTH CAROLINA PRESS Chapel Hill

This book was published with the assistance of the H. Eugene and Lillian Youngs Lehman Fund and the Authors Fund of the University of North Carolina Press.

© 2014 THE UNIVERSITY OF NORTH CAROLINA PRESS

Library of Congress Cataloging-in-Publication Data
Thigpen, Jennifer.
Island queens and mission wives : how gender and empire remade Hawai'i's
Pacific world / Jennifer Thigpen.
    pages cm. — (Gender and American culture)
Includes bibliographical references and index.
ISBN 978-1-4696-1429-8 (cloth : alk. paper) — ISBN 978-1-4696-1430-4 (ebook)
1. Hawaii—History—To 1893. 2. Hawaii—Foreign relations—Pacific Area. 3. Hawaii—
Politics and government—To 1893. 4. Hawaiian women—Political activity—Hawaii—
History—19th century. 5. Missionaries—Political activity—Hawaii—History—
19th century. I. Title.
DU627.T45 2014
996.9'02—dc23
2013035599

18 17 16 15 14   5 4 3 2 1

For Jamie, with Love and Gratitude

Contents

Illustrations

Acknowledgments

This book is, in part, about the "obligations of gratitude" that bound American missionaries to their Hawaiian hosts in unexpected ways in the nineteenth century. Writing nearly 200 years later, I find that the rules of reciprocity and gratitude still apply. Indeed, I have incurred a variety of obligations—debts I hope someday to be able to repay. In most cases, a simple "thank you" will not suffice, but it's a start.

A number of funding sources supported the research and writing stages of this project. I was the beneficiary of a number of grants and fellowships at the University of California, Irvine (UCI), including Humanities Center Research Grants, a Regent's Dissertation Grant, and a yearlong Chancellor's Club Dissertation Fellowship. These provided support at a critical time in my research, allowing me to teach less and write more. A University of California Pacific Rim Research Program grant offered the means to conduct research at archives in Hawai'i in the earliest stages of this project. A Mayers Fellowship from the Huntington Library in San Marino allowed me to spend a summer consulting the library's vast collections. At Washington State University, a New Faculty Seed Grant allowed me to devote all my professional energies and attentions to writing the manuscript. I offer my deepest thanks to these institutions for their support.

I have also been fortunate enough to have gained the support of mentors and scholars in my field. At UCI, Alice Fahs, Vicki Ruiz, and Dickson (Dave) Bruce provided steady instruction, guidance, and encouragement throughout the process. Alice offered unfailingly thoughtful insights into my work. She is not only a gifted historian but also a truly skilled editor. Under Alice's tutelage, I grew as a scholar and a thinker, and I am thankful that she continues be such a gracious mentor and friend. Vicki was an inspiration throughout the writing process, gently but persistently reminding me to allow my subjects to tell their own story. Vicki is also an enormously generous person, constantly offering her time, her attention, and her considerable expertise. As any of her current or former students will tell you, Vicki is never "too busy" to lend a helping hand. Dave persistently—but always cheerfully—kept me focused on my writing.

A number of scholars read my work at various stages and offered meaningful suggestions. Early on, Susan Yohn wisely encouraged me to think beyond a very "local" story and frame my discussion of the Hawaiian Islands mission in its much broader, global context. Sue Armitage and Susan Johnson read separate pieces, yet both urged me to attend more fully to the meeting of peoples and cultures in Hawai'i. Taken together, their comments and insights offered the delightful challenge of simultaneously expanding the scope of my research while maintaining a focus on the people who populate the narrative.

My colleagues at Washington State University have been a tremendous source of support. My department chair, Ray Sun, helped ease my departmental obligations at the writing-intensive stage of this project and also offered steady support along the way. Peter Boag read an early draft of the manuscript and offered important suggestions. I appreciate his mentoring and his friendship in equal measure. Sue Peabody provided thoughtful insights and encouragement at critical moments in the writing of this book. I am truly thankful for her help. My colleague and friend Jeff Sanders kindly read chapters as the manuscript was nearing completion. His suggestions allowed—and sometimes challenged—me to consider new perspectives on my subject. I thank Matt Sutton especially for his help. Matt has gone above and beyond in his support of me and of this book. In fact, it is very likely that he has read as many drafts of this book as I have. His incisive criticism of my work made this a better, stronger book and I am deeply indebted to him.

Finally, I thank my family. My husband, Jamie, has always believed that this book was a worthy endeavor and that I had something important to say. While I researched and wrote, he kept the home fires burning—sometimes, in the dead of winter, quite literally. He not only made our home a warm and welcoming place to return to at the end of the day, but he also reminds me that home and family are truly the most important things of all. Our children, Emma and Henry, also helped in the writing of this book, mostly by insisting that I not become subsumed by it. Together, they introduced just the right amount of silliness into my life as I approached the serious business of writing. I am truly grateful to all three of them.

Island Queens and Mission Wives

Introduction

In March 1820 the first company of American missionaries arrived in the Hawaiian Islands. At the insistence of the islands' aliʻi (ruling elite), the band was dispersed; while some remained on the island of Hawaiʻi, others sailed on to Honolulu. In July a small group traveled to Kauaʻi, where they also hoped to establish a mission. They brought with them a young man, Humehume, who the missionaries knew as "George Tamoree." He had traveled with the missionaries from Boston. On Kauaʻi, Humehume was reunited with his father, Kaumualiʻi, the ruling chief there.[1] Kaumualiʻi promptly presented the missionaries with a gift of food. Nancy Ruggles, a young missionary wife, reflected on the gift in her diary, observing: "Never before were our obligations of gratitude so great as they now are."[2] Ruggles rightly perceived the reciprocity—and obligation—implied in accepting such a gift. While Kaumualiʻi had reasons of his own to feel thankful that summer, Ruggles anticipated that the chief would expect a reciprocal gift sometime in the future. She might not have foreseen, however, that the gifts that missionaries and Hawaiian royalty exchanged in the first weeks and months of their relationship would pull both parties into an enduring cycle of exchange. This proved especially true on neighboring islands, where missionaries received a variety of gifts from the islands' aliʻi and were pressed to produce reciprocal gifts, particularly articles of clothing. Such exchanges, I argue, established the foundation for important diplomatic and political relationships that extended well into the future and would ultimately reshape the Pacific world.

American missionaries arrived in the Pacific with a set of strategies for Christianizing the Hawaiian people shaped by reigning American racial and gender ideologies. Early official narratives of the Hawaiian mission validated those strategies, telling a story of masculine intervention in a "heathen" land. My research demonstrates, however, that missionaries drastically underestimated the significance of the work that mission wives would undertake in the islands, and that they similarly misunderstood the power that Hawaiian women wielded in social, political, cultural, and religious matters. Such an oversight reflected missionaries' myopic ideology and proved an early—though not insurmountable—obstacle to missionaries' conversion plans.

Two of Hawai'i's highest-ranking women, Ka'ahumanu and Kalākua, offered early corrections to missionaries' misperceptions. Ka'ahumanu, who virtually ruled the islands at the time the missionaries arrived, interpreted her relationship to the Americans in her midst as one akin to that between ali'i and maka'āinana (common people). Indeed, missionaries learned that they would need Ka'ahumanu's permission to establish a mission on even a probationary basis. Similarly, in a show of her rank, Kalākua began making demands on the missionaries almost from the moment of their arrival. Hawai'i's royal women, in fact, used their power and status to compel mission wives to engage in what became an ongoing cycle of giving that endured throughout the missionaries' tenure in the islands.

If missionaries were unprepared for the kind of compulsory, reciprocal gift giving and exchange that would structure their relationship with ali'i, they certainly would not have anticipated that women—Hawaiian or American—would become largely responsible for shaping the future of the mission and the nature of Hawaiian-American interaction. Yet my research shows that relationships of exchange, originated and successfully maintained by women, determined the contours of the American mission in Hawai'i.

Island Queens and Mission Wives focuses on the creation and evolution of a multiethnic, global community in the Pacific. In particular, I narrate the dramatic story of cultural transformation that resulted as competing cultures came into close and sustained contact with one another within the context of an emergent Pacific world. While the cultural—and later, political—colonization of the Hawaiian Islands is well known, the exchange relationships forged among American missionary wives and Hawaiian women have been largely overlooked. I argue that women's relationships, organized around the exchange of gift items, became critical sites for the building and maintenance of important diplomatic and political alliances. Exploring the connections between women's work and colonization, this book addresses important questions about colonial processes not only in Hawai'i but also in many other locations across the globe.

This book supplements the existing literature on the American mission to Hawai'i in several ways. First, it seeks to "recenter" Hawaiians (particularly

- royal women compelled wives into gift-giving exchanges
*Women's relationships crucial for diplomatic/political alliances

ali'i) within the missionary drama and to situate Hawaiian interactions with American missionaries within the much larger context of the emergent Pacific world. In a second and related way, this book challenges the periodization that historians have often employed to understand the Hawaiian past. Such periodization did not develop solely as an outgrowth of Eurocentrism but was due in part to historians' traditional reliance on missionary documents. That is, while American missionaries viewed the period between 1820 and 1853 as Hawai'i's "mission period," the islands' inhabitants almost certainly did not. In fact, the missionaries were but one group among many foreign visitors who routinely visited the Hawaiian Islands beginning in the late eighteenth century. The idea that the missionaries' tenure in the islands constituted a particular, discrete, or important era in the islands' history developed only later, after the ramifications of the American missionary labors had become more clear. The traditional periodization, then, is informed more by our understanding of later historical outcomes than by our grasp of processes at work in the historical past.

While American missionaries ultimately gained a strategic foothold in the islands (and one that had long-lasting implications for Hawai'i's political, economic, and social future), this was not the inevitable conclusion, nor was it one that Hawaiians necessarily foresaw. Thus, rather than beginning with the so-called mission period, I begin my narrative earlier, in the 1780s, to coincide both with King Kamehameha's political assent and with an era of increasingly aggressive Pacific exploration that lasted well into the nineteenth century. Throughout the late eighteenth and early nineteenth centuries, ali'i were called upon to mobilize their skills as shrewd diplomats and political negotiators while dealing with a diverse, culturally foreign population with competing plans for Hawai'i and its people.

The argument I put forth rests in part on the premise that Hawaiians were neither "passive" nor "helpless" victims of Western colonialism. My research makes extensive use of the cache of English-language sources to identify instances of Hawaiian opposition to European and American aggression in the late eighteenth and early nineteenth centuries. In many cases, historians have overlooked such resistance. The sources I consulted, including not just American missionary documents but also accounts by European explorers such as George Vancouver and Otto Von Kotzebue, frequently—if inadvertently—pointed to the kinds of resistance foreigners encountered in their interactions with Hawaiians. My work is theoretically indebted to a historiography of colonialism that endeavors to grapple with the way in which power was constantly negotiated and contested in

— Recenter Hawaiians
— Challenge periodization of "missionary period"
   — begin w/ earlier events — not inevitable
— Hawaiians neither helpless nor passive

such contexts. For example, though missionaries later recounted their experience in the Hawaiian Islands as an unmitigated "success," their own records offer a more complicated and ambiguous picture, particularly the documents from the earliest years of the mission.

I am aware, of course, of the work of scholars who have argued for the centrality of Hawaiian-language sources to understanding and interpreting Hawaiian history. It is critical to note, however, that there are precious few of these sources for the period I examine because Hawaiians did not make much use of a written language in this period. The very few records that do exist are both fragmentary and scattered. With a few very small exceptions, the extant Hawaiian-language sources were written well after the period I examine and often by people who had been educated and Christianized by American missionaries, such as Samuel Kamakau, David Malo, and John Papa ʻĪʻī. These sources were later translated.

Throughout this book, I have made use of the work of the moʻolelo (histories) recorded by Hawaiian historians like Kamakau, ʻĪʻī, and Malo. I have handled these sources carefully in order to account for the passage of time as well as changes in interpretation or ideology that may have occurred in the intervening years. Indeed, I recognize the value of these translated sources, particularly for what they tell us about Hawaiian culture in the nineteenth century.[3] I have used them extensively in this way. I have also used them to corroborate—rather than to directly reflect upon—the events described by Western visitors. I have been similarly cautious in my handling of published missionary documents and memoirs, using those documents in the same way that I use Hawaiian histories.

Readers might notice that although I cite Hawaiian-studies scholars and discuss their scholarship, their approaches do not seem to have shaped this book. It is important to note that I also rely on and cite a variety of scholarly texts by a range of scholars representing many disciplinary perspectives throughout the manuscript without allowing their scholarship to shape or direct my analysis. My intent is to build on and make meaningful contributions to the existing literature rather than to replicate it. At the same time, it is important to note just how much Hawaiian-studies scholars have done to push all scholars to take seriously the concerns, interests, and motivations of Hawaiians in their interactions with foreigners. This is no small contribution; in fact, their work has done much to transform the way scholars of all disciplines approach and understand this topic.

I have approached all of my sources cautiously, vigilantly guarding against accepting—and repeating—Westerners' descriptions of Hawaiʻi

— Missionaries' accounts, explorers' accounts,
few Hawaiian-language sources
*Not so beholden to
prer. historiography of Hawaiʻi !!

and its people. My analysis is informed in important ways by Marshall Sahlins's assertion that "one cannot do good history . . . without regard for ideas, actions, and ontologies that are not and never were our own." I have thus endeavored to understand the historical subjects that appear in this study on their own terms and within their own cultural and historical context. Toward this end, I have relied not just on historical scholarship on Hawai'i but also on the foundational literature of anthropologists like Sahlins, Jocelyn Linnekin, and Greg Dening. I have also profited from Lilikalā Kame'eleihiwa's insightful, nuanced work. Finally, I have benefited from the work of historians of the American West (most notably Richard White and Daniel K. Richter) who have pioneered innovative methodologies for studying interactions between culturally distinct peoples.[4]

Third, this book expands on current scholarship by considering how Hawai'i's ali'i—beginning with King Kamehameha and ending with Ka'ahumanu—perceived and shaped their relationships with foreign explorers, travelers, traders, and missionaries. In order to accurately interpret these interactions, I draw on the theory and methods of scholars in the fields of cultural studies, gender studies, and anthropology. I examine the cultural ideologies that undergirded even the most basic daily interactions between Hawaiian royalty and their foreign guests. Lacking a common cultural language by which to communicate, ali'i and their guests often had to guess at meaning and intention. While such exchanges were rife with the possibility of miscommunication, a vast anthropological literature and a growing body of historical scholarship allows insight into these exchanges.[5] Where Hawaiian women of rank did not leave a written record of their feelings about their exchanges with missionary wives, for example, it is possible to interpret the manner in which they attempted to communicate their political authority.

Finally, the existing literature on Hawai'i in this period most often considers gender and colonialism in the Hawaiian Islands as separate, rather than intersecting, categories.[6] Where Hawaiian histories consider the political power of Hawai'i's high-ranking women in this period and mission histories explore the labor of mission wives, only rarely do texts connect "women's work" with the political labor of colonization. Island Queens and Missionary Wives examines the complicated colonial relations as they evolved in this period. Specifically, my research offers a careful exploration of missionary-Hawaiian contact to demonstrate that the intimate exchanges among and between women became central to the overarching story of colonization and conquest. Looking to the "intimate domains" of exchange generated around reciprocal gift giving, my research demonstrates that women were at the very center of the colonial drama in the nineteenth-century Hawaiian Islands.[7] Further, while my research focuses specifically on Hawai'i, these insights promise to help us rethink colonial interactions around the globe. Ultimately, this book seeks to help readers to not just better understand the role of women in colonization but also rethink the nineteenth-century transformation of the Hawaiian Islands, the nature of American expansion, and the development of an increasingly multicultural Pacific world.

Chapters 1 and 2 are intended to introduce readers to late eighteenth- and early nineteenth-century Hawai'i and New England, respectively, to establish the collision of cultures that ensued in the 1820s. Chapter 1 sets up the political, economic, and social context of the Hawaiian Islands in the years leading up to and immediately following Kamehameha's death. This chapter draws out the increasingly global and cosmopolitan character of the islands in this period and points toward the important political and cultural shifts that occurred on the eve of the missionaries' arrival. Though Kamehameha's rule coincided with a period of aggressive exploration in the Pacific, he laid the foundations for a politically and economically powerful Pacific nation. He did so first by unifying the Hawaiian Islands and, second, by cultivating political and economic relationships with travelers and traders. I argue that Kamehameha actively engaged with foreigners not only as a means by which to consolidate his political authority in Hawai'i but also to ensure the islands' long-term political viability. Further, this chapter shows that Kamehameha's active engagement with foreigners, begun in the late eighteenth century, served as an example of political diplomacy that lasted until well into the nineteenth century.[8] This chapter aims to reorient readers by situating them in Hawai'i at the beginning of the narrative and carrying them into a period of rapid Westernization that was already well under way before missionaries arrived in 1820. The effect is both to move Hawaiians out of the margins of a story that has traditionally privileged missionary perspectives and, in a related way, to place the American mission in its much broader Hawaiian context. Not only did Hawaiians not view the missionaries' tenure in the islands as a "mission period," but, especially in the earliest years, they also regarded and treated them just as they had the many other foreign visitors who traveled to Hawai'i in the eighteenth and nineteenth centuries.

Chapter 2 provides context for New England missionaries' enthusiasm for their work, elaborating on the Second Great Awakening and the missionary zeal that grew out of it, as scores of young men and women resolutely left

— Westernization already underway;
H. leaders actively engaged

the comforts of home to join the burgeoning foreign-mission movement. The awakening had a particular effect upon young women, opening up a new space for their religious participation.[9] Despite the mission board's explicitly gendered rhetoric, which posited men as "soldiers in the holy war" and their wives as "angels of mercy," the fervor of the awakening prompted a generation of women to dream of doing work that "mattered," even if it required great sacrifice. In this context, women like Lucy Goodale took their wedding vows in order to participate in the mission to the Sandwich Islands. Goodale agreed to marry Asa Thurston, a virtual stranger, just six days prior to departing for the Hawaiian Islands, a practice that proved a common pattern among missionaries to Hawai'i and elsewhere. Together in a hierarchical relationship, couples like the Thurstons set out to conquer the world. This chapter explores the gendered dimensions of mission organization, not only explaining the distinct roles assigned to men and women but also elaborating on the way in which this division of labor shaped the mission project. Moreover, I argue that missionaries' sense of the universality of mission gender ideologies set the stage for their interactions with the Hawaiians they hoped to convert.

Chapter 3 describes the world that the missionaries encountered when they arrived in Hawai'i in the spring of 1820. The situation there was drastically different than the one they had anticipated or planned for. Soon after landing, they learned that the islands were under new political leadership and that, in the wake of Kamehameha's death, the islands' *kapu* laws, which governed many aspects of everyday life, had been overthrown.[10] While missionaries were initially optimistic at their prospect for the successful conversion of the Hawaiian people, they became increasingly aware of the challenges they faced. Kamehameha's son, Liholiho, had inherited his father's place, yet his rule was complicated: Liholiho shared his authority with one of his father's widows. Before his death, Kamehameha named Ka'ahumanu *kuhina nui*, or coruler. While missionaries did not immediately grasp the islands' power structure, they would ultimately be compelled to acknowledge the royal woman's political authority. More immediately alarming to the missionaries was the discovery that they would be forced to compete for Hawaiians' attentions and loyalty. Missionaries came to resent the presence of other foreigners—Americans and non-Americans alike—in the islands, viewing them alternately as moral degenerates, interlopers, and political schemers. Yet the king and his governors seemed favorably predisposed to these foreigners, particularly the French and the English. Indeed, the ali'i seemed quite adept at negotiating—and sometimes exploiting—Hawai'i's

- Second Great Awakening → inspires women
- Gendered dimensions, gender Ideology important
- Forced to compete w/ other foreigners, political changes

culturally and politically variegated environment. The missionaries' arrival coincided with these significant changes and with the rise of Ka'ahumanu's increasing political and cultural authority.[11] This chapter explores both missionary strategies for the successful conversion of Hawaiians and Hawaiian mechanisms for negotiation and resistance within the context of an increasingly complicated and complex human tableau.

The foreign presence in the islands, coupled with male ali'i's disinterest in Christianity, required the band of American missionaries to reconsider their initial plans for the conversion of the Hawaiian people. Chapter 4 offers an examination of the kinds of gendered diplomacy that developed in the mission's earliest years in response both to the missionaries' failed efforts with Liholiho and other high-ranking men and their dawning recognition of the political authority of Hawai'i's royal women. Almost immediately after the missionaries arrived in the islands, Hawai'i's queens and other women of rank began making requests of the mission wives, mostly in the way of Western-style clothing and other garments, drawing missionary women into a role that would become vital to the success of the mission. I argue that these exchanges became critical sites for political diplomacy. These important relationships also created a space for the conversion of Hawai'i's royal women, who, missionaries hoped, would use their considerable influence to assist in the project of conversion throughout the islands. Moreover, Hawai'i's royal women proved quite adept at negotiating their relationships with missionary wives. Women of rank not only offered a public demonstration of their status in demanding gifts of clothing from missionaries, but they also continued to request certain kinds of gifts, specifically items that either enhanced their status or were easily absorbed and interpreted within the context of existing cultural beliefs and structures.[12] Ultimately, male missionaries came to both recognize Hawaiian women of rank as potential allies in their conversion efforts and rely on mission women to create personal and diplomatic relations critical to the mission project.

Chapter 5 elaborates on the ways in which Hawai'i's royal women publicly allied themselves with the American missionary cause and offers insight into the multiple meanings and motivations that might be attached to such alliances. While missionaries celebrated Ka'ahumanu's public declaration of her conversion in 1825 and the religious and cultural transformations of Hawai'i's royal women, the conversion stories so often repeated in missionary literature require deeper analysis and contextualization. This chapter traces the structure and language of missionary writings on the subject, juxtaposing these narratives with the multiple possible meanings of the

- Early efforts fail w/ elite men; develop gendered diplomacy → conversion allies
  - Elite women seek to boost status
  - Sites for political diplomacy

royal women's apparent conversions. While missionary writing focused on the symbolic destruction of Hawaiian religious and cultural forms, I argue that Hawai'i's royal women used their considerable political capital to create important diplomatic alliances and to erect protective political structures.[13] This chapter complicates missionaries' claims of a "Protestant triumph" in the Hawaiian Islands by interrogating the queens' intentions for allying with American missionaries. Moreover, the chapter points toward the long-ranging ramifications of the queens' political maneuvering in the nineteenth century. Hawaiian women of rank emerge not as simple victims of a project of American cultural imperialism but as shrewd political actors, laboring on behalf of the Hawaiian people.

— Meanings & motivations of elite women's conversions

— Create diplomatic alliances, protective political structure

CHAPTER 1 *Kamehameha's Kingdom*

In late November 1816, Hawai'i's King Kamehameha welcomed Russian naval officer Otto von Kotzebue to the islands. Kamehameha's demeanor during the visit was by turns equally cordial and cautious. The king scrutinized Kotzebue and his crew from a distance. According to Kotzebue, Kamehameha sent several boats to meet the *Rurick*. He conducted interviews with members of the crew before greeting Kotzebue onshore. At their meeting, Kamehameha impressed his Russian guests with his "unreserved and friendly behaviour." At the same time, the king evinced his wariness of foreign visitors by meeting the Russian vessel accompanied by "some of his most distinguished warriors." Kotzebue observed that "a number of islanders, armed with muskets," lined the shore. Kamehameha nevertheless acted the proper host, "conducting" his guests "to his straw palace." He attempted to set them at ease by offering them European-style chairs—rather than the more customary mats—to sit upon during their visit. Through an interpreter, the king reassured his guests of his intention to offer them generous provisions "gratis," just as he had previous visitors. Yet Kamehameha was also quick to demonstrate that he was no pushover, first by subtly invoking Captain James Cook's ill-fated eighteenth-century voyage to the islands and then by recalling the recent but unsuccessful Russian attempt to conquer the islands. On the latter point, the king was direct: "This shall not happen as long as [Kamehameha] lives!"[1]

Throughout the visit, the king simultaneously attempted to remind his guests of their vulnerable foreign status and to cultivate positive relations with them. He trod this line carefully, expertly balancing displays of his political authority with gestures of gracious diplomacy. In retrospect, Kamehameha's handling of the Russians emerges as emblematic of his leadership style, honed over the span of his reign and polished in his nearly constant interaction with foreigners from around the globe. Kamehameha, in fact, had ample opportunity to practice his political and diplomatic skills. By the time Kotzebue arrived in the islands in 1816, foreign ships—and their passengers—had become a more-or-less common sight in the islands, as

- King Kamehameha tried to both court & intimidate Russian visitors
- Foreign ships commonplace

visitors from Britain, France, and beyond made anchor at Hawai'i.[2] Though some came "merely" for purposes of trade or exploration, others arrived with more explicitly expansionist political and economic designs. All of them brought opportunities for more change. In response, Kamehameha developed a remarkably adaptive political style, which aimed not merely to endure foreign intrusion but also to secure Hawai'i's place within an emerging Pacific world.

This chapter describes some of the earliest encounters between the islands' ali'i—Kamehameha in particular—and their foreign guests during the late eighteenth and early nineteenth centuries and interprets them within the larger context both of aggressive Pacific exploration characteristic of the period and the internal political strife emanating from within the islands. The lasting negative effects of Western contact, well documented by historians, ethnologists, and anthropologists, can hardly be overestimated. Westerners introduced the idea of trade for money, a concept that spelled widespread destruction in the islands. The economic shift toward trade affected the islands' economy in a direct way, but related changes imposed deeper alterations. In their quest to repay mounting debts to traders, ali'i ordered maka'āinana to cut down virtually all the sandalwood trees. This wrought havoc on the natural landscape, causing poverty and malnutrition among maka'āinana.[3] Moreover, Westerners brought new microbes and disease with them, which ultimately decimated the population of Hawai'i. Some scholars, in fact, posit a precontact population of 1 million. Forty-five years later, the population of Hawai'i dwindled to just under 135,000.[4] These devastating realities powerfully shaped Hawaiian interactions with Westerners in the early part of the nineteenth century—particularly at the moment of American missionaries' arrival in the islands.

Yet in the earliest years of contact, Hawai'i's ali'i engaged in negotiations with Westerners from a position of power and authority. I argue that Hawaiians were not merely passive recipients of the changes initiated by foreign travelers, traders, and explorers; rather, King Kamehameha actively engaged in negotiations with foreigners with the intention of enhancing his own power while also increasing Hawai'i's political viability.[5] My research demonstrates that the king insisted that foreign guests recognize and observe his political authority even as he shrewdly remained open to Western influence, adopting both Western dress and custom. The king proved especially adept at mobilizing these symbols of Western civilization when they seemed beneficial or provided the opportunity to facilitate trade.[6] Yet Kamehameha also carefully retained and deployed important symbols of

Hawaiian culture in his interactions with foreign guests.[7] The king simultaneously and adroitly used both sets of symbols to communicate the legitimacy of his authority to an increasingly diverse, culturally foreign population with competing plans for the Hawaiian land and people.

Kamehameha's political and diplomatic strategies are not only important for explaining and interpreting the kinds of dramatic transformations that occurred in the islands during his reign; they also provide a means by which to interpret aliʻi's interactions with foreigners in the longer term. Though historians largely agree that Captain Cook's arrival in the islands represents neither the starting point nor the "most significant event" in the narrative of Hawaiian history, the years between his 1778 visit and American missionaries' arrival in 1820 were busy ones in the Pacific.[8] Beginning in the 1780s, the islands in general and Honolulu in particular became a popular stopover for fur-trading ships destined for China. Due in part to the king's savvy in dealing with foreigners, the islands became a "hub" of Pacific travel and trade. Some travelers, in fact, so enjoyed the physical and political environment that they took up permanent residence in the islands.[9]

By the time of Kamehameha's death in 1819, Hawaiʻi had taken on an increasingly global and cosmopolitan character. Indeed, throughout the nineteenth century, Hawaiʻi's aliʻi would be called upon to mobilize their skills as diplomats and political negotiators as the balance of power increasingly shifted to favor their Western visitors. Long before American missionaries arrived, in fact, aliʻi accrued a long history of engagement with culturally foreign populations, particularly those with competing plans for the islands and its peoples. This chapter helps to draw out a history of Hawaiian opposition to European and American aggression. That is, Kamehameha's political vision not only informed his interactions with foreigners from the late eighteenth century until his death in 1819, but it also formed a lasting example of political diplomacy in the islands. Hawaiʻi's high-ranking women, in fact, most closely emulated his political style in their interactions with American missionaries in the 1820s and beyond, as I demonstrate in the chapters that follow.

Kamehameha's interactions with Captain George Vancouver are particularly illustrative of the king's political savvy. When Vancouver attempted to make anchor in Hawaiʻi in January 1794, a small group of Hawaiians rowed out in canoes to meet his ship. Vancouver observed that a contingent of chiefs were assembled on the shore, "waiting in expectation" of his arrival. Kamehameha, flanked by some of the islands' "principal chiefs," greeted Vancouver with his "usual confidence and cheerful disposition."[10] This was

[handwritten margin note: —King K helps broader picture of elite interactions w/Westerners before missionaries ✗ elite emulate K]

Vancouver's fourth visit to the islands; his first had been as a midshipman on Captain Cook's crew thirteen years earlier in 1779.[11] Much had changed in the intervening years. Both men, riding the rising tide of Pacific trade and travel, had experienced an increase in personal status.

Vancouver moved quickly up through the ranks of the Royal Navy. A mere midshipman under Cook in 1779, he became a lieutenant in 1780. He served a variety of commissions in this capacity until 1790, when he was made captain of the *Discovery*.[12] He led an expedition with the joint aims of resolving property and trading-rights issues with the Spanish in the Nootka Sound and creating a detailed map of the northwest coast of North America for the specific purpose of confirming—or denying—the existence of a Northwest Passage. The two errands, though distinct, were nevertheless wedded by Britain's desire to gain an economic foothold in the Pacific, a territory upon which Spain had cast a "blanket claim to sovereignty."[13] France, Russia, and the United States also sent ships into the Pacific not simply to explore the region but to exploit its vast and seemingly untapped natural resources.[14]

Vancouver's explorations took him to locations throughout the Pacific—first to Australia and New Zealand, then through Tahiti and into British Columbia and Alaska and along the coast of California. He and his crew visited Hawai'i during three separate winters beginning in 1792. Though Vancouver arrived in Hawai'i informed by intelligence gained during his 1779 visit, the captain knew he would need to gain a greater sense of the islands' current political and cultural landscape. Moreover, Vancouver sought to establish positive relations with the islands' leaders.[15] During these visits, Vancouver not only gained important insights into the islands but also became increasingly convinced of Hawai'i's strategic importance to Great Britain.

Like Vancouver, Kamehameha also increased his status in the late eighteenth century. While Kamehameha was high-ranking by birth, it was not inevitable that he would come to rule the island of Hawai'i—nor would it have seemed likely that he would eventually become the first king of all the Hawaiian Islands."[16] Hawaiian men could improve their *mana* (power and prestige) in two ways: by mating with or marrying a high-ranking woman or through warfare.[17] Kamehameha would make strategically valuable partnerships, marrying (among others) Keōpūolani and Ka'ahumanu. Both were important bonds. Keōpūolani's ancestry made her one of the highest-ranking ali'i in the islands in her own right. Because of this, she was also a highly desirable marriage partner. This was particularly so for Kamehameha: producing offspring with Keōpūolani, as one scholar has noted, meant that "the whole lineage was uplifted."[18]

— King K made important marriages

Indeed, in this pairing, Kamehameha's "lineage was further glorified." It was Ka'ahumanu, however, who purportedly became Kamehameha's "favorite" wife. Not incidentally, she was also the daughter of Ke'eaumoku, a man whose authority Kamehameha repeatedly—and ultimately successfully—strove to usurp. After Kamehameha's death, Ka'ahumanu became the king's most politically powerful wife. During his life, however, Kamehameha relied on marriage as one means by which to enhance his authority over other chiefs—male ali'i—in the islands. For their part, Kamehameha's politically powerful wives seem to have absorbed and later adopted some of his most successful strategies of political diplomacy. They also made important adaptations of their own, as later chapters will demonstrate.

Kamehameha's successful partnerships helped to solidify his status, but it was on the battlefield that he made his reputation, accrued loyalties, and, in the late eighteenth century, gained chiefly authority. For example, when Cook attempted to "secure"—kidnap—Kalani'ōpu'u, the mō'ī (king) of Hawai'i island, to redress a theft, Kamehameha took part in the resultant bloody battle in which Cook was ultimately killed.[19] In the days following the melee, the "unfortunate" captain's remains—consisting mainly of his bones—were returned to his crew. The ship's surgeon, William Ellis, quickly observed that Cook's hair had been cut. It was rumored that the captain's hair was in Kamehameha's possession.[20] If Cook's crew took this as a confirmation of Hawaiian "savagery," Kalani'ōpu'u, who also happened to be Kamehameha's uncle, likely understood it in somewhat different terms: Kamehameha retained Cook's hair as a way to collect the foreigner's mana, and, in the process, enhance his own.[21] As the aging Kalani'ōpu'u prepared to step down in 1780, he appointed his son, Kīwala'ō, as his heir and declared Kamehameha guardian of the war god Kuka'ilimoku.[22] The appointment was an honor befitting Kamehameha's skill and stature.

Kīwala'ō and Kamehameha's relationship was a somewhat contentious one; their acrimony only intensified after Kalani'ōpu'u died in 1782. Kamehameha had defied Kīwala'ō before; after Kalani'ōpu'u's death, a handful of supporters encouraged Kamehameha to challenge Kīwala'ō's authority once again.[23] At issue was the division of land that inevitably followed the death of a high chief. Feeling that they had been disadvantaged in the redistribution, Kamehameha and his supporters battled to gain control over the island of Hawai'i. Kīwala'ō was killed in an early skirmish, and Kamehameha claimed control of Kona, Kohala, and Hāmākua, which were on the western and northern parts of the island. Yet the victory was hardly decisive.

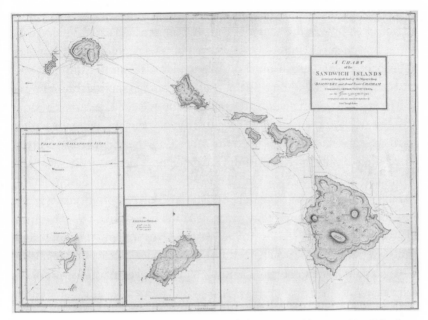

Vancouver's Chart of the Sandwich Islands, *ca. 1798*. (*Courtesy David Rumsey Map Collection, www.davidrumsey.com*)

The larger struggle lasted for the better part of a decade, as Kamehameha attempted repeatedly to dislodge his opponents from their districts on the southern and eastern sides of the island.[24]

While Kamehameha's rivals on the islands frequently eked out victories against him, Kamehameha nevertheless enjoyed a geographical advantage. European travelers doubtless remembered Kealakekua as the site of Cook's demise; nevertheless, they expressed a preference for the bay, citing its tranquility and security. The bay, located squarely within Kamehameha's territory, allowed him to capitalize on the opportunity to trade with Westerners who proved more than willing to supply Hawaiians with arms.[25] Yet Kamehameha was not so easily won over to the Western way of war; he soon found that even "muskets and bayonets" were unreliable and sometimes ineffective. Hopeful of at last securing a victory, Kamehameha turned to more-traditional means of warfare. In 1791 he built a *heiau* (temple) at Pu'ukoholā for his war god, Kuka'ilimoku.[26] The heiau, however, required a sacrifice. When Kamehameha completed the heiau's construction, he summoned Keōua, his remaining adversary on the island. Kamehameha's forces quickly put him down.[27] After a decade at war, Kamehameha was mō'ī of the island of Hawai'i.

— w/ geographical advantage & war-making eliminates rivals & rules big island

Such was the situation that Vancouver encountered when he and his crew arrived in Hawai'i in the winter of 1792. Kamehameha had consolidated his authority and successfully fended off even his most aggressive challengers. Vancouver spent most of his month-long visit attempting simply to gain an accurate understanding of the islands' complex political terrain and to ascertain its key figures. He quickly discovered that there was but one "aree de hoi" on the island of Hawai'i. Though he mangled the Hawaiian words ali'i and mō'ī and conflated their meaning, Vancouver clearly understood their significance. On Hawai'i, Kamehameha ruled.[28] He also came to understand that the new king harbored even broader ambitions. While Kamehameha labored to maintain his new position of authority on Hawai'i, he sought simultaneously to expand the reach of his power to encompass the remaining islands that lay to the West and North. From the intelligence Vancouver was able to gather, it became clear that Kamehameha already had his sights on the neighboring islands of Maui and O'ahu, which were under Kahekili's rule.[29]

Viewed within the context of political unrest present in the islands, Kamehameha might have regarded foreigners as either a nuisance or a distraction, and yet he also knew from experience that they could be counted upon for trade, particularly in the way of arms. Foreign visitors seemed useful in other ways as well; Kamehameha routinely encouraged skilled and well-traveled men to remain in the islands, tapping into their skills as sailors and translators and later as financial and political advisers.[30] From the perspective of a man on the political assent, then, Vancouver's visits in the early 1790s might have seemed auspiciously timed. In fact, Kamehameha effectively used his relationship with Vancouver as an opportunity to shore up his authority on Hawai'i and to exert control over rival leaders on neighboring islands. He did this first by developing positive relations with the explorer in the way of trade. Increasingly, however, Kamehameha capitalized on his status as mō'ī to monopolize trade with Vancouver, thereby cutting off rival chiefs' access to the British captain.

Kamehameha, then, regarded Vancouver as a valuable ally, and he wasted no time in establishing friendly relations with him. Vancouver confessed that he found the terms of trade in the islands in 1792 to be "exorbitant"; yet on that trip, he traded with some of the high chiefs rather than with Kamehameha himself. When Vancouver returned to winter in the islands a year later, the king went out of his way to reassure Vancouver of his generosity and goodwill. On this trip, as in future ones, the king proved munificent, indeed, providing his guests with the "refreshments" that seemed to be available in

—Vancouver recognized K's power, expansionism

— K uses Vancouver to boost authority, monopolize trade

such "abundant supply" in the islands.[31] Yet the exchange was hardly one-sided: Kamehameha also benefited, obtaining a variety of goods from the explorer. During one particular exchange, for example, Vancouver greased the wheels of diplomacy by presenting the king with a floor-length "scarlet cloak . . . adorned with tinsel lace." Kamehameha happily accepted—and even modeled—the gift on board the *Discovery*. Vancouver was delighted with the outcome of their exchange—and with good reason. He clearly viewed it as a "good opportunity to manifest our friendly disposition" toward Hawaiians. He hoped, too, to leverage—or even heighten—Hawaiians' "favorable opinion" of the British. The gesture was not wasted on Kamehameha, who, according to Vancouver, seized the opportunity to extract a promise of King George's "sincere friendship."[32] Yet Kamehameha also understood his burgeoning relationship with Vancouver not just as an opportunity to create positive diplomatic relations but also as a means by which to articulate and enhance his authority on Hawai'i. Kamehameha's handling of his European guests offered immediate political benefits, as subsequent chapters will make clear; however, his maneuverings also provided an example for the islands' ali'i to draw upon in their encounters with foreign visitors.

Kamehameha's exchange with Vancouver in the days following offers a case in point. The king ordered a number of gifts delivered to the *Discovery*. The king's generosity was such that when Ka'iana and Ke'eaumoku, both high chiefs on Hawai'i, arrived to deliver gifts of their own, Vancouver was forced to decline them. The *Discovery* already spilled over with hogs and a "profusion of vegetables"—all gifts from the king.[33] The decks of the *Discovery* were already so "encumbered with their good things" that there was simply no place to stow anything more.[34] Vancouver handled the shipboard negotiations with diplomatic caution, hoping to preserve friendly relations with the two chiefs. He publicly reassured the men that he had every intention of accepting their gifts, including "twenty very fine hogs . . . the instant the animals could be received on board."[35] Privately, however, Vancouver revealed his grasp of the islands' hierarchy and approached the exchange accordingly. The explorer resolved to "pay principle court to [Kamehameha] . . . as king of the whole island" and to treat Ka'iana and Ke'eaumoku with the "degree of respect and attention" their lesser status required. Though Vancouver rightly anticipated that "this sort of conduct might occasion some dissatisfaction" among the chiefs, he was hopeful that he could assuage their feelings in the future.[36]

Kamehameha, on the other hand, appeared less interested—at least for the moment—in political diplomacy than in asserting his authority on the

King K shows much generosity; Vancouver declines other chiefs' gifts - recognizes King K!

island. With all four men gathered on the deck of the *Discovery*, the king declared that Vancouver "had no occasion for hogs, or other productions of Owhyhee, from . . . any other chief." The hogs and other items, then, were no mere trinkets; rather, they operated as ostentatious displays of Kamehameha's authority.[37] Through his beneficence, Kamehameha hoped to articulate his ability, as mō'ī, to command—and dispense with—the islands' natural resources.[38] The lesson was intended for Vancouver as much as for the islands' high chiefs, who instantly grasped its meaning and importance. If the chiefs harbored hopes of expanding their authority on the island or of making trade relations with foreign guests, Kamehameha made the possibility difficult by cutting off trade opportunities with Vancouver. By acting as Vancouver's sole benefactor, Kamehameha effectively consolidated his authority on Hawai'i. With so much at stake, it was a point that bore repeating: in 1794, showing a rare degree of guile, Kamehameha insisted that dealing with local chiefs would be "troublesome and unpleasant." Moreover, such transactions might only "give rise to disputes and misunderstandings." According to Vancouver, Kamehameha "desired we would daily, or as often as should suit our convenience, make our demands known to him." Vancouver regarded this as a "considerate and friendly arrangement."[39]

At the same time that Kamehameha worked to capitalize on his relationship with Vancouver as a means by which to exert his authority over the island's ali'i, he was also compelled to make concessions to the explorer. In January 1794, for example, Vancouver arrived at Hilo Bay with the intent of achieving the "several purposes" that had brought him to the islands in previous winters. Vancouver anticipated a "very commodious" situation at Hilo, but he was disappointed to find that he had arrived too early in the season. As it was, the bay remained "intirely [*sic*] exposed to the northerly winds, which then blew very strong," making it impossible to land. The captain proposed that the ships relocate to Kealakekua and requested that Kamehameha join them. Kamehameha, however, "did not seem much inclined to accept" the invitation or to accede to his guest's change of plans. Instead, Kamehameha expressed his preference that the *Discovery*, *Chatham*, and *Daedalus* (a British naval-store ship) all remain at Hilo. According to Vancouver's account, the king reassured the explorer that he would personally see that "business" of reprovisioning was "properly performed."[40]

Vancouver found the proposed alternative unacceptable; he prevailed upon the king to change his mind, using virtually every tactic available to him to persuade Kamehameha to accompany the *Discovery* and its crew "to some place of secure anchorage." The explorer first reasoned with the king, then he appealed to his vanity and, finally, to his duty as ruler. Still, Kamehameha would not budge. Though his obstinacy on the matter was maddening and appeared somewhat inexplicable to Vancouver, Kamehameha's refusal was deeply grounded in Hawaiian cultural and religious belief. In fact, Vancouver's arrival interrupted the makahiki festival already under way. The makahiki, which spanned a period of about four months beginning in the middle of October and reaching into February, was traditionally a period of leisure, punctuated by dancing and sporting events. Work was kapu, as was war. The makahiki festival also entailed the collection of gifts of tribute, including dogs, tapa cloth, and feathers. The islands' ali'i collected the symbolic gifts intended for Lono and presented them to the islands' mō'ī—in this case, king Kamehameha. Tradition placed prohibitions on the king's movements during the festival period. As Kamehameha insisted, "it was not possible he could absent himself without the particular sanction of the priests."[41]

Vancouver nevertheless pressed the king to break the kapu on his movement. Relying on "artifice" to persuade the king, Vancouver claimed that he "attributed his declining my invitation to a coolness and a relaxation in the friendship he had formerly shewn and pretended to entertain." Moreover, Vancouver issued a thinly veiled warning, claiming he had little "doubt of soon finding among the other islands some chief, whose assistance, protection, and authority, would on all occasions be readily afforded."[42] Though Vancouver as much as admitted the idle nature of his threats, he nevertheless correctly predicted the outcome. Kamehameha relented, informing his priest of his decision to leave the district, thereby suspending the makahiki.

While Vancouver wrote that he deemed the "little difference . . . amicably adjusted," Kamehameha perhaps saw it differently: he argued that his absence marked an "unprecedented breach" of the islands' kapu laws and insisted that he "considered himself to be the last person in his dominions who ought to violate the established laws, and the regulations of the country which he governed." Yet Kamehameha was acutely aware of the potential cost of refusing Vancouver's request. The king's decision to delay the makahiki, then, was made under duress and in an effort to maintain his relationship with Vancouver. As the king labored to enhance his status on Hawai'i and to expand the reach of his political power in the islands, he continued to cultivate politically useful relationships such as the one he enjoyed with Vancouver.

After two years in the Pacific, Vancouver had grown increasingly convinced of Hawai'i's "importance . . . to Great Britain." The explorer wrote

— Vancouver does extract some
mutual concessions from King K

that he found the possibility of the "extension of [Great Britain's] commerce over the Pacific" and the "ready assistance" of the islands' inhabitants to be particularly attractive. Securing trade was, in part, what Vancouver had come to the Pacific to accomplish; his positive relationship with Kamehameha at last put him in a position to achieve his aims. On his final visit, Vancouver reintroduced a topic that "had been frequently mentioned" during the explorer's prior visits: cession of the island of Hawai'i to Britain. The explorer rationalized the ways in which cession would benefit Hawai'i's residents. In the narrative of his voyage, Vancouver castigated the " civilized visitors" who defrauded Hawaiians, paying them in trade with "commodities of no service or value." He reserved his greatest scorn, however, for those foreigners who participated in "putting fire-arms into the hands of uncivilized people."[43] It is unlikely that he shared these reflections with either Kamehameha or the islands' high chiefs. Instead, he stressed the altruistic nature of the relationship between Britain and Hawai'i. As Vancouver saw it, Britain's "benevolent monarch" aspired to only good things for Hawai'i and its people. He strove, among other things, "to render them more peaceable people in their intercourse with each other; to furnish them with such things as could contribute to make them a happier people"; and, moreover, "to afford them an opportunity of becoming more respectable in the eyes of foreign visitors." Related to the last, Vancouver raised the specter of foreign encroachment and positioned the British as Hawai'i's beneficent protector.[44] Late in February 1794, Kamehameha gathered with his chiefs on board the *Discovery* "for the purpose of formally ceding and surrendering the island."[45]

Yet despite Vancouver's interpretation, it is not clear that Kamehameha viewed their agreement as an acknowledgement of Hawai'i's "subjection, to the government of a superior foreign power."[46] Rather, Kamehameha's actions suggest that he perceived the arrangement as yet another means by which to build necessary diplomatic alliances and to enhance his defenses "against the ambitious views of remote or neighboring enemies."[47] As part of the agreement, in fact, Kamehameha expressed his desire that Vancouver would "leave the *Chatham* . . . for their future protection."[48] Vancouver demurred, insisting "that no such measure could possibly be adopted on the present occasion." Nevertheless, Kamehameha successfully negotiated Vancouver's assistance in constructing another vessel, the *Britannia*. In addition to the assistance the captain provided in "building the hull of the vessel," Vancouver allowed that he had provided "all the ironwork . . . oakum and pitch for caulking, proper masts, and a set of schooner sails." For all of this, Kamehameha appeared "exceedingly well pleased."[49] As well he might: from the king's perspective, negotiations with Vancouver had been overwhelmingly successful, resulting in British protection and British supplies.

While Kamehameha viewed his negotiations with Vancouver as a success, he also had continued reason to be optimistic about his political future. In 1795, several months after Vancouver's departure, Kamehameha won successive and decisive victories on neighboring islands, finally gaining control over Maui, Moloka'i, and O'ahu. During his lifetime, Kahekili remained Kamehameha's most credible rival for power, and the two men battled repeatedly. At Kahekili's death in 1794, however, his considerable kingdom—those "extensive dominions" that included the islands of Maui, O'ahu, and Moloka'i—were divided among his half brother and son.[50] Yet, as with the island of Hawai'i just over a decade earlier, the heirs disagreed violently over the terms of the land distribution. Kahekili's brother was killed in an early battle on O'ahu. His son, Kalanikūpule, though triumphant over his new rival, fared little better: he was set adrift in a canoe by some of the same British sailors who had helped him secure his recent victory.

Emboldened both by his recent agreement with Vancouver and by Kalanikūpule's weakened leadership, Kamehameha moved swiftly to gain control over the contested territory. He landed his fleet of war canoes—so numerous that they littered the beaches—first at Maui and then at Moloka'i. His troops claimed the first two islands without struggle; the conquest of O'ahu, however, where Kalanikūpule's forces had gathered, proved more difficult and more deadly.[51] Kamehameha's own chief Ka'iana defected in route from Moloka'i, joining Kalanikūpule's effort to defeat his former king. Kamehameha's troops, however, proved better equipped and better positioned. Armed with guns, they drove Kalanikūpule's warriors up the Nu'uanu valley. Those who survived the "promiscuous slaughter" on the valley floor were forced onto the steep cliffs above. Some escaped, but many others were forced over the cliffs onto the rocks below.[52] At battle's end, Kamehameha ruled over all the islands from Hawai'i to O'ahu. Only Kaua'i and Ni'ihau—the westernmost islands in the chain—remained to be conquered.

Kamehameha took up residence on O'ahu, contemplating his next move. Kaua'i and Ni'ihau lay just across the channel and offered Kamehameha the opportunity to unite the islands under one government. Yet Kamehameha had to consider not only his strategy for taking Kaua'i but also how to maintain his authority over the islands already under his rule. As Kamehameha expanded the reach of his authority, he continued to search for means by

- King K victorious over most of the other islanes

which to articulate his status in the islands and to translate his authority to foreigners who continued to deliver themselves upon their shores.

British captain William Broughton, for example, who had accompanied Vancouver as a lieutenant in command of the *Chatham* in 1792, returned to the islands in February 1796. While Kamehameha had welcomed British ships in earlier years, the timing of Broughton's visit was complicated. It was nearly a year after Kamehameha's victory at Nu'uanu and just less than two years since the king "ceded" the islands to Britain. Though Kamehameha likely interpreted their agreement more as a protective agreement than as a cession, his demeanor in 1796 suggests that he was well aware that the British might have seen things differently.[53] Kamehameha treated his visitors with all the respect required of political diplomacy, yet he continued to handle them gingerly. Throughout their visit, Kamehameha made regular and overt displays of his authority.

When Broughton and his crew landed early in the evening on February 6, Kamehameha acknowledged their presence by sending a message to the *Providence*. In it, he inquired whether the captain wished the king "to fire his great guns" in their honor. Broughton demurred, advising Kamehameha to "save his powder."[54] Kamehameha waited until the following day to make an official visit to the ship. According to Broughton, Kamehameha arrived in the morning, "attended by all his chiefs." They were impressively dressed in "cloaks and helmet caps." The king, too, was dressed for the occasion, though his appearance differed somewhat from his chiefs: "He himself wore European clothes, with a beautiful cloak composed of yellow feathers."[55] Though Broughton had seen the "cloaks and caps" ('ahu'ula and mahiole, respectively) on his earlier visits, his reference to them is hardly surprising.[56] Kamehameha's great cloak alone was made up of nearly 500,000 brilliant yellow feathers. The entire retinue, similarly clothed in traditional 'ahu'ula and mahiole, must have made quite an impression on Broughton and his crew. Yet while Broughton seems to have appreciated the garments' visual magnificence, it is less clear that he grasped either their cultural significance or the meanings the king likely hoped to convey by wearing them.

For Kamehameha—as for the other Hawaiians in attendance at the meeting—such garments were laden with particular, though evolving, cultural meanings. The chiefs' attire, for example, was almost certainly intended to convey their high status and rank in the islands. Broughton's reference to "caps and cloaks" suggests as much. Though warriors might wear helmets constructed of hair or other natural materials, they were prohibited from donning the 'ahu'ula to which Broughton referred. Hawaiians had long

—Seeks to articulate authority to foreigners – Capt. Broughton

– Attire intended to connote status, esp. feathers

regarded feathers as among their most valuable possessions. While some feathers were scarcer—and thus more precious—than others, feathered ornaments (including the mahiole, the 'ahu'ula, and the kāhili) belonged exclusively to ali'i. By themselves, then, such garments offered an indication of the wearer's status.[57] Worn in combination, the feathered mahiole and 'ahu'ula were understood as attire exclusive to the islands' high chiefs and kings."[58]

Similarly, Kamehameha's "beautiful cloak composed of yellow feathers" operated as more than mere ornamentation. If ali'i claimed exclusive possession of feathered garments, only the islands' most powerful elite could possess a cloak of the type and style Kamehameha wore. Its length and coloring in particular served as unmistakable visual representations of his rank and authority in the islands. The massive floor-length cape represented a veritable hording of island resources not just in the way of raw material but in labor as well. Kamehameha's cloak was constructed almost entirely of mamo feathers—among the most rare in the islands.[59] To preserve the scarce and precious feathers for the future, hunters captured the birds, extracted the best and most suitable feathers, and set the birds free again. Scholars have estimated that Kamehameha's great cloak would have required the feathers of at least 80,000 birds. The labor associated with capturing a sufficient number of feathers alone would have been extensive and time-consuming; the feather work necessary to complete the garment represented a similar draw in terms of human effort. It was complicated, complex labor undertaken by skilled craftspeople. Feathers had to be grouped by size, bunched, and tied before being attached to a net mesh (which provided the cloak's underlying structure). The task had to be repeated literally thousands of times. The scarcity of yellow feathers and the labor-intensiveness of the 'ahu'ula's construction meant that only the islands' most powerful men could command a garment like the one belonging to Kamehameha.[60] In fact, Kamehameha's all-yellow cloak was totally unique, reflective of his singular position of authority. It also, importantly, bespoke Kamehameha's proven masculine prowess as a warrior—a point he might have wanted to make clear to his guest.

Yet the king also came attired in what Broughton simply described as "European clothes." Indeed, while Hawaiians—ali'i in particular—had increasing access to Western-style clothing at the end of the eighteenth century, Kamehameha's use of "European clothes" on this particular occasion seems deliberate and aimed at a specific outcome. In fact, Kamehameha's mixed appearance reveals the multiple political and diplomatic

— Scarce, valuable feathers ⇒ singular position of authority

purposes he had in mind for his visit with Broughton and, moreover, helps to illustrate Kamehameha's growing political sophistication at the dawn of the nineteenth century. While the 'ahu'ula offered a ready means by which Kamehameha might communicate his status, he nevertheless ran the risk that his guests would not immediately apprehend its symbolic significance. Perhaps more important, Kamehameha understood that the garment might alienate—rather than ingratiate—his foreign visitors, thereby compromising Kamehameha's status with them.[61] European-style clothes, on the other hand, promised to achieve the opposite effect, emphasizing the similarities rather than the differences between Hawaiians and their foreign guests.[62] Viewed from this perspective, Kamehameha's adoption of Western-style clothing emerges as part of a larger diplomatic strategy. The king, in fact, increasingly employed this strategy as a means by which to establish himself as a "civilized" man—a credible and legitimate ruler of a "civilized" nation.[63] Drawing upon Kamehameha's diplomatic style over the course of the nineteenth century, Hawai'i's ali'i increasingly relied on European-style (and later, American-style) clothing to communicate both their status and their "civility" to foreign visitors.

In 1810 Kamehameha at last gained control of the entire chain of islands. Though the king had spent the intervening years since conquering Maui, Moloka'i, and O'ahu methodically preparing to take Kaua'i by force, he ultimately resorted to more pacific measures to achieve his aims. Hawaiian historian Samuel Kamakau's nineteenth-century account describes the flurry of communication that passed between Kaumuali'i (who ruled over both Kaua'i and Ni'ihau) and Kamehameha in the early part of 1810. While Kaumuali'i repeatedly declined Kamehameha's invitations to join him on O'ahu to negotiate a "treaty of peace," he nevertheless sent messengers in his place.[64] Once on O'ahu, Kaumuali'i's emissaries accepted a variety of gifts from Kamehameha, including "large *peleleu* canoes . . . feather capes and other gifts of value."[65] Kamehameha hoped the items would induce Kaumuali'i to agree to a meeting. Kaumuali'i, however, remained "doubtful of coming to Oahu, fearing to be served as Keōua had been" nearly twenty years before, when Kamehameha's forces killed him and seized control over Hawai'i island.[66] Kaumuali'i knew that at the very least, Kamehameha would demand that Kaumuali'i "give up the government" of Kaua'i and Ni'ihau. Recognizing that Kamehameha would take the islands by force if necessary, Kaumuali'i sailed for O'ahu aboard an American trading vessel.[67] When Kamehameha and his chiefs rowed out to meet Kaumuali'i, they came dressed for the occasion. Their canoes were resplendent "with feather cloaks and radiant with the colors of the rainbow."[68] Once again, Kamehameha relied on the 'ahu'ula to communicate his chiefly authority and his proven capacity as a warrior. Kaumuali'i, though similarly dressed "in the costume of chiefs," quickly surrendered to Kamehameha.[69]

Though historians often characterize the period following Kamehameha's unification of the Hawaiian Islands as a peaceful one, the king nevertheless continued to experience—and to defend against—challenges to his authority. Such challenges came as frequently from within as from without, as German physician Georg Anton Schäffer's dalliance in island politics helps to illustrate. The chief manager of the Russian-American Company, Alexander Baranov, authorized Schäffer to make contact with Kamehameha. Schäffer was to pose as a naturalist in order to gain the king's confidence. Ultimately, Baranov wanted Schäffer to negotiate the recovery of—or to receive compensation for—cargo from a Russian ship that had wrecked off the coast of Kaua'i, where the crew had stopped for supplies earlier in the year. Moreover, Baranov hoped that Schäffer could broker a more-permanent trade agreement with the king. Yet Schäffer arrived amid stiff competition for the king's favor. The king's own adviser, the Briton John Young, cautioned Kamehameha against Schäffer; American traders, jealously guarding their own interests, quickly joined in the chorus. Schäffer himself did little to alleviate suspicions regarding his true intentions. On Honolulu, he built a post as a base of operations and raised the Russian flag overhead. The king responded swiftly, ordering his chiefs to remove Schäffer from O'ahu.

Schäffer avoided violent confrontation by retreating to Kaua'i of his own accord. There he encountered Kaumuali'i, the denuded former king. The two men, like Kamehameha and Vancouver just two decades earlier, discovered the sympathetic nature of their ambitions. Kaumuali'i sought foreign assistance and protection; Schäffer wanted a Pacific base for trade. They quickly moved to establish a mutually beneficial arrangement. Kaumuali'i agreed to compensate the Russian-American Company for its lost cargo and, moreover, promised the Russians exclusive trading rights over the islands of Kaua'i and Ni'ihau. In exchange, Kaumuali'i placed the two islands under the protection of the Russian emperor, Alexander I. Within a month, Schäffer made additional promises, pledging ammunition and arms to enable Kaumuali'i to invade and take possession of Kamehameha's kingdom. Schäffer, of course, did not possess the authority to make such a treaty. Similarly, neither Kaua'i nor Ni'ihau were Kaumuali'i's to give away. Still, Kamehameha perceived the threat to his authority as credible and genuine.[70]

Challenges remain to King K's authority
—Westerners compete for attention
— Schäffer allies w/ deposed King

The political maneuvering taking place on Kaua'i helps to explain Kamehameha's interactions with Russian lieutenant Otto Von Kotzebue, who arrived in the islands soon afterward. Though Kotzebue worked to assure the king that Schäffer's "bad conduct" should not be "ascribed to the will of [the] emperor," Kamehameha could not be certain. He appropriately regarded Kotzebue and his crew with suspicion and made his authority evident. Kotzebue learned through an intermediary that the king anticipated a "hostile ship of war" and prepared accordingly. He issued "orders to station soldiers all along the coast"—400 in all, and armed with muskets.[71] When Kotzebue came onshore, he learned of the veracity of the king's claims: his men were, in fact, armed. Yet the king did not rely on this show of force alone to convey his kingly authority. Rather, the king worked to translate his status in other terms that his guest might understand. Specifically, Kamehameha went to great lengths to construct a Western-style persona in order to both articulate his own authority and to demonstrate Hawai'i's viability on the world's political stage.

Kamehameha's strategy appears to have worked. Kotzebue remarked with approval that the "king's camp" boasted "two snow-white houses, built of stone, after the European fashion." For the visit, the king produced "neatly made" European chairs and a mahogany table. Yet the lieutenant appeared aware that the king's display of European goods was largely for the benefit of his guests, remarking that the king generally preferred "not to forsake the customs of his country," residing in a "simpler" house that was more convenient and—in the king's view—more appropriate to the environment. Moreover, though Kotzebue "had formed very different notions of the royal attire," Kamehameha appeared for their meeting clad in decidedly Western apparel. Yet the "mixture of wildness and cultivation" that Kotzebue observed was the result not just of Hawai'i's ongoing interaction with the world beyond its shores but of Kamehameha's diplomatic strategizing.[72]

If Kamehameha hoped to translate his own—and Hawai'i's—legitimacy to Kotzebue, he also hoped that his message would not terminate with the lieutenant but would enjoy wider circulation among an even more powerful audience. Kotzebue's attempt to persuade Kamehameha to sit for a portrait with artist Louis Choris, who arrived on board the *Rurick*, provides insight into the king's aims. According to Kotzebue, Kamehameha at first "resisted [Kotzebue's] entreaties" to be painted, unwilling, as Kotzebue put it, "to be transferred to paper." Kotzebue presumed that the king's refusal was borne merely of superstition. "Probably," Kotzebue mused, "he connected some idea of magic with this art."[73] Yet Kamehameha's reluctance fell away once

All this explains King K's suspicion to Kotzebue

Kotzebue "represented to him, how happy our emperor would be to possess his likeness."[74] Indeed, the king recognized an opportunity when he saw one. He promptly agreed to sit for the portrait and dismissed Choris in order to prepare. When the artist returned, he discovered—much to his chagrin—that the king had changed from the malo and black tapa cloak he had been wearing in favor of Western-style attire. The king wore a white shirt, a red vest, and a yellow tie.[75] Choris was disappointed; he hoped to paint a more "authentic" portrait of the king and "begged him to change his costume." Kamehameha, however, was steadfast; he "absolutely refused" Choris's request.[76]

Choris ultimately made two portraits of Kamehameha—one sanctioned by the king and another that Choris was forced to paint from memory. Choris published the latter "unauthorized" portrait (along with other images he made during his travels) in *Voyage Pittoresque Autour du Monde*, a text that boasted a decidedly aristocratic list of subscribers, including the emperor of Russia and the kings of France and Prussia.[77] In his recollected portrait of the king, Choris—deliberately or not—departed from many of the conventions of royal male portraiture with which his audience would have been familiar. In keeping with his artistic vision, Choris not only depicted the king in traditional Hawaiian clothing but situated him amid Hawaiʻi's natural landscape. The effect was to cast Kamehameha as a "savage king" rather than a legitimate monarch as the king might have hoped.[78] Curiously, the tapa cloth Choris insisted upon as central to an "authentic" portrait of the king is only partially visible in the completed image. The painting does not capture the cloth's distinctive coloring or markings; rather, the cape's most significant feature—at least to European eyes—would have been the lack of buttons and characteristic formal high collar. Moreover, the cape, lacking these features, leaves Kamehameha's throat fully exposed. The king's upper torso is similarly, though only partially, on view. The effect is to train the viewer's attention on the king's bodily, physical presence. Choris also positioned Kamehameha amid Hawaiʻi's natural environment rather than indoors or in proximity to symbols of his royal identity or achievements. Such was hardly the masculine, commanding figure of a ruler that European audiences had come to expect. In fact, the "nativized" portrait that Choris made was one Kamehameha had actively worked to avoid.

At the king's insistence, however, Choris had also made a formal portrait of Kamehameha in his suit of clothes. Though Choris deemed Kamehameha's costume as more befitting a sailor than a king, it nevertheless diminished the marked differences between European and Hawaiian attire.

Portrait of Kamehameha I. While Louis Choris ultimately painted another portrait of the king—one that circulated more widely—Kamehameha only consented to sit for this portrait, which featured the king in European-style clothing. (Watercolor by Louis Choris, 1817; courtesy Bishop Museum, www.bishopmuseum.org)

Moreover, the finished portrait adequately conveyed Kamehameha's imposing size and his regal, masculine stature: Kamehameha's direct gaze and erect posture—both regular features of royal portraiture—offer visual cues as to the king's royal identity and demeanor. The king's age, indicated by his white hair and by the fine creases that line his face, also helped to emphasize his royal authority. Kamehameha's bearing and his attire in the finished portrait, in fact, shares some of the conventions of royal portraiture of the era. This was, perhaps, the king's object in altering his appearance.[79] The resulting portrait was a favorite of the king's and was widely circulated, as it still is even today.

When Kotzebue departed from the islands at the end of the year, he left with a favorable impression of both Kamehameha, whom he regarded as a man who ruled with "justice" and "rigour," and of the Hawaiian Islands, which, as he remarked early in his visit, had taken on "the mixed appearance of an European and Owhyee village."[80] While later foreign visitors shared Kotzebue's impressions of the islands, few had the opportunity to meet the king in person. Kamehameha perished in the spring of 1819.

Before his death, Kamehameha directed that the sacrifice to mark his passing should not be carried out. Instead, the chiefs should be kapu for the new king, Kamehameha's son and heir, Liholiho. Other rituals remained firmly in place, including the preparation of the king's body and the final placement of his bones, which remained secret.[81] Kamehameha's subjects lamented the loss of their king—the first ever mōʻī of the kingdom of Hawaiʻi. Jacques Arago, a Frenchman who arrived just months after Kamehameha's death, described the people's nearly palpable distress over Kamehameha's passing. The people's "too-poignant sorrow made them desert their huts"; they gathered together and filled "the air with groans" of sadness. Foreigners, too, lamented his loss, if for slightly different reasons. Arago regarded the king's passing as a permanent and irreparable harm to Hawaiʻi. "The people of this archipelago," Arago wrote, "were on the point of reaping the fruits of their courage and perseverance." Arago wondered if Kamehameha's death would effectively undo all that he had achieved during his rule.[82]

— Foreigners mourn his passing

CHAPTER 2 *Soldiers and Angels for God*

On a fall day in 1819, Mercy Whitney gathered with her new mission family at the Boston harbor in preparation for a journey to the Hawaiian Islands. Mercy was young—just twenty-six—and recently married. In the preceding weeks, Mercy had surprised her family by agreeing not only to wed Samuel Whitney, a virtual stranger, but also to accompany him on a mission to the Pacific for a term of no less than twenty years. Mercy and Samuel were not alone in taking such a leap of faith. Of the seven missionary couples preparing to board the brig *Thaddeus*, six had married in preparation for their journey. The mission's governing board—the American Board of Commissioners for Foreign Missions (ABCFM)—had clearly articulated its marital requirement. Missionary hopefuls like Samuel understood that if they were unmarried, they simply would not be assigned to the field. Similarly, women understood that they would only be allowed to participate in the growing foreign-mission movement as wives and "helpmeets" to full-fledged male missionaries.[1]

The group included seven male missionaries and their wives, five children, and four Hawaiians.[2] The small assembly of near strangers assembled to pray, to receive last-minute instructions before their departure, and to say goodbye to their families, friends, and loved ones. For the small crowd gathered to see the group off, the mood surely must have been mixed. Coupled with the dangers associated with a months-long sea voyage and the long term of mission service, it was possible—even likely—that the group would never be reunited with their families and friends. Moreover, missionaries could not predict whether Hawaiian Islanders would accept either the missionaries or their message. The solemn event closed with the mournful hymn "When Shall We Meet Again."[3] Yet the question laid more heavily on the minds of the loved ones who had gathered to see the small company off than on the missionaries and their wives. The men and women who set sail for Hawai'i were eager to set about their work and optimistic about the future. The ABCFM had offered the group a rare opportunity to effect "lasting good to the cause of Christ

— Missionary marital requirement

30

among the heathen." They considered it their "privilege" to serve, even at great sacrifice.[4]

Women's enthusiastic participation in these ventures seems surprising, given that they were expected to make all of the sacrifices expected of a full-fledged missionary but could take on only a limited official role in the mission project. Yet missionaries and their wives equally expected to give their all to and for the mission. Moreover, from the outset, they understood their roles and duties in gender-specific ways. Indeed, the board's requirements for mission work would have seemed entirely logical to this band of mission hopefuls, born and reared in the particular religious and cultural context of New England's Second Great Awakening.

This chapter explains New England missionaries' enthusiasm for their work in the Pacific by elaborating on the Second Great Awakening and the mission movement that grew out of it.[5] It also elaborates on the way in which mission participants understood their role or "place" within the mission in distinctly gendered terms. Though the fervor of the awakening coaxed a generation of young men and women to leave the comforts of home and family to work among the "heathen," men and women experienced the call to mission work in decidedly different ways. Moreover, they expected to serve different purposes within the mission. In this way, as in others, the American foreign-mission movement was a fundamentally gendered phenomenon.

In this chapter, I argue that nineteenth-century gender ideologies were not merely incidental to the American mission to Hawai'i and the larger foreign-mission movement out of which it grew; they were central to it.[6] The mission board employed gendered policies and gendered rhetoric that aimed to do more than simply describe—or even govern—the intimate relationships between men and women or the gender division of labor that "naturally" characterized their marriages. Rather, ideas about gender informed the basic structure and organization of the American foreign-mission movement from its earliest years. Mission concepts about the inherent, proper, and complementary roles of men and women, moreover, helped to shape missionary ideas about the practice and process of conversion. That is, ideas about gender provided a basis for understanding precisely who could do what in the service of Christ. Finally, missionaries' shared sense of the inviolability and universality of gender informed their understanding of the peoples they would encounter as part of their duty to Christianize the heathen world and set the stage for their interactions with them.[7] When American missionaries arrived in Hawai'i, they found that the gender ideology of

— Gender informs roles, duties, basic structure of the missionary movement & conversion

the mission did not translate easily. In some cases, their ideas about men and women's roles caused problems for the project of conversion.

Like her mission sisters and brethren, Mercy Whitney (née Partridge) was born in the last years of the eighteenth century in the geographical heart of New England's Second Great Awakening.[8] Mercy was reared in Pittsfield, Massachusetts, which was nearly equidistant from both Yale and Andover, two schools that emerged as institutional and intellectual centers of the revival and missionary movements in the American Northeast. She no doubt felt the effects of the religious revivalism that swept through the New England landscape throughout her young life. Born to a religiously devout family, Mercy was a member of the Congregationalist Church pastored by Heman Humphrey, a man deeply embedded in New England's religious leadership.[9] Though her family later expressed surprise at the depth of her religious devotion—indicated by her willingness to commit body and soul to the cause of Christianity—Mercy claimed that she had long harbored hopes of laboring in the mission field. In this way, as in others, Mercy seems much like the other female participants in the foreign-mission movement.[10]

Mercy was likely persuaded by preachers who stressed sinners' capacity to accept God's grace. If earlier models of Christianity emphasized sinners' helplessness in the face of God's omnipotence, this new brand of religion put the promise of salvation at the fingertips of anyone who repented. Moreover, though New England–style revivalism lacked the emotive power and democratic style of the parallel movements taking place in Kentucky and Tennessee, it nevertheless inspired believers to consider the power of human agency and the potential of humankind. If individuals could effect change in their own lives, it stood to reason that they could bring salvation to others willing to do the same—whether at home or abroad.[11]

Notions of human perfectibility fit easily with the philosophy of "disinterested benevolence" that grew out of the New Divinity Movement. As an outgrowth of the Calvinism of the latter part of the eighteenth century, the movement persuaded believers that faith alone was not enough. Rather, one had to actively participate in the work of salvation.[12] Such labor required more than mere service to the church. Instead, the New Divinity called upon believers to sacrifice on behalf of others. Many nineteenth-century Christians thus came to understand conversion and uplift of the "destitute and degraded" as a vital part of a genuine religious experience. Indeed, the ideal of disinterested benevolence established the very logic that undergirded volunteer societies and the larger foreign-mission movement in this period.[13]

Human ability, duty to sacrifice to others

Driven home again and again, the dual messages of "human ability" and the duty of Christians to sacrifice on behalf of others offered the necessary catalyst for the faithful.[14] This generation of believers felt called upon to act on behalf of both their own spiritual well-being and the spiritual lives of others. And act they did, participating in a wide-reaching foreign-mission movement that aimed to bring Christianity to the "heathen" toiling along the world's "rude shores."[15]

Women's willingness to participate in the mission movement can be explained at least in part by the promises implied in nineteenth-century American religious and cultural ideologies, which seemed to offer them a greater sphere of influence than they had previously enjoyed. Premised on democratic notions of the perfectibility of humankind, the Second Great Awakening suggested the breakdown of certain social hierarchies in American life, including those based on gender and race.[16] In the nineteenth century, such democratic impulses ran concurrent with an emergent domestic ideology that posited women's supposed innate piety and morality. Such ideas gained real cultural currency in America beginning in the eighteenth century and lasted well into the nineteenth, if not beyond. Together, the democratic and domestic ideals promised to clear a space for women's active participation in American religious life. Yet those ideals did not necessarily translate theologically, nor did they translate equitably.[17] From the beginning, the mission movement was conceived in gender-specific terms that located men at the center of activity and women at its periphery.

Though the ABCFM insisted that the work assigned to mission wives was "important," their labor was consistently described in ways that emphasized its supportive or complementary function. That is, the board assumed that men would perform the "real" and active work of conversion, while women would provide support—usually from the home. Moreover, the American mission movement did not view all men—or all women—equally. Instead, the board made important distinctions between the inherent capacities and capabilities of men and women based not only on gender but also on race.[18] These distinctions both effected the organization of religious life in America and shaped missionary ideas about and interactions with the people they would encounter as part of their labor.[19]

New England Christians' "discovery" of Ōpūkahaʻia, a Hawaiian native whom the missionaries called Henry Obookiah, offers a case in point. Missionaries and their supporters gleefully embraced Ōpūkahaʻia's story—and with good reason. Ōpūkahaʻia's tale was not simply one of individual uplift; it also seemed to confirm what Christians believed they knew about

—2nd GA: democratic impulses, breakdown of some hierarchies, woman's innate piety (domestic)

Soldiers and Angels for God / 33

—Still, women as supportive/complementary

the world's heathen. While Ōpūkahaʻia was a remarkable man in his own right, American missionaries regarded his story largely in terms of what it said about their evangelical prospects. Moreover, the narrative worked in important ways to shape missionaries' expectations of the Hawaiians they encountered in 1820 and beyond. The narrative characterized Ōpūkahaʻia's "native" state as one of childlike innocence but, just as important, emphasized his capacity for uplift.[20] According to his memoir, which was published in 1818, Ōpūkahaʻia fled his home country and worked his way to America on board an American ship.[21] Edwin Dwight, a student at Yale College, stumbled across the young man on the campus in 1808. Dwight reported that the young Hawaiian wept, apparently in despair over his own ignorance: he confessed to Dwight that he could neither read nor write.[22] He was similarly unschooled in the Gospel. According to Dwight's account, "when the proposition was made that he should come the next day to the college," Ōpūkahaʻia seized the opportunity "with great eagerness." Dwight reported that he helped to educate Ōpūkahaʻia, and the Hawaiian became his "best and kind friend." Dwight arranged for Ōpūkahaʻia to live with a cousin, Timothy Dwight (the president of Yale College), while he attended to his studies. This "pious and good family" also hoped to educate Ōpūkahaʻia in the Gospel and to expose him to the word of God. The narrative held that though Ōpūkahaʻia at first "believed but little," he proved an apt pupil and made rapid progress.[23]

Ōpūkahaʻia's story did more than simply heighten New England Christians' perception of the problem of "paganism" in the world; it helped to focus their evangelical energies by suggesting a place and a people in need of Christian uplift. The young Hawaiian seemed to embody both the problem of savagery and the promise of Christian civility properly and effectively imparted. Further, Ōpūkahaʻia's story suggested to readers that the "heathen" were both in need of Christian salvation and capable of receiving it. For many Christian readers, Ōpūkahaʻia represented a living example of the civilizing effects of Christianity. His story promised to help mobilize religious-minded men and women eager to go "into all the world" to "preach the Gospel to every creature."[24] In fact, many Christians later credited Ōpūkahaʻia with providing the impetus for the American foreign-mission movement.

In 1810, just two years after Ōpūkahaʻia had been "discovered" on the Yale campus, a group of seminary students—the Brethren—seized the opportunity to make a case for an American foreign mission. The Brethren included "mission-minded" men like Samuel Newell and Samuel J. Mills, who had long been troubled by the perceived problem of "heathenism" in the world. They had, in fact, debated the issue for a number of years—at least since 1806—and sought ways to spread Christianity across the globe. It was not until 1809, after Samuel Mills met Ōpūkahaʻia and participated in his conversion, that the Brethren's plans began to crystallize.[25] In 1810 the group formally sought the advice and counsel of the "fathers in the church" regarding the feasibility of a foreign mission by submitting a petition to the General Association of Congregational Clergy.[26] The association quickly approved the Brethren's petition and moved to convene a board, name its members, and draft a constitution for its governance. Just two years later, the board gained its official charter. With that, the ABCFM and the American mission movement were born.

If the "church fathers" acted quickly, it was because they understood that the time was right for foreign missions. New England's evangelical community had long awaited such an opportunity but had worried that there were simply not enough young men willing and able to participate in such an ambitious undertaking.[27] By 1810, however, the climate had changed, evinced by the surprising number of young men—and young women—who volunteered themselves for service. Throughout New England, moreover, a donating public signaled its willingness to fund missionary endeavors by providing gifts both large and small. In November 1811 the board received a donation in the amount of $1.25—from "two widows." A later $10.00 gift came from a reader of the *Panoplist*, a publication aimed at a Christian readership. Before long, the board was accepting larger donations from organizations that included the "Female Charitable Society in Sheffield," the "Foreign Mission Society of New London," and the "Boston and Vicinity" foreign mission society. The board took its successful fund-raising as a positive sign of its readiness to begin its work in earnest. "In our own country," the board observed, "the missionary spirit is excited."[28] The board sought to harness that excitement and to leverage Christians' growing and nearly palpable sense of duty to spread Christianity across the globe.

At the ABCFM's helm were men who had been both influenced by and influential in the religious revivals of the Northeast.[29] They conceived of a foreign-mission movement that was not only embedded in the particular religious climate of the Second Great Awakening but also informed by emergent American political ideas about the place of the United States in the world and the legitimacy of U.S. expansion.[30] The board, in fact, easily attached its rhetoric of salvation to an already-existing discourse of empire. As early as 1810, the ABCFM articulated its belief that Christ would not only "have the heathen as his inheritance" but should also take "the uttermost parts of the earth for his possession."[31] In short, the board took as its mission the obligation to spread Christianity to every corner of the globe. It also shared and acted upon set of ideas about the universality and supremacy of American cultural values. Men like the Reverends Samuel Worcester and Timothy Dwight shared a sense of duty to "save" the "heathen" living in places like India, what is now the American West, and, ultimately, Hawai'i.[32] Yet theirs was a particular brand of salvation—having as much to do with dispensing "civilization" to the remotest parts of the world as with spreading the Gospel. The two, in fact, were inextricably bound together in the early American mission movement. Moreover, ideas about civilization bore deeply gendered imprints, shaping the ABCFM's concept of the duties of missionaries who fell under its authority and helping to define the relationships among missionaries and non-Christians around the globe.

The ABCFM sent its first company of missionaries to India in 1812. The entire enterprise was a disaster. Landing in India was more complicated than any of the missionaries had envisioned at home, and indeed, the missionaries quickly realized that "the British East India Company was formed" for entirely "commercial purposes" and without any regard to the "religious condition and destiny of millions." The missionaries were thus forced to plead their case to company officials for the establishment of a mission. They were unsuccessful, and the ABCFM ordered them to return home. Disheartened, perhaps, but undeterred, the missionaries determined to find some other site "not subject to the Company's control." At about this time, missionary Samuel Newell's wife, Harriet, grew ill and died. From there, the mission deteriorated further. Some of the missionaries left the service of the board for health reasons, while others left for theological ones. Within a few years, the India mission virtually fell apart.[33]

Yet neither missionaries who remained in the field nor the mission board at home appeared defeated by their failure to successfully Christianize the "heathen" in India. In fact, their failures seemed to inspire the board to invest its efforts—and its funds—into a redoubled mission project around the globe. In 1818 the ABCFM printed and distributed a text entitled *The Conversion of the World*, written by Samuel Newell and Gordon Hall, who had participated in the failed experiment and paid a personal price for it. Nevertheless, Newell and Hall lamented that "Idolatry and superstition" prevailed "over the greatest part of the human race" and pointed to several specific locations around the globe that were "peopled with human beings in the most deplorable state of wretchedness and ignorance." They maintained faith in the mission project, declaring: "[T]he gospel of Christ is the

+ Salvation tied w/ civilization, gender

remedy." Newell and Hall presented the problem of irreligion in terms of its scope: by their calculations, despite missionaries' best efforts, there remained "six hundred millions of the human race, to whom Christ has not yet been preached." If heathenism persisted around the world, it was due to heathens' childlike ignorance of the Gospel. If only there were more missionaries able and willing to go wherever they were most needed, the authors argued, the "six millions" might be saved.[34]

If The Conversion of the World provided a reading Christian public with a sense of the sheer magnitude of the problem of irreligion, another text offered a more personal account that stressed the effects of God's saving grace. Moreover, it was a case with which many New England Christians were already familiar. In 1818 the ABCFM published The Memoirs of Henry Obookiah. Though his story had already been told as part of The Narrative of Five Youths, which chronicled New England Christians' efforts on behalf of Ōpūkahaʻia and four other Hawaiians, Ōpūkahaʻia's story took on new meaning and new urgency in 1818. Indeed, while Ōpūkahaʻia's "discovery" in New Haven came at a critical moment for the formation of the ABCFM, his death of typhoid came at an equally important moment for the organization of a mission to Hawaiʻi. His memoir, published at his death, operated as a story of Christian uplift and transformation. The narrative detailed Ōpūkahaʻia's journey from paganism to spiritual enlightenment and from savagery to civility, often conflating the two. As Ōpūkahaʻia embraced the Gospel, he seemed to become not only more Christian but more civilized. The mission board congratulated itself on its part in changing Ōpūkahaʻia from the "clumsy . . . and dull" young man, ignorant of God's word, whom Dwight had first encountered at Yale to the handsome, polished, and thoroughly Christianized individual depicted in the published Memoirs.[35] The narrative suggested that, owing as much to his own discipline and intellect as to missionary determination, patience, and forbearance, Ōpūkahaʻia found salvation. Having learned and accepted the word of God, he died a saved man. Yet, according to the memoir, Ōpūkahaʻia perished before he attained a much more earthly but no less noble goal: spreading the Gospel to his countrymen in Hawaiʻi.

The Memoirs circulated widely in New England immediately after its publication. In fact, the thin volume became a best seller. The text assisted in spreading awareness about Hawaiʻi and its people and also served as a fundraising tool: proceeds from its sale were directly applied to the mission itself and to support a Foreign Mission School in Connecticut. The Memoirs spoke to New England Christians generally but resonated most deeply with

— Anecdotes including O's, of conversion, Civilization
— bestseller

mission hopefuls. Ōpūkahaʻia's story both allowed and encouraged young men and women to connect the concepts of benevolence and Christian uplift with one of the "six millions" Newell and Hall had written about. Yet men and women often differed in the way they connected with these ideas. As missionary descendent Albertine Loomis observed in a late-edition introduction to the *Memoirs*, many men who read the book "sent generous gifts to the American Board to help finance a mission to the Sandwich Islands." Women, on the other hand, "read it and let it be known that they would go gladly to the Pacific if only young missionaries who needed 'companions' would look their way."[36]

Men and women, in fact, had different paths available to them when it came to the foreign-mission cause. For those who hoped to provide aide, men more often had the means to make significant contributions. Women, of course, also gave money, but they did so more often as members of benevolent societies and thus donated not as individuals but as part of a collective with a shared interest in the missionary cause. For those women who sought direct access to the mission, their participation was shaped by reigning American cultural ideas about men and women's basic and inherent capacities. Those ideas were nurtured further within the ABCFM, which defined the nonnegotiable rules of engagement for its members. Men who wanted to be assigned to the mission field needed three things: an education, a trade, and a bride. Of women, the board only required a husband and demonstrable piety. Though men had to acquire more training for their engagement in the mission, they nevertheless enjoyed greater direct access to the missionary's "path of duty" than did their female counterparts.

In fact, the mission movement seemed to favor men like Samuel Whitney, who was perhaps best described as a "man of medium capacity."[37] Whitney was born to a somewhat poor but respectable family; nevertheless, as a young man, he had grown "disobedient, and wicked." Relatively speaking, Samuel Whitney had a late conversion. Coming to his faith in his twenties, he determined to improve his condition and to devote himself to God—and to "the missionary cause."[38] Fortunately for Samuel, the president of Yale College, Timothy Dwight, actively and earnestly believed in the democracy of the Second Great Awakening. That is, Dwight believed in young men's capacity to improve their situation in this life in addition to the next. Under Dwight's leadership, Yale became a veritable training ground for some of the mission movement's most active male members.[39] Samuel studied at Yale for two years, even earning support from the "Education Society" there.[40]

Yet Samuel was a work in progress. Even those who liked him personally described him as both an unrefined man and an unremarkable pupil. One letter writer discretely predicted that Samuel would make a "respectable, but not distinguished," teacher.[41] Nevertheless, Samuel—like the other male members of the first company—had the opportunity to make his own destiny. In 1819 he learned that the ABCFM was actively organizing a mission to Hawai'i. Though he had not yet completed his training at Yale, Samuel appealed to the board for a position as a schoolmaster.[42]

Knowing the board's requirements, the men who wrote letters on Samuel's behalf spoke to his training. Samuel, however, had less education and was thus slightly less qualified than the other men who were ultimately deployed to the Hawaiian Islands.[43] In the first company, all of the male missionaries had pursued at least some formal education. Samuel Whitney attended Yale, as did the Reverend Asa Thurston. Thurston also attended Andover Theological Seminary, where Hiram Bingham also trained. Indeed, six of the seven male missionaries in the first company had acquired theological or seminary training in preparation for their work.[44] The pattern remained for missionary men of subsequent companies, who held degrees from Yale, Dartmouth, and Princeton, among other institutions. These men, too, had either seminary training or had attended—if even briefly—the mission school at Cornwall.[45] Male mission hopefuls, in short, understood that in order to participate in a foreign mission, they would need adequate training for the work the ABCFM expected of them.

Male mission hopefuls also knew that the governing board actively sought individuals with the skills necessary for a successful mission. In stating its goals, the board insisted that it would use "preachers, catechists, school masters and the press" in an effort to "propagate the gospel among unevangelized nations."[46] The occupational makeup of missionary companies sent to the Hawaiian Islands is, in fact, revealing. It not only indicates the ABCFM's sense of its own needs and priorities in terms of Christianizing Hawaiians, but it also suggests some of the purely pragmatic reasons why, in the first years of the Hawaiian Islands mission, the board regarded men as more desirable candidates than their female counterparts. It also illustrates the board's plan for conversion and demonstrates the way in which gendered assumptions about education and missionizing were mutually reinforcing. That is, men had greater access to the kinds of training the ABCFM was looking for in its missionaries, and thus they enjoyed greater access to direct mission work.

— Most had some higher ed or seminary training

— Gendered views on education, missionizing

The board, for example, was careful to send a physician with the first three companies, presumably to care for the continued health and safety of its members.[47] Thomas Holman filled that role in the first company. Though Holman's stay in the islands was exceptionally brief, missionaries in the islands and the board at home learned by experience that the presence of a physician could smooth the way for relations between the missionaries and Hawai'i's ali'i, who valued the skills that physicians brought with them. Moreover, missionaries quickly learned how useful a doctor might be to the newly formed mission families. Within a year of the missionaries' arrival, four of the seven missionary wives gave birth. Holman, however, was not there to attend the wives. After a number of disputes—having to do with personal matters as well as the issue of pay—Thomas and Lucia Holman severed their ties with the mission and returned to America in the summer of 1820. The board sent a physician with each of the next two companies; Abraham Blatchley accompanied the second company, while Gerrit Parmele Judd was a member of the third.[48]

The ABCFM also sent printers to attend to the business of creating a Hawaiian-language Bible. Missionaries to Hawai'i and elsewhere generally and vigorously agreed on the value of a printed Bible in spreading the Gospel. The mission board sent Elisha Loomis with the first company of missionaries to Hawai'i—along with a printing press—to accomplish just such a task. Yet missionaries Gordon Hall and Samuel Newell had warned that the "indiscriminate distribution" of the Bible would prove "but little better than throwing it away." They fretted that in the absence of clergy trained to interpret and teach the Gospel, true conversions would be few and far between—if they came at all. "*There is no instance on record of a nation being evangelized by the Bible,*" they insisted, "*without the preaching of the Bible.*" The board concurred, clearly envisioning evangelizing and education as critical and related elements of the missionaries' work.[49] The first companies were, in fact, predominated by ordained or licensed clergy and teachers. Hiram Bingham and Asa Thurston—members of the first company—were both ordained prior to their departure. Samuel Ruggles deployed as a teacher. Samuel Whitney was also a teacher, though he was later licensed to preach and was ultimately ordained.[50]

In its earliest years, then, the ABCFM consistently assigned the officially sanctioned work of the mission—preaching, teaching, printing, and healing—to its male members. The correlation was hardly coincidental. In keeping with nineteenth-century ideas about the proper and inherent roles of men and women, men enjoyed almost exclusive access to the kind of education and training the board was looking for in its missionaries. Yet even sufficiently educated and trained men were not assured a place in the mission; young men needed wives in order to qualify for the work.

The ABCFM worried in particular about protecting the morality of male missionaries. The board fretted over the seductive influence of native women on single, sexually vulnerable missionary men. The board's anxiety suggests the way in which nineteenth-century American gender ideologies were also wrought up in ideas about race.[51] Though the board's thinking about its own missionaries most often reflected larger cultural notions about the virile and aggressive masculinity inherent to men and the passivity of women, the marital requirement revealed a budding concern over the possibility of men's moral frailty. Moreover, by casting mission wives as likely guardians of male virtue, the board opened the door to a new interpretation of women's place within the mission. At the same time, the marital requirement pointed to and perhaps reinforced a set of racial distinctions based on ideas about gender. White women's assumed sexual virtue illuminated the supposed moral degeneracy of native women, thereby clearing a space of Christian women's participation—either as protectors of male virtue or elevators of native women's sexual morality.[52]

Either way, missionary men knew the board's policy: without a wife, they could not be assigned to the mission field. Yet just weeks prior to the mission's scheduled departure for Hawai'i, most of the missionary hopefuls were still unattached. Only Daniel Chamberlain, in fact, was married. While their unmarried status presented a problem, it was not an insurmountable one. Young women like Mercy Partridge who were eager to participate in the foreign mission often made their availability as brides known to clergy members in their community. Interested men might then make discrete inquiries with local pastors about the availability of a woman willing to marry a young missionary and accompany him to the mission field. On this basis, suitable matches could be made.[53] The board fully supported such a method of introduction; in fact, it generated a list of young women likely to agree to such partnerships—women who were "'missionary minded' as well as being young, pious, educated, fit, and reasonably good-looking."[54] Such was the case for Mercy Partridge and Samuel Whitney. The pastor of Mercy's church, Heman Humphrey, formally introduced the pair six weeks before the *Thaddeus* set sail for the Hawai'i. The couple married a few weeks later on October 4, 1819.[55]

In the pioneer company of missionaries, such marriages were the norm rather than the exception. Subsequent companies followed a similar pattern.

— Protective of male missionaries' morality — wives
— Moral degeneracy of native women
*Women/men eager to marry for these purposes specifically!!

Portraits of Mercy and Samuel Whitney, who joined the first company of missionaries to the Hawaiian Islands. (Samuel F. B. Morse, artist; courtesy Mission Houses Museum Library)

While clergy brought the Whitneys together, other couples met by way of close mutual friends or family. This was precisely the case for Lucy Goodale and Asa Thurston. Lucy's cousin William introduced the two in the fall of 1819. Upon meeting Lucy, Asa informed her that "a mission to the Sandwich Islands was to sail in four or six weeks. "At length," Lucy recalled, "having prepared my mind, the proposition was made." Their courtship lasted all of three weeks. In six weeks' time, the couple had met, married, and set sail on a dangerous and life-altering journey.[56] Women, of course, sometimes refused their suitors; such was the case with Hiram Bingham's first proposal to a woman who decided it was "not her duty to go," much to Hiram's distress. Fortunately for Hiram, Sybil Moseley was on the lookout for a groom. The two met at Hiram's ordination in September 1819.[57] Thus, virtually all the women who set sail for Hawai'i in 1819 accepted their grooms on little more than a recommendation.

Eager to participate in the foreign-mission movement but prevented from becoming full-fledged missionaries, women like Mercy Partridge found and exploited an alternative—though culturally respectable—means of access. Mission-minded women, in fact, skillfully negotiated the sometimes conflicting ideas regarding women's role in society that emerged in the late eighteenth and early nineteenth centuries. On the one hand, they remained confined by an ideology that suggested a particular and proper domain of women's activity: the home and the family. On the other hand, they benefited from an emergent democratic ideal that promised to widen their sphere of influence and activity. Offering themselves as wives in order to participate in the mission field, missionary-minded young women expressed little resistance to the domestic ideal. In fact, they actively described themselves in gender-specific terms, positioning themselves in reference to the role the board envisioned for them.[58] That is, missionary women actively sought out mission work as a means by which to meaningfully participate in American religious life while still observing the gendered norms of the day.[59]

As the small band prepared to commit themselves "to the winds and the waves, for conveyance to far distant Islands of the Sea, there to spend the remainder of [their] days," the ABCFM drafted a set of instructions to guide their labors. The board was particularly careful that there should not be any confusion about the roles that each member would play, offering clear directives to the missionaries and their wives. The board reminded its missionaries that they committed themselves to the "arduous" and "momentous" work in the "high and holy service of Christ"; they were expected to comport themselves accordingly. While the board assumed that the principles would be familiar to the small group, they nevertheless insisted that they could not be "too often reiterated, or too strongly enforced." In short, the board instructed missionaries to "aim at nothing short of covering those islands with fruitful fields and pleasant dwellings, and schools and churches; of raising up the whole people to an elevated state of Christian civilization." In keeping with their training, and in line with such an ambitious charge, the board members tasked the men of the mission with giving Hawaiians both the Bible and the "skill to read it." The board acknowledged that the labor ahead of the missionaries was "great and difficult"; at the same time, it reminded the group of their commitment to the cause: "You have given yourself to him for this service; you have made your vows, and you cannot go back."[60]

Though the ABCFM's instructions to "the beloved females of the mission" were much more brief than those they offered to the men, the providential committee clearly articulated their vision of women's role within the mission. The board leapt at the opportunity to remind women of their essential nature by insisting that women's designation as "help meet for man" was more than a merely temporal one. Indeed, it was a role for which the "sovereign goodness . . . fitted them." Favorably comparing mission wives to "helpers of the apostles" who had "labored much in the Lord," the board spelled out the duties women could expect to perform in the mission field. They were perhaps disappointingly similar to the ones they might fulfill as wives at home in New England. Mission wives, the board suggested, might best help the mission by simply assisting "the brethren." In addition to the "various cares" for which they were responsible in the home, women might employ "their affectionate offices" and "cheering influences." Both appeared important to the functioning of the mission. Yet the board also implied that women's very presence in the mission field might be a positive and beneficial one. Though the board explicitly denied women an official place in the mission, they nevertheless left a space for their participation by hinting at the "salutary and vivifying influence" women might impart to the islanders the missionaries hoped to convert.[61] Yet even this suggestion painted women's role in the mission as a passive rather than active one. The board clearly regarded the men of the mission as the primary agents in the task of converting the "heathen" to a more Christian, civilized state. Mission literature produced in this period reveals that even in an era of supposedly "feminized" religious culture, men were regarded as the only legitimate arbiters of religious doctrine.[62] Where the men of the mission—whether teachers, doctors, or clergymen—expected to assume an assertive stance in converting their heathen subjects, women would serve a supportive role from their place in the home.[63]

The organization of the mission appeared much on the minds of New England clergy, who reiterated the ABCFM's message in the weeks leading up to the missionaries' departure. In September, the Reverend Heman Humphrey delivered a sermon to mark the occasion of the ordination of the Reverends Hiram Bingham and Asa Thurston. In it, he directed the men of the mission to search their souls for affirmation of their ability and willingness to take part in such a challenging undertaking as the one before them. While Humphrey took up a language of deference and subservience to God, he nevertheless portrayed missionary men as actors—and sometimes aggressive ones—in the drama of Christianizing the Sandwich Islands. Humphrey reminded the missionaries that as God's servants, they "offered [themselves] for the missionary service." Yet Humphrey also relied on a rhetoric of aggressive manliness to describe their work. He dubbed the men of the mission "soldiers of the cross, in the holy war" and exclusively charged them with the task of "assail[ing] the strongholds . . . of pagan idolatry."[64] Male missionaries, he insisted, had a vigorous labor ahead of them. Clearly, the job of Christianizing was not for the faint of heart, nor for the "weaker sex."

Thomas H. Gallaudet also marked out the distinctive paths of the men and women who would live and work among Hawaiians, though he spoke at greater length on the role of women who recently committed themselves to the mission cause. Echoing the board's sentiments, Gallaudet reminded his listeners that woman had been "sent by heaven as an help-meet for man." As such, women were "designated to share and soothe" their husbands' sorrows and to "lighten [their] cares." In the mission field, a wife had an even greater role, however. Gallaudet envisioned the mission wife as one who might "invigorate by her kind remonstrances" her husband's "languishing efforts in the path of duty." Though women possessed "less active courage" than the men they married, they nevertheless had an important role to play in the home, keeping "bright the lamp of domestic piety" to embolden their husbands "in the tumultuous bustle of the world."[65] Gallaudet thus underscored for his listeners the proper but complementary roles men and women might play in the mission. Gallaudet's meditation on the duties of husbands and wives could not have come at a more appropriate time. The October 11 gathering was not solely a "meeting for prayers, with reference to the Sandwich Islands Mission"; it was also the occasion of Hiram and Sybil Bingham's wedding. The message likely resonated deeply with the newly married couple, as well as with the rest of the small band as they set off to Christianize the world.

CHAPTER 3 *When Worlds Collide*

The little band of missionaries found ample time to reflect on their new situation on board the *Thaddeus*, their home and "abode" for the foreseeable future. The first days at sea were rough. In November, one mission wife remarked that the weather was "boisterous" and the wind "contrary."[1] Weather conditions not only threatened to hamper the pace of the journey; it also made the missionaries and their wives seasick. Moreover, some of the company began to realize just how far from home they were. Sybil Moseley Bingham confessed that three months into the journey she felt "truly like a pilgrim and a stranger" with no "abiding place." As she lamented: "[A]ll the objects of my heart" seemed "far, far away."[2] Bingham and her new mission family, however, did not give in to despair; instead, the journey seemed to provide new opportunities for the group to recommit itself to its evangelical project. In January, as the *Thaddeus* rounded Cape Horn and the mission band "gaze[d] upon" the region's "rude coasts," Bingham reflected on the work to be done in Hawai'i. "Here, as there," she wrote, "'No gospel's joyful sound' is heard." She regretted that the "poor souls" the missionaries passed knew "no other scepter than that of the Prince of darkness." Yet Bingham was hopeful that "the day is hastening when they shall."[3]

Bingham carried this confidence with her into the spring, when the *Thaddeus* sailed near the coast of Hawai'i. On March 30, 1820, Bingham reported that Thomas Hopu, one of the mission's Hawaiian assistants, called out to the slumbering missionaries: "Land appears!" After a trying sea journey, the mission band came into "full view" of Hawai'i, "that dark pagan land so long the object" of missionaries' "most interested thoughts." The excitement on board the *Thaddeus* must have been nearly palpable. As Bingham wryly observed: "[T]here was but little sleep." In the morning, a small crew went ashore to "inquire into the state of things." They returned with news that stunned all those still gathered on board. "Kamehameha is dead!" they reported. "The government is settled in the hands of his son, Liholiho . . . the taboo system is no more . . . the idol gods are burned!" It took some time for the missionaries and their wives to absorb the astonishing news.

Confidence & excitement

They could only interpret the changes as a sign of God's will. "The Lord," it seemed, had "gone before" the missionaries, clearing a space for their work in the islands.[4]

Despite the missionaries' optimism regarding the success of their endeavor, they faced numerous challenges. First, the Hawaiians—maka'āinana and ali'i alike—expressed little interest in Christianity. The king and his chiefs, in particular, appeared indifferent to the missionaries' project and proved difficult to convert. It was not simply, as American Board of Commissioners of Foreign Missions corresponding secretary and mission historian Rufus Anderson later wrote, that Hawaiians, "having abolished one religion without any religious motives," felt "in no haste to come under the restraints of another."[5] In fact, the king and his chiefs seemed exceptionally tolerant of—if not more interested in—the French Catholics who had recently arrived in the islands. Second, and a related point, was the fact that the missionaries had to compete with other groups for Hawaiians' attentions. By the time the first company of missionaries arrived in 1820, the islands were virtually teeming with foreigners from around the globe who arrived with political, economic, and religious interests.[6] Many had already established relationships with the islands' ali'i. Third, missionaries also encountered an unfamiliar gender hierarchy, one that compelled them to negotiate directly not just with the islands' new kuhina nui (coruler), Ka'ahumanu, but with other women of rank. American missionaries' arrival coincided, then, with both a period of rapid transformation already well under way and the rise of Ka'ahumanu's growing political authority.

As under Kamehameha, Hawai'i's ali'i in the early part of the nineteenth century continued to engage with foreigners from around the globe, who came not only with different aims for Hawai'i and its people but also with different cultural styles for conducting those exchanges. The French, who arrived in the islands just ahead of the missionaries, provide an excellent example of both the distinct and "variegated" character of the foreign presence in Hawai'i and Hawaiians' skillful negotiations with their foreign guests. Like Kamehameha, ali'i continued to absorb some of the changes that foreigners brought with them while steadfastly negotiating their relationships with outsiders on the most favorable terms possible. These negotiations sometimes left little space for the American missionaries, who were relative newcomers to the islands.

When the small band of missionaries departed from Boston, they had no way of knowing that Hawai'i's powerful King Kamehameha had already perished. The missionaries, in fact, fully expected to find "the old

Louis Choris's portrait of Kaʻahumanu. The portrait, which Choris titled Cohoumanou, reine des iles Sandwich, was first published in 1822 and circulated among an elite European audience. (Lithograph by Norblin, after Louis Choris; courtesy Bishop Museum, www.bishopmusum.org)

King Kamehameha ruling the Islands with despotic power, and zealously upholding idolatry." Upon landing in Hawaiʻi, however, they learned that Kamehameha's young son, Liholiho (also called Kamehameha II), ruled as the islands' mōʻī. Yet the young king's authority in the islands was far from absolute. At a ceremony held days after Kamehameha's death that conferred the new king's title, the deceased king's favored widow, Kaʻahumanu, disclosed to Liholiho that Kamehameha had named her kuhina nui (chief counselor). Kaʻahumanu declared: "We two shall share the rule over the land." As kuhina nui, Kaʻahumanu became coruler of the Hawaiian Islands.[7] Endowed with this new role, the already-powerful Kaʻahumanu increased her political influence overnight.

Kaʻahumanu and Keōpūolani, Liholiho's mother, wasted no time in urging Liholiho to abolish the ʻaikapu (sacred eating) and to establish ʻainoa (free eating) throughout the islands. Under Kamehameha's reign, the kapu laws governed virtually every aspect of daily life and helped to protect—and in some cases, reify—aliʻi's power.[8] The ʻaikapu prohibited men and women, including aliʻi, from eating together. Moreover, women were prohibited from eating coconuts, bananas, pork, and other flesh foods.[9] Though Kaʻahumanu and Keōpūolani applied persistent pressure upon the king,

Kaʻahumanu (former wife) co-ruler

encouraging him to participate in free eating, Liholiho was slow to accede to their wishes, and for good reason: as mōʻī, Liholiho had a great deal to lose in the abolition of the kapu system. Moreover, he knew that he lacked widespread support in this and other matters. Liholiho thus proceeded cautiously to assure the stability of his newly acquired authority.[10]

Nevertheless, Kaʻahumanu and Keōpūolani began their campaign just one day after Kamehameha's death. Mission and Hawaiian historians alike later took great interest in the establishment of free eating, though they did so for different reasons and arrived at different interpretations. While I explore the meanings that missionaries ascribed to these events in chapter 5, this chapter focuses on Hawaiian historical accounts to center those perspectives. Samuel Kamakau recounted that almost immediately after Kamehameha's passing, Keōpūolani "ate coconuts which were taboo to women." She also engaged in mixed-sex eating when she "took food with the men." The very next day, when Keōpūolani greeted Liholiho at the ceremony marking his reign, she "put her hand to her mouth as a sign of free eating." As Kamakau later reflected, "this was a strange thing for [her] to do" since she stood to benefit from the kapu laws. Moreover, he recognized the long-reaching significance: what motive would the common people have to observe the ʻaikapu if the aliʻi no longer did? According to historical accounts, Keōpūolani later dined with Liholiho's younger male sibling, Kauikeaouli, who would become Kamehameha III. According to Kamakau, Liholiho still was not persuaded; he looked on as the pair engaged in a flagrant violation of the ʻaikapu. Several months later, Kaʻahumanu prevailed upon Liholiho to join her at a feast at Kailua, insisting that a "ti leaf tabu" would be declared upon his arrival. According to Kamakau, the ti leaf tabu effectively negated old kapus and meant that "any new [kapus] would not have power." Liholiho at last assented. He knew "what was going on at Kailua" and elsewhere on the island; the ʻaikapu was eroding under his rule, not just with Kaʻahumanu's approval but at her urging. When Liholiho arrived at Kailua after a two-day sea journey, "hogs and dogs were immediately baked, other provisions were made ready, and chiefs male and female . . . sat down and feasted together." During the fete, Kaʻahumanu pressed Liholiho to "make eating free over the whole kingdom." The king consented, issuing orders for the abolition of the ʻaikapu. At the same time, Liholiho ordered that the heiaus be destroyed and the idols burned.[11] Though the ʻaikapu was, in fact, already in decline, having been broken by elite and common women alike on many occasions, Kaʻahumanu and Keōpūolani urged Liholiho to strike a profound symbolic blow against Hawaiʻi's religious system.[12] Moreover, they did so at almost the precise moment that the missionaries set sail from Boston. Yet it was only in retrospect that missionaries recognized the royal women's role in overturning the 'aikapu. Yet, as chapter 5 will show, missionary writers' interpretation of the women's actions was strikingly at odds with those put forth by Hawaiian historians.

Though the missionaries misidentified the source of transformation, they were nevertheless overjoyed to learn that Hawai'i's religious system had been dismantled. Indeed, it seemed to presage the introduction of Christianity to the islands. Yet the missionaries quickly discovered that they had their work cut out for them, kapus or no kapus. Just after landing, a number of Hawaiians paddled out to investigate the anchored ship and its inhabitants. Hiram Bingham reported that the missionaries were likewise curious, "but the appearance of destitution, degradation, and barbarism, among the chattering, and almost naked savages" was almost more than the missionaries could bear. According to Bingham, many of the missionary band were moved to tears at the sight. Some looked away. Yet the "spectacle" before them seemed to steel their resolve and sense of purpose. Bingham confessed that he struggled with his initial response, only to emerge recommitted to the project. "Can such beings be civilized? Can they be Christianized? Can we throw ourselves upon these rude shores, and take up our abode, for life, among such a people, for the purpose of training them for heaven?" If the need to "save" the islands' "heathen" had begun to seem abstract during the missionaries' months-long sea voyage, the presence of flesh-and-blood Hawaiians galvanized Bingham. "Though faith had to struggle for the victory," Bingham wrote, "these interrogatories could all be answered decidedly in the affirmative."[13]

Missionaries interpreted Hawaiians' interest in the ship and its occupants and the news of the islands' recent religious upheaval as positive and encouraging signs. While the "swarms" of Hawaiians who paddled out to the *Thaddeus* unsettled the missionaries, such attention and interest seemed to bode well for their future prospects in the islands. Moreover, many of the missionaries saw the hand of "divine providence" in the overthrow of the islands' kapu laws, ensuring their success there. Hiram Bingham recalled the missionaries' response upon hearing the news. "[O]ur hearts [were] surprised, agitated and encouraged beyond every expectation," he wrote. "The hand of God! How visible in the beginning to answer the prayer of his people for the Hawaiian race!"[14]

The mission band seemed so entranced by this vision of the Hawaiians' easy conversion that they seemed only peripherally aware of the obstacles

—Missionaries encouraged by Kapu abolition;
interest in ships

that stood in their way. Most immediate was the problem of gaining approval to begin the work they had come to do. More than a week after landing in Hawai'i, the missionaries were still on board the *Thaddeus*, awaiting permission to land. Negotiations on this point were stalled not as a result of the Hawaiians' "great indolence and total disregard to the worth of time," as some of the mission band suspected, but because of the natives' lack of interest and, in some cases, skepticism regarding the missionaries' intentions.[15] Indeed, ali'i had inherited a healthy skepticism of foreigners from Kamehameha. One of the king's interpreters, the diminutive Frenchman Jean Rives, advised Liholiho against admitting the missionaries at all. The king seemed to take Rives's advice into consideration, hindering speedy approval. While the missionaries were frustrated at the delay, they failed to recognize that the matter of their admission was hardly a pressing one for ali'i, who were in no hurry to reach a conclusion on the matter. In fact, Englishman John Young advised the missionaries that the ali'i might take upwards of six months to make a decision on their situation. Young had served as an adviser to Kamehameha and acted in the same capacity under Liholiho, and he was thus in a position to guess at the missionaries' most likely outcome—if not to help shape it. Yet the missionaries felt that they had waited long enough to begin God's work; Hiram Bingham confided that they were "unwilling to wait six months for permission to debark."[16] Growing impatient, the missionaries pressed for a resolution.

The missionaries made three separate attempts to gain permission to land and establish a mission. According to Bingham, the missionaries "visited the king and chiefs" in the first part of April in an effort to "make their acquaintance and secure their confidence." The missionaries asked that some of the mission party be allowed to remain at Kailua while the rest traveled on to Honolulu. Bingham revealed the missionaries' intention to focus their evangelical attentions on the king when he wrote that the arrangement "would be far better" than for all the missionaries to "leave the king, and go to Oahu, or for all to remain with him at Kailua, which he was proposing to leave ere long." Liholiho, however, was suspicious of the missionaries' motives, believing that "all white men" preferred O'ahu. In fact, he believed that "the Americans" aimed to "have that island." Liholiho thus denied their request, but he did not send them away. Instead, the king offered the missionaries permission to land at Kailua temporarily. The missionaries were "disheartened" at the outcome, but not discouraged.[17]

On April 10, the missionaries made a second attempt. On that day, "all the brethren repaired to the shore to do what was practicable to get the royal permission" to proceed with the plan they had previously outlined. Instead, the king said that he "should wait till the return of Kaahumanu. She had gone on a fishing excursion."[18] The missionaries, unfamiliar with the islands' power structure, appeared surprised and somewhat suspicious when it appeared that the king could not make a definitive resolution about whether or not they would be allowed to stay without first conferring with Ka'ahumanu. Indeed, one report published in the *Missionary Herald* relayed that though the assembled council of chiefs regarded the missionaries' requests as "reasonable," they nevertheless "hesitated to say it might be so." According to the report, the chiefs "pretended to be waiting" for Ka'ahumanu to grant the missionaries' request.[19] The missionaries had little choice but to wait.

As fortune would have it, Ka'ahumanu arrived later in the afternoon. Yet while the missionaries regarded her return as a "very favorable event," they persisted in their belief that the king or another male chief would ultimately decide their fate. Missionary accounts suggested that the high-ranking Maui chief Ke'eaumoku—or Governor Cox, as he was also known—might act on their behalf. Ke'eaumoku arrived at "about the same time" as Ka'ahumanu. According to the missionaries, Ke'eaumoku not only enjoyed "great influence" but also spoke English and was "considered as a substantial friend of the whites." The missionaries regarded his return as fortuitous: it came "at the very moment when the important question was pending . . . and when we thought that his influence was most needed."[20] The missionaries perceived Ke'eaumoku's influence to be so great that they counted his return a sure sign of their success. "The Lord," Bingham later recalled thinking, "is on our side."[21]

Despite the missionaries' hopes, however, the matter was not resolved. Ke'eaumoku, in fact, simply did not possess the authority necessary to approve the missionaries' request. They would have to present their case to Liholiho and Ka'ahumanu, who, as the islands' corulers, would decide the matter together. Yet just as the missionaries prepared to do so, "two native dancers and a band of rude musicians, singing and drumming," interrupted them. The missionaries determined that the performance was "probably at the king's order." Diplomacy compelled them to wait patiently until the dancing concluded to state their request. According to Hiram Bingham, when the dancing was at last complete, Liholiho demanded that the missionaries spell out "the useful arts with which the missionaries were acquainted," as well as the missionaries' "qualifications to promote [the] temporal good" among the Hawaiian people. The missionaries obediently

— Missionaries had to wait for Ka'ahumanu —co-ruler ct

complied, arguing for the myriad benefits of a Christian mission. The missionaries "gave [their] aloha" and left Liholiho and Ka'ahumanu to "hold a consultation by night." After nearly two weeks of waiting, the missionaries hoped they were at last near "a favorable answer."[22]

The following morning, nearly two weeks after the missionaries' arrival in the islands, Sybil Bingham wrote that they were "still on board the *Thaddeus*." The delay seemed curious to her. She felt "not the least hostility on the part of the natives; on the contrary," she regarded them as quite "friendly." In this circumstance, it was "difficult to say why we are so delayed."[23] Later that day, however, the missionaries at last gained permission to establish a mission—but only on a probationary basis. The group would be allowed to remain in the islands for one year. Though they regarded this as a "very short probation for such an experiment," the missionaries did not press for a greater commitment; nor did they ask for any greater concessions. Indeed, as Hiram Bingham later noted, "this was as much as it was prudent to ask at the time." The group likely recalled what had happened to the first band of American missionaries who had been deployed to India, and they wished to avoid a similar outcome.[24]

As part of their agreement with the missionaries, ali'i made specific requests regarding the division of the missionaries. While they allowed some of the missionaries to continue on to Honolulu as the missionaries proposed, Liholiho stipulated that Dr. Thomas Holman be stationed at Kailua "on account of his art."[25] The missionaries determined that "one of the ordained missionaries" should remain at Kailua in order to "maintain the standard of the gospel" there. They elected the Reverend Asa Thurston to the post. Thomas and Lucia Holman remained on Hawai'i with Asa and Lucy Thurston, while the remaining missionaries and their Hawaiian assistants sailed on to Honolulu to establish a mission there.[26] Though the missionaries, having so recently bonded, were displeased with the thought of such a separation, they understood that they were not in a position to ask for anything more. Mercy Whitney joined Sybil Bingham in admitting that the separation would be "painful" and "trying." The women harbored emotional as well as practical concerns. In April, as the missionary men hammered out an agreement with Ka'ahumanu and Liholiho, several of the mission wives were pregnant. Dr. Holman's "royal appointment" meant that some of them would likely be without a doctor when the moment of "travail" arrived. Still, both women ascribed the arrangement to the "will of God."[27]

This event constituted the missionaries' first set of negotiations with ali'i and suggested the missionaries' tenuous place in the islands. The protracted

- Finally, permission for a 1-year mission;
dictate where missionaries will set up (separated)

discussion over the relatively straightforward question of whether or not the missionaries would even be permitted to stay in the islands revealed a simple but troubling fact: Hawaiians were not the eager converts that the missionaries had hoped for or expected when they had departed from Boston. Where Ōpūkahaʻia's example had suggested a people ready and eager for the gift of Christianity, the Hawaiians that missionaries encountered in the first days after their arrival seemed entirely apathetic about the prospect of adopting the missionaries' new religion.[28]

Moreover, while the missionaries credited "divine providence" for permission to establish a mission, they nevertheless had to acknowledge the very real politics of mortal intervention: God may have paved the way for their work, but there was little doubt that Hawaiian men—and women—had cast the final vote in allowing the missionaries to remain in the islands, even on a temporary basis. The realization did not come easily to the missionaries. Indeed, they had to grapple not only with Hawaiians' ambivalent orientation toward the mission but with the unfamiliar gendered hierarchy they encountered in Hawaiʻi. In the official account of these early negotiations—the one published and circulated in New England—the missionaries reported that Keʻeaumoku should be credited with intervening on their behalf. Yet in Hiram Bingham's account, which was published much later, the missionary admitted that Liholiho had not simply "pretended" to await Kaʻahumanu's return. Indeed, perhaps only after reflecting upon his greater experience with aliʻi did he accede that her agreement on the matter was "indispensable" to the missionaries.[29]

In the earliest days of the mission, American missionaries gained insight into an unfamiliar hierarchy. Prior to their departure from Boston, the missionaries might have anticipated that they would have to formally defer to the queen's rank; yet they nevertheless believed that legitimate negotiations about matters of importance to the missionary project would transpire among men. They did not envision negotiating with powerful and politically legitimate women; nor did they imagine that the queen's cooperation would be deemed absolutely crucial.[30] This initial negotiation, then, offered valuable lessons about a power structure in the islands that missionaries would have to learn to negotiate and suggested a foreshadowing of things to come.

Similarly, Liholiho's reluctance to deal with the missionaries and his misgivings about their intentions might have suggested prior relations and allegiances. The missionaries must have noticed, for example, the names of some of the Hawaiians with whom they negotiated. While the vast majority of Hawaiʻi's aliʻi retained their Hawaiian names, others, like "Billy Pitt"

(Kalanimōkū) and "Governor Cox" (Keʻeaumoku) were commonly referred to by English-language names they had acquired in their years of interaction with foreign visitors prior to the missionaries' arrival. The missionaries almost certainly understood the derivations of such names; yet it is less clear that they grasped, in the first days and weeks after their arrival, their significance in terms of connoting the important relationships between the islands' aliʻi and foreign travelers, traders, and explorers.[31] In short order, however, the missionaries became acutely aware of the presence of other foreigners—American and non-American alike. Once in Honolulu, Sybil Bingham observed that there were "many white residents" on the island. While some feigned "outward respect" toward the missionaries, she nevertheless gathered—correctly—that many of them desired" neither us or our message."[32] Moreover, the missionaries could not have missed the fact that some foreign residents—such as the Englishman John Young, the Frenchman Jean Rives, and the Spaniard Don Francisco de Paula Marin—were favorably situated with regards to Hawaiʻi's aliʻi. The American missionaries were not the only foreigners who hoped to exert some influence—religious or otherwise—in the islands, a fact that was much more clear to the islands' aliʻi than to their newly arrived missionary guests.

In fact, recent French intervention in the islands promised to complicate the missionaries' plans for Hawaiʻi's conversion. The French corvette the *Uranie*, captained by Louis de Freycinet, put in at Hawaiʻi in early August 1819, just a few short months after the death of Kamehameha. The captain quickly established a meeting with Liholiho; he hoped to confer with the new king "upon the interests of the French government." During their meeting, the captain reminded Liholiho of the alliance between Hawaiʻi and Great Britain, formed by Kamehameha and George Vancouver more than two decades earlier. Freycinet assured Liholiho that Great Britain and France were also allied; thus, Freycinet was "disposed" to provide "assistance in maintaining peace" in Hawaiʻi while also assuring the king's authority.

Further, Freycinet confessed that he had learned that "some of the chiefs" harbored "bad intentions" with regards to Liholiho. Freycinet was right: Kamehameha's recent death suggested the possibility that some of the islands' chiefs, disaffected by Kamehameha's conquest of the islands, might regain some of their authority. Many of Hawaiʻi's aliʻi shared with the captain and his crew a view of Liholiho as a weak and politically vulnerable leader. As Jacques Arago, a French writer and artist who arrived on board the *Uranie*, averred: "[A] rebel who was the enemy of [Kamehameha] trembled even in the moment of success." Not so with Liholiho, who, in

- Other westerners; many resent the missionaries

- French trying to make inroads w/ Liholiho (who was seen as weak)

stark contrast, appeared as an unthreatening man of "repose." Arago feared that "such a King" would prove totally incapable of "preserv[ing] his crown" against an insurgency.[33]

Freycinet pledged his loyalty to Liholiho and assured him that he planned to make his loyalty to the king known to the islands' mutinous chiefs. Freycinet reported that Liholiho was "well pleased" with this show of support; he called an assembly of chiefs so that Freycinet might make a public "declaration" asserting his allegiance to Liholiho. When the chiefs gathered later that same day, Jean Rives served as the event's interpreter.[34] Through Rives, Freycinet warned that civil war would be bad for the islands' trade relations. "The merchant ships that for so many years sought the Islands for the purposes of carrying on trade," Freycinet intoned, would "no longer wish to call there." Moreover, he threatened, foreign "friends of their King" would act swiftly "against anyone who failed to recognize his authority." Freycinet was pleased to declare that his address "seemed to produce the effect that had been expected."[35]

If Liholiho was "well pleased," Ka'ahumanu appeared less so. The royal woman was skeptical of both the captain's intentions and his effectiveness. She feared that Freycinet's announcement would serve not to stabilize the political situation in Hawai'i but to fuel the rumors, "already spread slyly about," that the French sought control over the Hawaiian Islands and that Liholiho had already ceded the islands to the king of France.[36] Yet Ka'ahumanu appeared alone in her outspoken wariness of the French captain.

During Freycinet's short visit, in fact, some of the ali'i actively sought out relations with the French, creating entanglements that would last well into the future. Kalanimōkū, for example, was baptized as a Catholic aboard the *Uranie* in July. While there remains enormous disagreement about Kalanimōkū's intentions with regards to his spiritual life, historians largely concur that the chief received a Catholic baptism. Freycinet recalled that during one of his many visits to the ship, Kalanimōkū observed the ships' chaplain, the Abbé de Quélen, and inquired about his function. Learning the ecclesiastic's purpose, Kalanimōkū reportedly "begged" the chaplain to baptize him. Kalanimōkū allegedly reported that his mother "had received this sacrament . . . on her deathbed"; he hoped to be baptized, too. The chaplain agreed to the request. The ship's captain made the necessary arrangements for the ceremony, which grew to include not only the novice but also an audience of royal spectators, including Liholiho and Ka'ahumanu. In fact, the party was so large that they could not be accommodated in the boat Freycinet sent to ferry them to the ceremony. "A number of single and double canoes, filled with men and women making up his court," trailed behind. As the party came aboard, the *Uranie* observed the royal processional with an eleven-gun salute.[37]

Freycinet set an elaborate stage on board. "The quarterdeck," Freycinet wrote, was "decorated with flags"; some also bedecked the floors "so that the princesses would have a suitable place to sit." The crew produced chairs so that Liholiho and Ka'ahumanu might be seated according to the European—rather than Hawaiian—style. Freycinet even produced an altar. Once the royal party was gathered comfortably on deck, the chaplain "proceeded in accordance with the customary ritual" to baptize Kalanimōkū. Freycinet described Kalanimōkū as "deeply moved" by the ceremony.[38]

Arago attended the ceremony and captured the shipboard scene in a sketch he made of the event. Though the image seemed to confirm many of the details of Freycinet's account, including the seating arrangements, the décor, and even the presence of the altar, Arago offered a somewhat different version of events. Far from the enthusiastic convert of Freycinet's reckoning, Kalanimōkū as described by Arago was a man of "cunning and perfidious character" and an "enemy" of Liholiho. In Arago's view, Kalanimōkū was less interested in baptism than in "serving foreign interests" while also preserving his own "high station." Arago painted Kalanimōkū as a pretender and an opportunist: the chief "embraced Christianity" only as a means by which to ingratiate himself to his European visitors and to "secure to himself their friendship."[39]

Moreover, Arago understood such maneuvering as growing out of the complicated and contentious political situation in the islands. Arago foresaw a power struggle on the horizon: Kalanimōkū was not the only chief vying for position during a turbulent period of political transition. Arago pointed to Kaumuali'i—the disaffected ruler of Kaua'i—as another source of challenge to the new political regime. Kaumuali'i, Arago wrote, had grown wary of the "yoke that seemed to be imposed on him" by Kamehameha "and resolved to shake it off." As Arago saw it, Hawai'i's chiefs were "preparing for a general contest." It would not be long until Liholiho's power fell into "other hands." Yet if Arago identified problems emanating from within the kingdom of Hawai'i, he also pointed toward Hawai'i's growing political vulnerability from without. Arago hinted that the British were merely waiting "patiently" for civil war to provide the opportunity to claim the islands for themselves. In such a context, Arago argued, Kalanimōkū could not be trusted. He would plan the "ruin of his own country" to assure his own "road to future greatness."[40]

Portrait depicting Kalanimōkū's baptism aboard the Uranie. *(Crepin after Jacques Arago, engraved by Lerouge & Forget, 1824; courtesy Bishop Museum, www.bishopmuseum.org)*

Hawaiian sources confirm the political discord that existed in the islands, but they deny Kalanimōkū's complicity with Freycinet. Native historian John Papa 'Ī'ī, for example, took note of the presence of foreigners and suggested that Kalanimōkū sought baptism under the sway of their powerful influence. 'Ī'ī reported that it was John Young who "told Kalanimōkū that a true Christian was on board" the *Uranie*; it was he who "inspired" the chief to be baptized. Yet 'Ī'ī pointed even more directly at Rives as "the person who encouraged Kalanimōkū" to receive baptism. For 'Ī'ī, Rives's loyalties were clear: "He was born in the country whose warship it was." Samuel Kamakau negated Kalanimōkū's participation in the rite with even greater force, writing that the French captain and clergyman expressed interest in baptizing Kalanimōkū into the Catholic Church only after they learned that he was a high-ranking ali'i—suggesting that they harbored political rather than "merely" religious aims. Moreover, according to Kamakau, Kalanimōkū was never aware "whether what he was doing was right or wrong." Kalanimōkū only understood what was happening, Kamakau protested, "when he felt the water upon him and the sign of the cross." For Kamakau, Kalanimōkū had been the victim of duplicitous and scheming foreigners. Indeed, he

Hawaiian historians deny chief's complicity w/ French, baptism; French had political motives

compared them in skill to men who possessed the clever capacity to "hook the breadfruit, especially that of the topmost branch."[41]

In fact, the truth is likely to be found in some combination of these various accounts. Kalanimōkū experienced political displacement during the redistribution of land that followed Kamehameha's death. While Kamehameha retained control over the land—and an exclusive monopoly over the sandalwood trade—during his lifetime, many of the high chiefs hoped to gain a share of the king's bounty at his death.[42] Where Liholiho was reluctant to dilute the monopoly, aware of the loss of revenue and status it entailed, Ka'ahumanu recognized an opportunity to enhance her own position. In the transition after Kamehameha's death, Ka'ahumanu not only advocated for the redistribution but also absorbed the important political role Kalanimōkū had played under Kamehameha. In this context, Kalanimōkū reached out to his foreign guests in an effort to cultivate useful political friendships and alliances.

Kalanimōkū, in fact, enjoyed a friendly—if not familiar—relationship with the French captain, visiting the *Uranie* prior to his baptism in order to conduct trade and to establish cordial relations with Freycinet. Moreover, despite native protests that the French baptized Kalanimōkū without his consent, the chief hardly behaved like a man distraught over having been deceived. Freycinet reported that the chief and his party—including Liholiho—remained on board the *Uranie* for "refreshments" after the rite was complete. Their celebration lasted into the evening. When the royal party disembarked at dark, they were all quite drunk, according to Freycinet, and armed with additional gifts of brandy from the captain. As the royal party made their way to shore, the captain offered a second salute to his new friends.[43]

Moreover, Kalanimōkū's brother, Boki—the governor of O'ahu—was baptized shortly thereafter when the *Uranie* anchored at Honolulu. As ranking chief on O'ahu, Boki was on hand to greet the French captain as he came ashore. The chief was accompanied by two foreigners: William Heath Davis, an American closely connected to the sandalwood trade, and Francisco de Paula Marin. In addition to nurturing political relations with the ali'i, Marin also cultivated an impressive array of European fruits and vegetables. Upon meeting the trio and touring the island, Freycinet grasped immediately O'ahu's bustling and cosmopolitan character. Freycinet bemoaned that he had not visited O'ahu first, given that he might have "obtained without the least trouble all of the supplies that we had so much difficulty in getting at the other two islands," Maui and Hawai'i. Freycinet wasted no time

—In reality, Kalanimōkū was quite friendly w/ French

—Oahu: cosmopolitan

This image of Oʻahu in the early 1820s not only shows a number of ships in the harbor but also depicts European and American-style structures alongside Hawaiian ones. (© Mystic Seaport, #1956.2111)

conducting necessary business with merchants and other ships at Oʻahu, obtaining foodstuffs and other staples. Yet Boki had business of his own to conduct. According to Freycinet, when the chief learned that his brother had been baptized on Hawaiʻi, he insisted "that he should be allowed the same favor." Like Kalanimōkū, Boki gained Quélen's approval, and on the August 27, Boki boarded the *Uranie* accompanied by his wife and a small entourage of foreign guests to receive a Catholic baptism. While Freycinet believed that Boki sought baptism simply because his brother received it, Arago saw ulterior motives. Once the rite was complete, Arago wrote, Boki "returned on shore with a full sense of the advantage he had derived from it."[44]

Though Kamakau characterized the French as duplicitous schemers, intent on deceiving Hawaiʻi's aliʻi, he nevertheless pointed toward the larger context in which Kalanimōkū and his brother Boki engaged with foreigners. If the French were interested only in capturing the "breadfruit" that rested at the upper branches, they benefited from the islands' destabilized political situation. "On a rainy day," Kamakau wrote, breadfruit appeared presumably like the aliʻi: "thick with gum and sticky," rendering them both easier to capture. That rainy day, Kamakau had to concede, had come once again to Hawaiʻi. As in Kamehameha's day, the island's chiefs in 1819 were "divided" and its leadership uncertain. Yet if foreigners seemed poised to take advantage of Hawai'i's ali'i, high-ranking chiefs like Kalanimōkū and Boki responded by molding the relationships they formed to their own political and economic advantage.[45]

When the missionaries arrived the next spring, then, they encountered a politically destabilized, fractious environment that was characterized by relationships—not just between ali'i and foreigners, but among the ali'i themselves—that they could barely discern or understand. Though the missionaries at first focused on the possibilities suggested by the perceived religious void in the islands, it was nevertheless the case that both the contentious political situation in the islands and the presence of foreigners complicated the missionaries' plans for the easy conversion of the islands' inhabitants. Moreover, missionaries' earliest interactions with Hawaiians revealed the much larger project they would have to undertake in their efforts to Christianize the islands' inhabitants. Everywhere the missionaries looked, they found work to be done: Hawaiians would have to be educated not just in the Gospel but in living a Christian way of life. Ironically, the overthrow of the kapus served to underscore this point for the missionaries: theirs was not simply a matter of replacing one religion with another, or even of converting Hawaiians religiously, but of transforming them culturally.[46] From the missionary point of view, their work could not begin soon enough.

Having successfully negotiated an agreement for their stay in the islands, the missionaries deposited the Holmans and the Thurstons on Hawai'i; the remaining members departed Hawai'i for O'ahu near the middle of April. The group landed at Honolulu on April 14 and reported, somewhat hopefully, that their anchorage there marked the end of the "eventful voyage of 18,000" miles. While they hoped to establish a permanent mission on the island and at last set about the work of saving souls, the missionaries were disappointed to learn they could "not do much business" until Boki returned. When he at last arrived in port, the missionaries learned "that through the influence of strong drink" he was rendered "unfit for business."[47] Ali'i's perceived fondness for "strong drink"—including not only the regional 'awa but also the rum, brandy, wine, and gin that foreign traders brought to the islands—promised to create real difficulty for the mission. As Hiram Bingham scowled, "intemperance" was "as stubborn a foe as any species of idolatry."[48]

In the long term, of course, Bingham was concerned about the prospects of coaxing the chief to worship. This was crucial to their success: the

Missionaries entered destabilized world w/ complex relationships

- Boki (gov. of Oahu) plastered!

missionaries aimed making conversions first among the islands' ali'i in the hopes that the habit would "trickle down" to maka'āinana. Yet Bingham also worried about the mission's much more immediate problem: obtaining suitable shelter. The missionaries had gained temporary lodging in "native-built houses," but they hoped for something more substantial and permanent.[49] In the first days after the missionaries' arrival on O'ahu, Boki appeared "dilatory" regarding the construction of "houses to accommodate the mission." Though it took some time and the pressure of a public meeting, in June Boki at last "commenced . . . the building" of a mission.[50]

Yet the glow of victory on this point was short-lived: internal problems "marred the happiness" the missionaries experienced. In July William Kanui, an assistant to the mission and one of the "five youths" the American Board of Commissioners for Foreign Missions had celebrated so enthusiastically in Boston, "fell to immoral practices" and was excommunicated from the Congregationalist Church. His loss was a real as well as symbolic one for the mission: not only had they lost one of their earliest and most "promising" converts, but the seeming ease of his apostasy also potentially pointed toward the difficult work of conversion that lay ahead.[51]

Worse than losing a new convert, however, was the defection of two of their own. The same month, Thomas and Lucia Holman left their mission station in Hawai'i and traveled to Maui. Ostensibly, the Holmans left the mission station as a result of Lucia's poor health; yet the couple had appeared disagreeable almost from the outset of the journey, and their difficulty relating to the other missionaries and adjusting to a missionary's life began on board the *Thaddeus* and continued into the summer. When the Holmans left Hawai'i island in July, just a few months after their arrival, they did so on their own accord and without the board's approval; nor did they consult members of the mission family, even those stationed with them on Hawai'i. The Holmans faced swift disciplinary action, but the damage had already been done. By the start of 1821, Thomas had been excommunicated from the church; Lucia was placed under suspension. They set sail for Boston later that year.[52] The loss was devastating to the remaining missionaries, less for the impact on individual missionaries themselves than for the threat to the larger mission project.

If the missionaries worried that the breakdown of mission order and hierarchy represented by the loss of three of their cohort set the project off on shaky footing, they were likewise concerned about how Liholiho might interpret their movements. The Holmans' departure meant that the Thurstons were alone in the missionizing project on Hawai'i; their new status

— One couple leaves mission; threat to greater
project
on big island

left them feeling isolated and anxious. Yet if they followed the Holmans to Maui, where Kalanimōkū also resided, they risked incurring the king's displeasure.[53] Not only had Liholiho stipulated that some of the missionaries remain on Hawai'i, but he also retained a lingering rivalry with Kalanimōkū. The missionaries could not appear to have traded their alliance with Liholiho for one with a rival chief. By the end of the year, however, the decision was made for them. Liholiho "and what may be called his court removed from Kailua to Honolulu." Liholiho and Ka'ahumanu arrived at last in the early part of 1821, just as the missionaries approached the anniversary of their landing in Hawai'i.[54] The missionaries' probationary period was nearly expired; they dearly hoped that Liholiho and Ka'ahumanu would see fit to renew their charter. Hiram Bingham viewed the king's relocation as an opportunity to demonstrate the missionaries' intentions "to do him good" and to "elevate the nation" of Hawai'i.[55] Moreover, the king's proximity promised greater opportunity for his education and conversion.

Yet the missionaries ought not to have mistaken the king's intentions. Liholiho's relocation was not motivated by his desire to have greater access to Christian instruction but rather was possibly spurred by the importance of creating a stable seat of government. Whatever his motives, the king was reportedly in no shape to take to either the *palapala* (lessons in English) or the Gospel. When Hawai'i's minister of foreign affairs, Robert Crichton Wyllie, made a report on the effects of spirits in the islands, he reported that Liholiho "was seldom in his senses" during a two-year period spanning from 1821 to 1823. Indeed, Wyllie declared, the king seemed to "have lost all self command." His remarks were based largely on the diary of Don Francisco de Paula Marin, who made note of the king's fluctuating state of sobriety. "This day the king is not very drunk," Marin wrote on March 12, 1821. In May, however, "the king began to drink"; in late May, he was "drunk all the day." Liholiho became so prone to drink that, as one historian has wryly noted, it became easier for Marin, like other foreigners, "to note the days when the king was sober."[56]

The high chiefs' fondness for spirits was a practical problem to be sure: it was difficult to entice the chiefs to worship on days they had been drinking. The chiefs' intemperance also nagged at the missionaries as a moral problem to be solved.[57] Yet whether or not Liholiho was drinking seems, in retrospect, the least of the missionaries' worries. The king, in fact, rarely stayed in one place for very long. Though O'ahu was ostensibly the seat of government, Liholiho made frequent trips through the islands and was rarely available for the kind of religious or educational training the missionaries had in

King Liholiho moves but still not interested & drunk!

mind for the islands' high chiefs.[58] A year into the mission, Kaumuali'i—the high chief on Kaua'i—stood out for his significant progress in learning to read. In this, Bingham later declared, Kaumuali'i "exceeded" the rest of the chiefs, including Liholiho and Ka'ahumanu.[59] Moreover, though the missionaries boasted that both "chiefs and foreigners" pledged their support for the construction of a new church in the fall of 1821, attendance at worship remained sporadic. Neither of the island's high-ranking men—Liholiho and Boki—attended services with any regularity. Missionaries could not count them as converts, nor could they rely on them to set an example for the island's maka'āinana.

The missionaries faced other troubles as well. While they retained friendly relations with some of the island's other foreign guests, they knew that they were not well liked by many of the travelers and traders who came to the islands to conduct business with ali'i or to engage in individual transactions with maka'āinana. Hiram Bingham complained that "the masters and mates, in the Merchant, Whaling, and Naval service" frequently exerted an influence unfavorable "to the peace, reputation, or success of the missionaries."[60] Bingham was not alone in viewing foreigners as adversaries to the mission. Rufus Anderson reported that "unfriendly foreigners" schemed to "undermine the confidence of the rulers and people in the mission." The foreigners, Anderson charged, not only introduced the idea that the missionaries came to enslave Hawaiians but also insisted that friendship with the American band would jeopardize Hawaiians' continued relationship with the English.[61] Liholiho, however, seemed determined not to let the missionary presence interfere with already-established diplomatic or trade relations. In 1821 he made a number of shipboard visits to foreign vessels anchored near Honolulu; he likewise invited guests to visit him and entertained them at home.[62]

Liholiho, then, exhibited only sporadic interest in what the missionaries had to offer, attending to the palapala only occasionally and to public worship infrequently. Though the missionaries quickly established regular worship services and set up "little schools" for the purposes of instructing Hawaiian islanders, they witnessed only slow and halting progress in the islands. A year into the mission, the missionaries had to admit that their strategy for converting Hawai'i's high chiefs simply was not as successful as they had predicted it would be. Here, on "heathen ground," Hawai'i's chiefs proved difficult to convert. If the missionaries hope to succeed in their project of "saving" the islands' inhabitants, they would simply have to find another way.[63]

CHAPTER 4 *Gendered Diplomacy*

Though missionaries' later interactions with Hawaiians proved somewhat frustrating, their initial exchanges seemed promising. Within days of the missionaries' arrival in the Hawaiian Islands in 1820, Kalākua, a widow of the late Kamehameha, came aboard the *Thaddeus*. She was joined by Kalanimōkū, the same chief who had recently been baptized as a Catholic. In the days leading up to their shipboard visit, the missionaries remained anchored off the north shore of Hawai'i, waiting for permission to land. During that time, Kalākua and Kalanimōkū provided sustenance for the missionaries, sending generous gifts of fruit, poi, meat, and cheese. Having endured a months-long sea voyage, the band of missionaries eagerly received the gifts. As one missionary later acknowledged: "[F]resh provisions relish well after living almost a half a year on salt food."[1] Kalākua's visit, however, was not motivated by simple benevolence. The queen, in fact, also brought a piece of cloth aboard. According to mission wife Nancy Ruggles, Kalākua promptly "requested . . . a gown like ours."[2] She was "very particular" that the dress should be prepared in advance of their upcoming meeting with King Liholiho.[3] The missionaries relied upon their interpreter, Thomas Hopu, to explain the restrictions of the Sabbath. "It was the Lord's day," Ruggles demurred. The making of the dress could not begin until the following day at the earliest.[4]

Kalākua's visit to the *Thaddeus* illustrates the vital role of gift giving and exchange in the early period of Hawaiian-missionary contact. As this example demonstrates, gifts served as a primary means of communication between these culturally distinct peoples.[5] In this early exchange, Kalākua relied on the symbolic language of gifts to convey meaning and intention for her interactions with the missionaries. Moreover, both in the act of giving and in requesting a gift of her own in return, the queen attempted to establish the basis for future relations with the missionaries.

In the earliest days of contact, however, Hawaiians and missionaries appear to have had only the most tenuous grasp on the intended meanings of the gifts offered and received from the other. Nevertheless, they shared an

— Initial interactions had seemed promising —
gifts as basis of relationships, communication,
reciprocity

65

interpretation of gift giving as an exchange-oriented activity. That is—as anthropologists later understood—a gift rarely terminates with the recipient; rather, it must be repaid or reciprocated. In this way, gifts create a nearly infinite "cycle of exchange," pulling individuals and groups into continued and sustained contact with one another.[6] Gifts, then, not only function as a means of communication but also serve as active agents in the production of social relationships, even between disparate social groups. In fact, the gifts that missionaries and Hawaiian royalty exchanged in the first weeks and months of their relationship pulled both parties into an enduring cycle of exchange that established the kinds of important diplomatic and political relationships critical to the islands' political future.[7]

In this chapter, I argue that the Hawaiian and American missionary women who came into close and sustained contact with one another in mid-nineteenth-century Hawaiʻi shaped the direction of the mission and the fate of the islands. Indeed, women stood at the very center of the Hawaiian-missionary drama. Hawaiʻi's royal women, in fact, virtually compelled mission wives to participate actively in the mission. Despite missionary notions about women's "place" in the mission, my research reveals that mission wives came to play a central role in sustaining critical diplomatic relations with some of the island's most powerful rulers, including queens and other women of rank.

Gift giving and exchange, I show, functioned in several distinct but related ways. First, gift giving provided a means by which aliʻi might articulate their political authority. Aliʻi demonstrated their power by both giving gifts to missionaries and demanding repayment from them. Second, gift giving emerged as an approved avenue of activity for mission wives who were, in many instances, compelled by Hawaiian women of rank to engage in an activity that became critical to the mission's success. Missionaries came to view the gifts they provided to Hawaiʻi's highest-ranking women—particularly gifts of clothing—as important tools for the conversion of Hawaiians. Third, because gift giving brought women into close and sustained contact with one another, the exchange of things seemed to offer the possibility of producing personal relationships among women—an outcome that the American Board of Commissioners for Foreign Missions would likely have endorsed. Yet I argue that these exchanges also created critical opportunities for political diplomacy.[8] From the earliest days of contact, Hawaiʻi's royal women and missionary wives engaged in an exchange relationship that forever altered the lives of its participants.

Gifts, then as now, are laden with meaning. In their exchange—their conveyance from one party to another—gifts may signal many things, and meanings are sometimes simultaneous.[9] Some American missionaries understood the lavish gifts they received in the first days and weeks after landing as gestures of welcome or extensions of peace and goodwill. Others interpreted the gifts as tribute from a subordinate group to their acknowledged superiors. As such, many missionaries viewed the gift as just and fitting. By shifting perspectives, however, one can see that alternate interpretations abound. Hawaiians, in fact, attached different meanings to the gifts they proffered in their first contact with American missionaries, depending in large part on the status of the giver. Missionaries were unfamiliar with the hierarchies that governed Hawaiian social relationships and probably misunderstood the distinctions between the gifts they received from aliʻi and those from makaʻāinana. Particularly as the mission period progressed and missionaries developed a close association with aliʻi, it seems possible and even likely that makaʻāinana provided gifts to missionaries as a signal of their respect. Aliʻi, on the other hand, likely had different motives for giving. While it is quite possible that aliʻi extended tokens of kindness to their missionary guests, high-ranking Hawaiians may also have been attempting to convey other sentiments to the band of missionaries. Rather than signaling their own powerlessness or subordination, as the missionaries at first inferred, Hawaiian royalty who welcomed their visitors with gifts attempted to convey their elevated status as beneficent donors, much like Kamehameha had beginning in the late eighteenth century. In so doing, aliʻi pointed to the relative dependence of their guests and established the imbalance of power that would structure Hawaiian-missionary relations in the years to come.

Nancy Ruggles and her mission brothers and sisters were grateful for the offerings of fresh food they received in the first days and weeks after landing in the islands, and they continued to have reasons to be thankful. The missionaries received a seemingly endless bounty of provisions, mostly in the way of gifts from aliʻi. The gifts were undeniably generous; their quantity and abundance attested to this. Samuel Ruggles, the mission's schoolteacher and husband to Nancy, acknowledged as much in the days after the missionaries' landing. "The natives" appeared "very kind," Ruggles wrote, and expressed "their generosity by sending us hogs, potatoes, melons, and various kinds of fruit."[10] Yet Samuel Ruggles's interpretation was unusual: mission diarists rarely described kindness and generosity as motivating factors in the supply of missionary wants. To the contrary, the first band of missionaries more commonly interpreted gifts of this kind as tokens of gratitude from Hawaiians. Writing shortly after the missionaries' arrival,

Elisha Loomis offered a somewhat more characteristic missionary perspective on such gifts. "The widow of Kamehameha sent us a present of fresh fish, cocoanuts, sweet potatoes, bananas, sugar cane, [and] bread fruit," Loomis recounted, "expressing much satisfaction that we had come to bring them good things."[11]

This interpretation was in keeping with missionary beliefs about both the value of their work and the subjects of their labor. Missionaries promised to introduce Christian salvation to the inhabitants of the "rude and dark shores" of Hawai'i; they also intended to bring literacy and "civilization" to the chain of islands.[12] These, to the missionary mind, constituted tremendous gifts. They were thus not surprised to receive gracious hospitality from Hawaiians in return. Offering a window into missionary perceptions on the value of their labor, Mercy Whitney recalled that "one of the brethren" believed that the Hawaiians who came to greet the missionaries regarded them as "apostles."[13] Given such self-perception, missionaries initially appeared disinclined to interpret gift giving in any other way but as an expression of gratitude from Hawaiians, royal and common alike, in anticipation of the greater gifts they would soon receive.

Nevertheless, the missionaries had much to be grateful for, as the gifts of shelter and food might have reminded them. In journal accounts of their earliest days in the islands, they commented frequently on their "blessings" and noted their thankfulness at the supplies that they received.[14] Missionaries, however, frequently misplaced their gratitude, and in so doing, they risked their relations with the islands' ali'i. After a month's residence in the islands, Mercy Whitney reflected on the "abundant blessings" that came in the way of gifts from their Hawaiian hosts. Whitney, moreover, went so far as to note the names of specific donors. Yet Whitney pointed to God—rather than to their Hawaiian donors—as the source of those blessings. As Whitney saw it, "the Lord" supplied the missionaries' "daily wants, almost without care."[15] Such an interpretation was perfectly consistent with missionaries' faith in God's divine intervention. For the missionaries, God did not work in "mysterious ways" but in a completely logical and explicable manner, enabling them to do their work in spreading the Gospel. It would not have been a leap for the missionaries to believe that God had supplied appropriate—even abundant—provisions for the mission. This is not to suggest that the missionaries were not thankful for the gifts they received or that they did not express gratitude to their hosts; rather, I argue that they ultimately credited God for the "supply of their wants."[16]

Pointed to God for generous gifts

Although the missionaries often identified God as the ultimate source of such gifts, they continued to benefit from Hawaiian generosity. They profited in particular from the largesse of aliʻi, who gave gifts both great and small. In the first weeks and months after their arrival, missionaries received a host of gifts, ranging from fruit, potatoes, and sugarcane to an "elegant" fly brush.[17] The gifts that aliʻi provided to American missionaries during the initial stages of contact suggest the political and diplomatic savvy developed in the decades leading up to the missionaries' arrival under Kamehameha's rule. While missionaries had only limited exposure to Hawaiians prior to their voyage, Hawaiians had extensive contact with Westerners and had become quite adept at dealing and negotiating with foreigners who visited the islands. As a result of these interactions, Hawaiians not only developed an affinity for Western goods but also became shrewd bargainers. Moreover, as Kamehameha's example shows, Hawaiians in the nineteenth century clearly grasped the potential political benefits of their dealings with foreigners.[18] That being the case, aliʻi could behave generously toward their foreign guests in order to both grease the wheels of trade and develop politically beneficial foreign relations.

Moreover, high-ranking Hawaiians' engagement with their foreign guests must be interpreted within the structure of nineteenth-century Hawaiian culture, where social inequality dictated the rules of social interaction and exchange. Prior to Western contact, such interactions between aliʻi and makaʻāinana were organized around a system of reciprocal obligation.[19] In this reciprocal relationship, aliʻi distributed land for use by makaʻāinana; in return, makaʻāinana paid tribute in the form of labor. While some scholars have used such exchanges as evidence that the relationship between commoners and chiefs was a feudalistic one, others have demonstrated their familial and reciprocal nature.[20] Aliʻi, for example, provided willingly for makaʻāinana, and makaʻāinana in turn provided for aliʻi in the way of food and clothing. Such a system of reciprocal obligation became a useful structure for exchange between aliʻi and their missionary guests. That is, in the early part of the 1820s, aliʻi likely understood their relationship with American missionaries as one akin to their relationship with common people. After all, the missionaries sought many of the same favors—particularly in the way of land use—that the makaʻāinana sought from the aliʻi. As a result, the gifts from high-ranking Hawaiians came with a set of obligations mirroring the reciprocal relationship between aliʻi and makaʻāinana. Additionally, gift giving and generosity operated as a means by which aliʻi could display their mana.[21] By liberally distributing gifts of food and other necessary items, Hawaiian royalty provided for the needs of their guests and also created a debt between the two parties. Both of these outcomes promised to enhance the status of ali'i.

In proffering gifts and foodstuffs, then, ali'i attempted to indicate and clarify the missionaries' status as guests or subject peoples who would be allowed to stay in the islands as long as they remained in the rulers' good graces. Moreover, Hawaiian royalty implied in their gift giving that the missionaries were guests who could scarcely care or fend for themselves, requiring a host's indulgence and continued assistance. Hawaiians thus situated themselves as the benefactors to a befuddled group of guests that had suddenly landed upon Hawaiian shores. Fruit, meat, poi, and cheese were not mere gifts of "aloha," then, but were offered as part of a larger lesson about the ordering of relations in the islands. In their generosity, ali'i deftly articulated the unequal status of the two parties engaged in this exchange.[22]

Hawai'i's royal women appear to have been quite fluent in the related discourses of obligation and reciprocity, and they seemed prepared to interact with the American missionaries on this basis. The example of Kalākua's visit on board the *Thaddeus* is illustrative of precisely this point. Kalākua used the medium of gifts to communicate her power in relation to her missionary guests. As a woman of rank, Kalākua would have felt entitled to the products of subject people's labor. The directness and timing of her request suggest as much. Moreover, the royal woman made her gift just as the missionaries were preparing to set sail for Kailua to visit Liholiho, to whom they planned to plead their case for establishment of a permanent mission. Kalākua was surely keenly aware of the missionaries' precarious position in the islands—perhaps even more aware than were the missionaries themselves. Given the royal woman's rank and position of influence, mission wives were not, as Kalākua rightfully perceived, in a position to deny her request.

Moreover, Kalākua was remarkably direct in her exchange with the missionaries. Her frankness, in fact, suggests that she was quite practiced at dealing with foreigners. While missionaries at first misunderstood the subtext of her request, Kalākua nevertheless understood the exchange as an opportunity to establish the terms of her relationship with the group. If Kalākua had attempted to imply their status as guests in the transfer of gifts to the missionaries, she also reminded them of their subordinate status in her demand for a very specific kind of gift *from* the missionaries. The gift of food effectively created a debt between two parties and established the unequal basis for their social relationship.[23] This first request from Kalākua was likely intended to communicate a particular ordering of power relations in the islands. The specificity of her request only emphasized her point. Though historians have sometimes viewed Hawaiians as simple victims of Western imperialism, this example strongly suggests that in 1820, Hawaiians did not view themselves in this way.

Yet the mission wives who participated in these exchanges came to view them not just as a means by which to repay whatever debts they incurred while in Hawai'i but as a way to engage directly in the mission project and to advance its aims. Mission wives and their husbands ultimately came to see the pragmatic value of mission women's work in procuring gifts for Hawaiian women of rank. Gifts, they understood, could be used simultaneously to both ingratiate the missionaries to Hawaiians and achieve key conversions.

Hawaiian women of rank thus successfully required missionaries to alter both their strategies for conversion and the focus of their attentions. While missionaries had initially intended to conduct their project of Christianizing and civilizing the Hawaiian Islands from the pulpit and in conversation and consultation with the king, their Hawaiian hosts clearly had other plans and attempted to make their alternate agenda plain from the outset.[24] That is, Hawaiian women of rank redrew the boundaries of missionary-Hawaiian contact by initiating contact with mission wives in the way of gift giving and, particularly, the exchange of clothing.

Moreover, the intimate setting these exchanges required allowed American missionaries virtually unprecedented access to some of the most powerful figures in the islands: Hawaiian women of rank. While exchange with foreigners was common in the islands well before 1820, these interactions were unique, owing not only to the changed political landscape upon which they took place but also to the nature of the gifts themselves. Kamehameha, for example, gave generous gifts of food and other provisions to George Vancouver during the Englishman's visits to the islands in the late eighteenth century. Yet he did so in an official capacity and also, significantly, in public spaces. The kind of repayment the king expected was similarly political and similarly public; Kamehameha, in fact, crafted opportunities for Vancouver to demonstrate the increasingly exclusive nature of their political friendship, as I demonstrated in chapter 1.

Though women of rank gave gifts of food in a public setting, the gifts of clothing they requested—or required—in exchange demanded a greater level of intimacy and frequency of contact. New gowns or dresses required multiple fittings and brought Hawaiian and mission women together repeatedly. Mission women frequently called upon Hawaiian women of rank to take measurements, conduct fittings, or sew. As the frequency of exchange increased, it became more common for royal women and missionary wives to spend protracted periods of time together.[25] The exchange of clothing, moreover, drew missionary women into the private spaces of the Hawaiian home. Missionary wives often visited the queens at home and became privy to the inner workings of their private lives. If mission wives were surprised to find themselves in such intimate spaces, they nevertheless took advantage of the opportunities it afforded them to make themselves useful to the mission. Recall that prior to their departure, men like Heman Humphrey and Thomas Gallaudet spelled out the very limited role that mission wives could play in the mission project.[26] In addition to their function as help-meets and domestics, the board assured women that they might assist in the conversion of Hawaiians by acting as exemplars of Christian femininity. In their efforts to cultivate close relations with Hawaiian women, mission wives filled a role sanctioned by the mission board.[27] Yet—contrary to the board's aims—in their ongoing interactions with high-ranking Hawaiian women, mission wives expanded their role and their importance to the mission project while highlighting the significance of Hawai'i's high-ranking women to the missionary aim of Christianizing the Hawaiian Islands.[28]

Mission women, of course, had other approved avenues of access to mission work. As Gallaudet opined in 1819, a religious-minded woman could act as a "help-meet for man" by becoming "the partner of some humble missionary."[29] Yet mission wives were also encouraged to extend their role in sex-specific ways. Should a mission wife long for more, for example, she might care for the sick or ailing.[30] Sybil Moseley Bingham's husband heartily agreed with such a vocation, writing that the "Christian female" only rarely observed "a better opportunity to make an impression, powerful and salutary, than in attending a missionary husband at the couch of a sick patient." Sybil Moseley Bingham's chance to "make an impression" arrived in 1821, when Ka'ahumanu became ill. The queen traipsed so close to the "borders of the grave" that the missionaries held out little hope for her survival. According to Hiram Bingham's account, Sybil Moseley Bingham "sat down by the side of the sick queen, and with unfeigned sympathy for her sufferings and danger, bathed her aching temples." Hiram Bingham credited his wife with restoring Ka'ahumanu's health; yet he also delighted in the way in which her labor opened the door to greater personal intimacy with the queen. Sybil Moseley Bingham's nurturing care "bound a silken cord around [Ka'ahumanu's] heart, from which I think she never broke free."[31] The "silken cord" to which Hiram Bingham referred was meant to describe the presumably singular bond shared by women. In his use of this

— Royal & missionary women spend more time together; women take advantage of i

gendered colloquialism, Bingham pointed toward a sphere of influence that could only be occupied by women—and was also sanctioned by the board. As Kaʻahumanu's influence in the islands grew and as missionaries fumbled in their relationship with Liholiho, who remained indifferent to them, the opportunity to cultivate meaningful relations with the queen might have appeared particularly attractive.

Yet Hiram Bingham may have misinterpreted what he took to be his wife's special bond with—and unique influence over—Kaʻahumanu. Though the missionaries retrospectively marked Kaʻahumanu's illness and recovery as a pivotal, transformative moment in the relationship between the royal women and mission wives—and, consequently, in the missions' history—a later exchange between Sybil Moseley Bingham and Queens Kamāmalu and Kaʻahumanu in 1822, several months after Kaʻahumanu's illness, reveals the complicated nature of these relationships. Indeed, they continued to be organized around Hawaiian hierarchies.[32] In March, Kamāmalu made a request for clothing. Kamāmalu was a woman of considerable power; daughter of Kalākua and wife to Liholiho, she certainly perceived herself to be in a position to make demands upon the missionaries. That Sybil Moseley Bingham rushed to satisfy the royal woman's wishes suggests that missionaries also acknowledged her authority. Kamāmalu, Bingham wrote, "sent us a whole piece of cloth to be made up for her in shirts." At the queen's direction, Bingham and another missionary wife called to take the royal lady's directions. The women "chatted quite familiarly," but try as they might, Bingham and her companion were unable to persuade the queen to use the cloth for gowns rather than shirts. The queen deemed the latter "much more comfortable" and stood by her request.[33]

Sybil Moseley Bingham's journal offers an interesting account of the exchange. Bingham carefully observed the "familiarity" that passed between herself and Kamāmalu. Moreover, she deliberately noted the pleasant tone of their conversation. The two women engaged in the affectionate "salutation of joining noses" at the commencement of their meeting.[34] As cordial as the relationship appeared, however, the queen remained steadfast in her desires: she wanted shirts for comfort rather than dresses that would meet the standards of propriety desired by the missionaries.[35] Within two days, Bingham had completed one garment and was ready to deliver it. In contrast to the "familiar" and relatively warm exchanges of just a few days before, however, Bingham complained that the queen's attention was focused not on the missionary's arrival but on a game of whist.[36] Distracted, the queen hardly acknowledged Bingham, who reported that she received only "a nod

— Relationships continue to be hierarchical

of cold civility" for all of her efforts.[37] Bingham disguised her frustration, waiting for a few awkward moments before making her departure.

If Bingham felt hurt and disappointed by her dealings with Kamāmalu, she fared little better in her interaction with Ka'ahumanu, upon whom she called next and with whom she believed she also shared a close relationship. Bingham was no doubt irritated to find Ka'ahumanu "with some of her women and one or two chiefs . . . engaged in the same manner as the company we left." Once again, Bingham had to compete with playing cards for the royal woman's attention. Barely able to attract Ka'ahumanu's interest, Bingham finally persuaded the queen to try on the garment she had made to see whether it fit. The queen was disappointed in the results: the garment was too small. Before Ka'ahumanu dismissed the missionary, she allowed Bingham "the satisfaction of knowing some alterations were needed." In her diary, Bingham confided her frustration at having been curtly dismissed by the royal women; nevertheless, she kept her feelings to herself.[38] Bingham's discretion in this regard suggests that she clearly understood that her role in this exchange was to provide something—a reciprocal gift—in order to balance some of the debt missionaries had incurred in the two years since their arrival. In this way, the relationship between Hawai'i's royal women and the mission wives resembles those between ali'i and maka'āinana. That is, the gifts of labor extended in the construction of garments seem to have been understood by both parties as a kind of expected payment or tribute to ali'i. Moreover, while missionaries were doubtless frustrated by this arrangement, they nonetheless understood these exchanges as necessary to establishing favorable relations with the islands' politically and culturally powerful ali'i.

This relationship proved significant to the missionary endeavor, and in fact it took on heightened importance as missionaries' relations with Liholiho and his governors faltered and as Ka'ahumanu's political authority grew. While missionaries perceived Liholiho as a weak leader prone to drink, they initially held out hope for his conversion. Yet by 1822, two years after the missionaries' arrival, the king continued to demonstrate little interest in Christianity. Moreover, he and Boki, governor of O'ahu, continued to look to the English for protection and political alliance. Ka'ahumanu, by contrast, became an advocate for the missionary cause.[39]

For example, in 1823, just months before Liholiho embarked on an expedition to England aimed at creating a formal political alliance, Ka'ahumanu welcomed the second company of missionaries to Hawai'i. She also seized the opportunity occasioned by the king's absence to bring the islands into compliance with missionary moral codes, directing Honolulu's residents to observe the Sabbath by insisting that they refrain from travel and work on those days. Liholiho and his wife, Kamāmalu, contracted measles and died abroad in 1824. Governor Boki escorted their bodies home aboard the *Blonde*. Liholiho left the throne to his much younger sibling, Kauikeaouli. In the wake of Liholiho's death, Ka'ahumanu effectively assumed political power over the islands.[40] Ka'ahumanu continued to provide support for the missionary project by helping to translate Protestant morality into Hawaiian law, aligning the latter more closely with the moral tenets of Christianity.[41] In 1827 the queen publicly opposed Governor Boki by allying herself with the American missionaries against the French Catholics who had recently arrived in the islands.[42] Recognizing Ka'ahumanu's considerable political authority—authority that might be exercised to the benefit of the mission—the missionaries came to view Ka'ahumanu's conversion as vital to the larger goal of Christianizing the Hawaiian Islands.[43]

Thus, by the time the third company of missionaries arrived in 1828, the group understood the importance of maintaining amicable terms with their Hawaiian hosts and the beneficial nature of those relations. If, upon reflection, the missionaries understood that they would be allowed to stay "to do good," eight years into the mission, they clearly acknowledged their duties in relation to the royals.[44] Missionaries even began to entertain requests they otherwise deemed unreasonable or "impracticable" because, in the words of Laura Fish Judd, a member of this third installation, "we do not like to refuse."[45] In her reprinted memoir, Judd recounted an exchange between herself and Ka'ahumanu. According to Judd, Ka'ahumanu "insist[ed] that we shall live with her; she will give us a house and servants and I must be called by her name." Judd's response suggests that she shrewdly understood that refusal was not an option. As she recounted later, she trod carefully; even though she believed the plan to be "unworkable," she was careful not to give offense, diplomatically offering an alternative she hoped the queen would find acceptable. More significant, perhaps, is the way in which Judd understood the tactical importance of diplomacy on this and other matters. As Judd recalled, mission wives needed the "wisdom to choose wisely between duties to be done, and what is to be left undone."[46] If it was "impracticable" to satisfy the queen's wishes in this regard, there were other means by which to appease her.

Clearly, missionary women took their perceived responsibility to Hawai'i's royal women seriously and understood its import to the mission. Missionary wives threw themselves into the labor required to fulfill royal women's requests for clothing. Indeed, Judd described Sybil Moseley Bingham's dedication to such efforts, noting that she "looked thin and care-worn" as a result of her labors on behalf of her family and the royals. In addition to her normal domestic obligations, Bingham once filled "an order from the king" that included "a dozen shirts, with ruffled bosoms, followed by another for a whole suit of broadcloth!"[47] Judd significantly characterized the king's request as "an order," suggesting that, by time of her writing, missionaries had begun to interpret his requests in such a way. The fact that Bingham had not refused, despite her other considerable obligations—both to her own family and to the mission—is equally important.[48] High-ranking women and men favored Western-style dress and continued to make regular requests of missionary wives in this regard. Mission women focused their efforts on providing this particular gift to the Hawaiians, even to their own detriment or exhaustion.

Hiram Bingham later reaffirmed the exertion of missionary wives' work in this regard, noting that "such demands from the king, his wives and other chiefs . . . required some sacrifices, and caused, during the first years, some expenditure of health and strength on the part of those who were willing thus to toil."[49] Such a description of missionary labor, of course, grew out of the larger discourse of sacrifice that gave meaning to their work. Missionary labor was animated at least in part by the extent to which Christian missionaries willingly sacrificed for the benefit of a degraded "other."[50] At the same time, it is clear that these women regarded the provision of clothing as a priority. If missionaries were inclined to sacrifice, and if they felt some ability to choose the realm of such sacrifice, it is important that they so readily volunteered this particular labor.

While it might appear that, in fulfilling their obligations, mission wives engaged in a kind of coerced labor, missionaries also viewed their labors on behalf of the royal women as a means by which to ingratiate themselves to their hosts and to cultivate relations between the mission and the islands' powerful aliʻi. In addition to fulfilling their obligations to the aliʻi, missionaries also viewed these exchanges as a way to advance the larger aims of the mission. Hiram Bingham later reflected on the mission's strategy and recalled that immediately after receiving the kings' permission to establish a Protestant mission in the islands, the missionaries "made it a daily object to gain their confidence, to make ourselves acquainted with their language, habits, and modes of thinking." Moreover, the missionaries endeavored "to adapt our instructions to their capacities and most urgent wants." Hiram Bingham judged such tactics "as the best means of access to their minds and hearts."[51] His wife apparently shared this attitude. Though Sybil Moseley Bingham was occasionally put off by what she took to be the dismissive attitude of the islands' women of rank, she nevertheless acquiesced to their desires in the larger interests of the mission. In her dealings with Ka'ahumanu and Kamāmalu, for example, Bingham astutely recognized that it was better to swallow her pride and "gain some" than to give up in frustration and "lose all."[52] Far from resenting the labors they performed for elite Hawaiian women, mission wives willingly participated in these exchanges with the explicit goal of converting Hawaiian islanders.

Such attitudes regarding gifts of clothing gained currency during the first years of the missionaries' stay in the islands. Mission wives articulated a sense of obligation and also came to understand what might be accomplished in providing gifts of clothing to women of rank. Sybil Mosley Bingham seemed willing enough to continue to supply the royal women's needs in this regard, but she appeared more than happy to furnish another of their requests. " [The queen] and some others much wish to have bonnets," Bingham wrote. She regarded this as "a pleasant circumstance."[53] Pleasant, indeed: since their arrival, missionaries had been troubled by the garland-adorned heads of Hawaiian women. While mission wives rejected fashion for its vanity, "proper" clothing and attire seemed to signify a great deal about the "civility" of the wearer. A proper New England lady, for example, kept her head covered—preferably with a bonnet—in the interests of decorum and modesty. For missionaries, a covered head had an added religious injunction as well: a pious Christian woman covered her head as a sign of her submissiveness to both God and men. An uncovered head, or one adorned with flowers, would have suggested immodesty, vanity, and a lack of proper deference.[54] Mission wives thus met Hawaiian women's interest in acquiring bonnets with real enthusiasm. Bingham and some of the other mission wives wrote letters to women at home in New England asking if they would send "presents that would please these wahines."[55] Bingham seemed to understand the allure of such items and was prepared to use them to her advantage. "I have hinted to the Queen," she wrote, "that perhaps some of the good ladies in America, since she was attending to the palapala, would probably send her one."[56] Enticing the queen to the palapala, Bingham used the promise of a nice bonnet to advance a more spiritual cause.

Although Sybil Moseley Bingham clearly observed the rules of reciprocity and strived to meet her obligations to the queen, she nevertheless recognized an opportunity when she saw one. Royal women's desire for dresses

-Partic in exchanges w/ conversion as goal
-Clothing as civilizing - a good sign

and gowns indicated the possibility of the transformation of Hawaiian women; missionary wives were only too happy to sate the elite women's desires for Western dress if it meant that they would cast aside the traditional tapa they seemed to prefer, and if it ensured that they would remain properly covered. The request for hats put the promise of transformation that much closer to the missionaries' grasp. Moreover, Bingham indicated that she fully intended to use the lure of desired objects to secure the queen's continued attention to her lessons. Bingham clearly recognized the power of a well-placed item. She had a hat of her own to dispose of and planned to put it to strategic use. "I will present mine," Bingham wrote, "where I think it will do the most good."[57]

It must have been deeply gratifying to the missionaries to witness—and have a hand in—the transformation of the royal women. Missionaries continued to wish that elite Hawaiian women would dress more like them, donning the sober colors and inexpensive fabrics they wore as an indication of their modest means and humility instead of the lavish materials and bright colors the women of rank seemed to prefer. Nevertheless, mission wives appeared satisfied when Hawaiians adopted European-style clothing—in whatever color—because it covered their nudity, which the missionaries took as a sign of Hawaiian incivility or worse. Missionaries continued to fret over Hawaiians' supposed immodesty, and nudity remained a special cause for alarm for the mission wives. Clarissa Richards—a member of the second company of missionaries—recorded her first impressions of Hawaiian islanders upon her arrival in April 1823. "I saw them," she wrote, "wretched, degraded, ignorant . . . and yet my heart bled for them. They were destitute of clothing except a narrow strip of cloth twisted about their loins." In her reflections, Richards connected Hawaiian nakedness with their supposed degradation. She was not alone in her interpretation: Sybil Moseley Bingham had also decried the "spiritual and literal nakedness" of Hawaiians upon first landing a full three years earlier.[58]

It is not hard to imagine, then, that the opportunity to clothe Hawaiians presented itself as profoundly important to the mission. In the expected reciprocation of gifts, the missionaries found a surprising foothold. By providing clothes for royal women, mission wives fulfilled their obligations to supply desired objects while also realizing some of their own goals for the transformation of the Hawaiian people, thereby advancing their own cause. If missionaries were concerned about both the spiritual and physical nakedness of Hawaiians, and if Hawaiians were at first reluctant to take part in religious conversion, the missionaries could at least work to solve the more

—Missionary wives happy to supply clothes → attention
Closeness, fix sinful nakedness

visible problem before them by providing gifts of clothing in the way of bonnets, dresses, shirts, and suits.

Moreover, missionary wives attempted to use desirable items as a means not only to encourage the observance of Western habits of dress but also to entice the Hawaiian women of rank toward Christianity. Sybil Mosley Bingham was quite forthright as to her intentions to use clothing as a leverage. Dangling the promise of a new bonnet before the queen in exchange for a promise that she would continue "to attend to the palapala," Bingham quite clearly saw this exchange as an opportunity both to demonstrate gratitude and to use well-placed gifts to benefit the mission. The aims and effects of such a placement of gifts, then, were multiple. Giving aliʻi Western clothes thus might have appeared to Hawaiians as a requisite payment for their generosity and protection; to the missionaries, however, clothing and other items served to advance the mission objective of civilizing their hosts—an important first step on the way to providing them with the gift of Christianity.[59]

Despite the mission wives' hopes for the transformative power of clothing, the Hawaiian subjects of their reform efforts represented more than blank slates upon which new cultural norms could be written. Hawaiian women of rank felt themselves in a position to ask for whatever favors they desired: not only were they situated in positions of considerable power, but they had consistently provided for the missionaries' well-being. Given this arrangement, missionaries had little to no control over how their hosts used the garments they gave as gifts. The mission wives, who also served as seamstresses, could provide elaborate simulations of American and European-style clothing, but they could never insist that the royal women actually wear the garments, nor could they make suggestions as to style or appropriateness. Moreover, the missionaries clearly hoped that they could lead by example, encouraging Kaʻahumanu, Kinaʻu, and Kamāmalu to don "appropriate" attire as a positive first step toward more "civilized" living and Christian salvation. The missionaries sincerely hoped that the trend would grow in popularity, trickling down to servants, attendants, and other common women.[60] Yet while Hawaiʻi's high-ranking women delighted in the novelty of Western-style clothing, they nevertheless seemed to appreciate them as novel and exotic garments rather than as symbols of civility and Christianity. The royal women, then, were not immediate or full converts in the way that the missionaries hoped.

Still, the royal women enjoyed the gifts of dresses and gowns—and even the bonnets—that the missionary wives provided. Women of rank made specific requests for these items and wore them at important functions. At the same time, they felt no obligation to wear them in the prescribed manner or even to wear them consistently. Laura Judd reflected that the bonnet Kaʻahumanu wore when she came to greet the third company of missionaries was "worn doubtless in compliment to us, as the common head-dress is a wreath of feathers or flowers." Despite her public adoption of Western fashion, Kaʻahumanu continued with a more-traditional practice of wearing a garland about her head.[61] This was similar to the mixed apparel that missionaries observed in their earliest days in Hawaiʻi. Lucia Holman elaborated on royal women's attire just days after the missionaries' arrival in 1820. Though one woman was beautifully dressed in striped calico and another in black velvet, their attire struck a discordant note. Each wore a "wreath of yellow feathers curiously wrought around their heads."[62] Common women, too, persisted in their habit of garland wearing, much to the frustration of the missionaries, who hoped to alter their patterns of dress and to hold them up as positive examples of conversion. The problem appeared to be at least partially one of interpretation. While the missionaries saw clothing as a means by which to uplift Hawaiian women, the subjects of their reform perceived it more "as ornamentation than [a way] to cover nakedness."[63]

Hawaiian women—royal and common alike—also continued to adorn themselves in the pāʻū, made of tapa cloth. Missionaries complained bitterly about the "tappers" the Hawaiian women wore. They decried the pāʻū for its style and, in a related way, for its failure to function as a mechanism of modesty. An early nineteenth-century visitor to Hawaiʻi described the pāʻū as the "principle part of dress of women." Hawaiian women wore the pāʻū by wrapping a length of tapa cloth "several times around the waist."[64] The pāʻū, then, clothed the lower part of the body but left the torso and chest exposed. The missionaries found this mode of dress to be unacceptably immodest. Yet, just as the dresses and bonnets the missionaries peddled were embedded with cultural meanings, the pāʻū was loaded with important information. In ancient Hawaiʻi, the production and distribution of bark cloth was class based, with common people engaged in its production as tribute to aliʻi. Tapa cloth was produced from tree bark, and its production was labor intensive and consisted of many steps, including soaking, beating, scoring, and coloring the cloth. Moreover, due to its fragility, tapa cloth lasts only a short time. High-ranking women, too, produced bark cloth, though the cloth they produced was regarded with deepest respect. The pāʻū that high-ranking women produced was intended to be a simulation of those worn by the goddesses and was thus considered sacred. Thus Hawaiian women—particularly those of high status—proved reluctant to trade these garments for the ones that missionaries preferred.[65] In this context, the conflict over "tappers" takes on new and heightened meaning.

The perceived problem of immodesty thus persisted in the Hawaiian Islands. If Hawaiian women of rank could not always be counted upon to wear appropriately modest clothing, common men and women offered even less promise. If the missionaries' earliest descriptions of the Hawaiian people focused on Hawaiian nakedness, equating their physical state with their supposed mental and spiritual degradation, they believed that little had changed after more than a decade in the islands. The missionaries continued to worry about the state of Hawaiians' souls and obsessed over their seemingly intractable nudity.[66] Although some Hawaiian islanders had learned that the missionaries thought "it not right to expose their nakedness" and became somewhat more "modest" in their attire, they nevertheless refused to cover their entire bodies.[67] This troubled the missionaries. Native Hawaiians regularly appeared half clad: if breasts were covered, the lower half was not, and vice versa.[68] Moreover, Hawaiian women simply could not be induced to lay aside their garlands in favor of Western-style bonnets. Even after the missionaries attempted to teach young Hawaiian girls how to make their own bonnets, Hawaiian girls continued to "ornament their heads with garlands" and could not be "persuaded to leave them off." The missionaries, relying on their own influence, strategic gift giving, and royal women's example to reform Hawaiians' outward appearance, might have begun to feel as though they were fighting a losing battle.[69] Despite the missionaries' best efforts, Hawaiians appeared difficult to reform.

In both their dress and their demeanor, Hawaiian women of rank often reminded the missionaries of their relative positions of power in the islands by continuing to cast themselves in the role of beneficent hosts. Laura Fish Judd recalled one such occasion in her memoir. According to her account, Kaʻahumanu teasingly reprimanded Hiram Bingham for what she took to be his shortsighted gratitude. Hiram Bingham had thanked Kaʻahumanu for the "nice things" she had sent earlier in the day, remarking that she had "been very thoughtful today." Kaʻahumanu "looked him in the face, and asked with an arch smile, 'Ah, is it today only?'"[70] By 1828, the time of this exchange, the missionaries had begun to establish cordial—even warm—relations with Hawaiʻi's ranking women and had developed an almost affectionate rapport with Kaʻahumanu. The mission, in fact, enjoyed increasing influence in the islands under Kaʻahumanu's reign as kuhina nui. Nevertheless, Kaʻahumanu's lighthearted rebuke was certainly not entirely in jest. The queen, in fact, offered a pointed reminder of her ongoing generosity toward the missionaries, lest they begin to take her good graces for granted. Moreover, Judd, who recalled the exchange some thirty years after it allegedly occurred, seemed to understand the importance of gratitude in constructing and maintaining relationships with ali'i. Indeed, they had emerged as vitally important to the success of the mission.

Yet these relationships remained complicated. In 1829 Laura Fish Judd risked incurring the queen's displeasure by declining a gift from her. The timing of the exchange is significant: with the queen's support, the missionaries had just completed a "new thatched church" in Honolulu. During a visit, Ka'ahumanu wondered aloud what Judd and her mission sisters Sybil Moseley Bingham and Mary Ward planned to wear to the church dedication.[71] The queen's inquiry was somewhat coy. In fact, Ka'ahumanu harbored a hope that she and the mission women could "dress alike" for the occasion and had already selected the fabric for their dresses. "She ordered the woman in waiting to bring in the material" so that the mission women might give their approval. To Judd's dismay, it was made of "heavy satin" and brightly colored— "pink, white, and blue." The mission women consulted one another but felt compelled to decline her offer. They explained that they were "supported by the church and by the earnings of the poor." Judd later stressed that it would be improper for them to don clothing made of such expensive material. Ka'ahumanu insisted that it was a gift and pressed the women once again to accept. Without a hint of irony, Judd reported that mission women could not possibly feel "comfortable in such unaccustomed attire." The mission women were "sorry to oppose her wishes," but they declined nevertheless. In response, Ka'ahumanu appeared "taciturn all afternoon."[72]

As the women prepared to depart later that evening, Ka'ahumanu "resumed her cheerful manner, and asked what we would like to wear on the forthcoming occasion." The women, grateful that the queen had provided an opportunity to mend fences, offered their skills as seamstresses and reiterated their willingness to "make something handsome for her" (likely from the disputed material). At the same time, they restated their wish that their own gowns be made of simple black silk. The queen "made no reply" and instead wished them goodnight. The missionaries were surprised and delighted when, the following morning, they received a new gift from Ka'ahumanu: "two rolls of black silk, with an order to make her dress exactly like ours."[73]

The missionary women must have felt tremendous relief at receiving Ka'ahumanu's gift. They well understood the diplomatic expedience of accepting the first gift, yet its form made that virtually impossible for them. They indeed knew that the consequences of their refusal could be serious: a rift threatened to jeopardize not only the queen's friendly relations with the mission but also her appearance at the church dedication. By offering a second gift and making a renewed request for a gown, Ka'ahumanu offered a remedy to both problems. The black silk in this case served as a show of diplomacy. Though the queen insisted that she did not understand the missionaries' claim that it was "not proper for good people to wear good things," she nevertheless honored their request.[74] Moreover, in requesting a gown like those worn by the missionaries as a counter gift, Ka'ahumanu indicated her willingness to publicly observe missionary ideals of female modesty and decorum. The queen would fulfill her promise to attend the church dedication, and she would arrive dressed like a true Christian. The missionaries might well have taken this as a signal of the queen's continued goodwill and her commitment to the Christian mission.

While some would argue that the relationships that developed around the exchange of gifts were often calculated in terms of their immediate diplomatic or political usefulness, the effects of exchange were often unexpected and had long-ranging significance. In insisting that missionaries acknowledge their considerable political and cultural power, for example, Hawai'i's royal women created a situation that forced male missionaries to recognize the important role that women—American and Hawaiian alike—might play in achieving the mission's goals. Demanding gifts that required repayment and specifying things that, within the context of the mission at least, only mission wives could supply, Hawaiian women of rank drew mission wives into the very center of Hawaiian-missionary relations. In these interactions, mission wives became responsible for maintaining diplomatic relations with some of the island's most powerful figures. Moreover, in their continued and sustained exchange of things with royal women, mission wives opened up new avenues for the conversion of the islands. By 1829 conversions like the one that Ka'ahumanu appeared to have experienced seemed critical to the mission's success. Pinning their hope on such conversions, American missionaries charged their wives—and the royal women—with an important task. They could only pray that the conversions were genuine.

— Ka'ahumanu makes a concession to missionary modesty etc.

CHAPTER 5 *Hawaiian Heroines*

In December 1825, just over five and half years after the missionaries' arrival in the islands, Kaʻahumanu took communion in the Kawaiahaʻo Church in Honolulu. Mercy Partridge Whitney was among those in attendance at the service; afterward, she eagerly reported that Kaʻahumanu—along with seven other Hawaiians—had "united with the church." Moreover, she recalled, "they all received an English name in addition to their native one, in the ordinance of baptism." On that day, Kaʻahumanu became, to the missionaries, Elizabeth Kaʻahumanu.[1] Though American missionaries were cautious when it came to conversions—having, as Hiram Bingham put it, "no faith in baptismal regeneration"—they believed this one to be genuine.[2] Mercy Whitney, for example, vouched for the depth of the queen's conversion when she observed just a few weeks later that the royal woman behaved "like a mother to us all." The metaphor was a common one: from the mission's earliest days, missionaries and their wives described their hope that aliʻi would become like "mothers and fathers" to the mission. Yet the results among Hawaiʻi's high-ranking men had been disappointing. In contrast, as Mercy Whitney reported, Kaʻahumanu "endeared herself" to the missionaries not only "by her attachment to the mission" but also by "her consistent walk and conversation as a Christian."[3]

Despite a disappointing and sometimes trying first year in Hawaiʻi, the years thereafter proved somewhat more productive. By 1825 the missionaries had made what they considered to be a few key conversions, most notably among Hawaiian women of rank. The missionaries were deeply gratified by these successes and seized upon ranking women's dramatic and highly symbolic activities in the 1820s to produce stories heralding their successful conversions. Mission writers circulated those narratives to a reading—and donating—public in America. The literature they produced had dual effects. First, it highlighted Hawaiian women's role in the Christianization of the Hawaiian Islands by illustrating their transformation from "savage heathen" to "civilized" Christian women. By the middle part of the nineteenth century, published stories that centered on the successful conversion

84

of Hawai'i's high-ranking women—lauded as "heroines" to their people—abounded and were held up as proof of the spread of Christianity and civilization in Hawai'i, as well as, not incidentally, of the efficacy of the missionaries' work on behalf of the Hawaiian people.[4] In a second and related way, the conversion literature suggested, sometimes quite overtly, a new space for white women in the American foreign-mission movement. Where the ABCFM originally envisioned that women would serve the mission as "helpmeets"—that is, as wives and mothers—the missionary experience in Hawai'i demonstrated the much larger and more vital role that American women might play in the conversion of the world's "heathen."[5]

This chapter explores the conversion narratives that mission and other writers produced in the period spanning from the mid-nineteenth century to the early years of the twentieth to reveal the increasingly gendered nature of Christian conversion in the Hawaiian Islands. The narratives generated in this period measured a female convert's piety not solely by her willingness or desire to be baptized into the church but also by the manner in which she reformed her personal and intimate life to align more closely with the tenets of Christian femininity. In fact, the conversion literature situated the adoption of Western gender norms as a convert's critical first step on the path to a Christian life. Yet while mission writers triumphantly claimed true women and true Christians for the mission, conversion stories obscured the way in which Hawaiian women of rank understood the relationship between the new cultural forms the missionaries insistently pressed upon the islands' inhabitants and the new religion American missionaries brought to the islands.[6] Further, they masked the role of Christianity in the royal women's lives. This chapter explores not whether Hawai'i's high-ranking women became "true" Christians but, rather, the context and circumstances of their adoption of the new religion and its related practices. I argue that the conversion narratives that grew out of the Hawaiian mission experience are important for what they say about missionaries' attitudes about their civilizing and Christianizing project; at the same time, royal women's orientation toward their mission guests and toward Christianity in particular must be read against the backdrop of a turbulent Pacific world and with the royal women's larger personal and political aims in mind.[7]

The notion that Hawai'i's queens and women of rank had played a crucial role in the process of Christianizing the Hawaiian Islands emerged as a convention of the missionary literature in the middle part of the nineteenth century and had gained widespread acceptance among a Christian reading public by the early part of the twentieth century. Though missionaries acknowledged the number of lesser players in the drama, they reserved their highest praise for Hawai'i's elite women. Mission historians drew attention to three Hawaiian "heroines" in particular: Keōpūolani, Kapi'olani, and Ka'ahumanu. Each of these women exerted power and influence in their own right; for this reason alone, they might have captured the missionaries' imagination and attention. Yet they became important to the literature for their seeming embrace of Christianity and for the manner in which they aligned their lives more closely with the tenets of Christian femininity. These royal women became important signifiers of religious conversion and cultural transformation of the Hawaiian Islands and suggested the potential for the salvation of "heathen" peoples around the globe.[8]

In an 1825 published memoir, the Reverend William Richards, a member of the second company of missionaries to the Hawaiian Islands, reflected on Keōpūolani's death. Keōpūolani was one of Kamehameha's widows and mother to Liholiho. She also held the highest royal rank. More important to missionaries, however, was the fact that Keōpūolani died a Christian convert. Just a few years prior, in 1823, Richards and the Reverend Charles Stewart, also a member of the second company, had been assigned to help establish a mission in Lahaina on Maui, where the royal woman lived out the last years of her life.[9] She made a fitting subject for the missionary's text: during the early part of the so-called mission period in the islands, Keōpūolani demonstrated an increasingly positive orientation toward Christianity.

Readers of missionary literature perhaps best knew Keōpūolani for her role in encouraging Liholiho to break the kapu laws to establish 'ainoa throughout the islands in 1819, as I have described in chapter 3.[10] Though the missionaries expressed a deep gratitude toward God and credited "divine providence" for affecting such a profound change in the islands, they could not deny Keōpūolani's role in dismantling the islands' cultural and religious system and opening up a space for the acceptance of Christianity. The kapu laws governed nearly every aspect of native life and mandated reverence for those of the highest rank. Indeed, as Richards reminded his readers, Keōpūolani's status was such that "in her early life, she never walked abroad except at evening and all who saw her walking at that hour prostrated themselves to the earth."[11] Though Keōpūolani was also obliged to observe the kapu laws (such as those that prohibited her from eating with men), it was nevertheless true that she benefited from the kapu system in that it helped to reify her status.[12]

Richards, however, insisted that though Keōpūolani "was always remarkably strict" in observing the kapus, she always behaved mercifully and justly in her dealings with those who defied or broke them. Moreover, Richards emphasized her role in dismantling a system from which she derived real benefits. He declared that "it was a greater sacrifice" for Keōpūolani "to renounce the old system" than for "those who were less venerated." He encouraged his Christian readership to interpret Keōpūolani's willingness to see the kapu laws overturned as a selfless sacrifice aimed at elevating her people even at the expense of her own status. In this way, her actions were akin to the "disinterested benevolence" that led the missionaries to the islands and that motivated mission wives to give so selflessly of themselves in their efforts to reform Hawai'i's women. Richards viewed Keōpūolani as a gentle ruler with her subjects' best interests at heart and also as a woman whose mind and heart seemed "prepared" for Christianity even before the missionaries arrived.[13]

Yet, as a practice, the 'aikapu was already in decline well before Keōpūolani and Ka'ahumanu advocated for its eradication. Not only had Hawaiians—ali'i and maka'āinana alike—broken the kapus, but they also had witnessed foreigners regularly engaging in free eating without sanction.[14] While there is little evidence that Hawaiian women found the practice "humiliating," as some historians have claimed, the missionaries viewed this arrangement as demeaning to women.[15] In fact, more recent scholarship suggests that ali'i increasingly adopted the practice of free eating because the Westerners they had seen enjoy the 'ainoa seemed immune to the kinds of disease decimating the population in Hawai'i.[16] Though mission writers celebrated the overthrow of the 'aikapu as both a triumph over "superstition" and as a way in which women's status in the island might be elevated, the ali'i who led the charge may have viewed the change with less symbolic than practical value.

Mission writers also praised Keōpūolani for her rejection of polygamy, a practice that vexed them as a nagging remnant of heathenism. Having already begun the process of conversion, the literature suggested, Keōpūolani took a bold next step in 1823 to cast aside this common marital practice. According to mission accounts, Keōpūolani, who had two husbands, initiated a conversation with one of her mission teachers—Tauā, a Tahitian who accompanied English missionary William Ellis on his tour of Hawai'i—on the subject. As Richards reported, Tauā advised Keōpūolani that it was more "proper for a woman to have one husband" and, more to the point, that "Christian females never have more than one husband."[17] In reply, Keōpūolani asserted that though she once "followed the custom of [her] country" by keeping two husbands, in the future she wished to "obey Jesus Christ and to walk in the good way." She declared Hoapili her "only husband"

— BUT Kapu system was already eroding

— Also praised Keopulani's efforts against polygamy

and vowed to "cast off" Kalanimōkū, to whom she was also married. Much to Richards's satisfaction, Keōpūolani made good on her promise: she sent for Kalanimōkū and explained that she had "renounced" the "old religion, the religion of wooden gods." Instead, she "embraced the new religion, the religion of Jesus Christ." She ended her relationship with Kalanimōkū, explaining that as a Christian, she was obliged to "have only one husband."[18]

Missionaries in the field fretted endlessly over Hawaiian islanders' most personal and intimate relations—including marriage, sex, and child rearing—and worked to reform them. Hiram Bingham, as a leader of the mission, held fast to his belief that it was the missionaries' job to correct Hawaiians' "uncouth and disgusting manners" and to improve "their modes of dress and living" to remove them from "grossness, destitution and wretchedness."[19] American missionaries described Hawaiians' intimate practices—including the practice of polygamy—as barbarous and degrading and a symptom of their incivility. This was particularly so for women whose sexual purity, missionaries believed, was compromised by the multiple sexual relations implied by nonmonogamous unions.[20] Yet Hawaiians, who did not share missionaries' views about gender and sexual morality, proved resistant to change. Two years into the mission, ali'i and maka'āinana—male and female alike—persisted in the practice of keeping more than one spouse.[21] Thus, missionaries viewed Keōpūolani's embrace of monogamous marriage as more than a symbolic victory; rather, Richards and other writers seized upon her story as an example of the concrete and measurable effects of missionaries' Christianizing efforts in Hawai'i.

Because historians must rely heavily on mission documents to piece together Keōpūolani's purported rejection of polygamy, it is critical to treat her words and actions with caution. Most historians accept that Keōpūolani "cast off" her second husband; nearly every description of Keōpūolani derived from mission documents makes at least a passing reference to the break.[22] But the matter of whether or not she made the kinds of explicit links between her acceptance of Christianity and the termination of her martial relationship to Kalanimōkū is less clear. It would have been within the bounds of Keōpūolani's power to terminate her marriage for other reasons as well.[23] While missionaries viewed marriage as a lifelong, monogamous, and hierarchical contract between a man and a woman, Hawaiian practices—particularly among ali'i—suggest a different orientation toward marital unions. Marriage, in fact, was an important means by which to enhance one's mana. Though this was particularly true for men, high-ranking women also made strategic marriages.[24] Yet the missionaries had

— Hawaiians slow to modify marital practices

— Marriage had a political element to it

cause to publicize the account as a victory for Christ and for the mission. Keōpūolani—the most powerful woman living in the islands—personally rejected an enduring social practice, one that Stewart declared "inconsistent with the principles of Christianity."[25] This offered a powerful testament to the efficacy of the mission to reform and restore the royal woman's character.

In the late summer of 1823, Keōpūolani, already frail from a lifetime of illness, grew very ill. The royal woman, schooled by missionaries, expressed her apprehension of dying without "having learned enough of the good word (of God) and of the right way to go to heaven."[26] Though Richards claimed that "others gave evidence of their piety earlier than Keōpūolani," hers was nonetheless a compelling story of Christian transformation. In the hours before her death, Keōpūolani slipped into a coma. The unconscious woman was baptized into the church. Richards dubbed her "the first fruit of the mission" and reported that her death reflected "a loss of no small magnitude" to the project of Christianizing the Hawaiian people. As Richards observed, the royal woman "stood high in the affections of the people." Consequently, "her influence was of special value to an infant mission."[27] Richards and other mission writers thus took special care to chronicle the royal woman's conversion. In so doing, they pointed to the importance of Hawai'i's royal women in the islands' purported transformation from a "pagan" to a Christian land.

Keōpūolani may have represented the mission's "first fruit," but the missionaries eagerly laid claim to other successes as well. In 1866 Rufus Anderson, who served the ABCFM throughout the nineteenth century, published a work devoted to Kapi'olani, another woman of high rank. The book, titled *Kapiolani, the Heroine of Hawaii: or, A Triumph of Grace at the Sandwich Islands*, celebrated Kapi'olani's conversion in the early years of the mission and established her experience as emblematic of the kinds of profound cultural and religious transformations the missionaries enacted in the islands.[28] Anderson collected and amassed missionaries' impressions of the royal woman to demonstrate that, in just a few short years under their tutelage and with God's grace, Kapi'olani had been transformed from a woman of "dissolute" habits to the "heroine" of the book's title.[29]

Anderson and other writers underscored Kapi'olani's Christian metamorphosis by elaborating on Hawaiians' "natural" and supposedly degraded state, a designation from which even the islands' highest-ranking women were not immune. The degeneracy of native peoples was a trope of nineteenth-century conversion narratives and one with which both readers and writers were likely familiar. Mission writers roundly agreed with William Richards, for example, who declared that in 1820 "there was scarcely a person on the islands more degraded than Kapiʻolani." In the early days of the mission, "she gave herself up to intemperance and every species of degradation."[30] Indeed, in an address to the Woman's Board of Missions for the Sandwich Islands near the end of the century, Persis Taylor asserted that when missionaries visited the high-ranking woman at home just after their arrival, they were mortified to find Kapiʻolani and her husbands reclining on their "mats." All three, Taylor insisted, were "nearly nude, and in a state of beastly intoxication." While the missionaries had come to expect as much from the likes of Liholiho and Boki, they were culturally less prepared for such conduct from the islands' high-ranking women.[31] As alarming as Kapiʻolani's private conduct appeared to the missionaries, however, they were rather more concerned with her public demeanor. Taylor reported that the missionaries first encountered Kapiʻolani on the beach, where she was "basking in a noonday tropical sun." Much to the dismay of the missionaries, who valued feminine modesty almost above all other qualities, Kapiʻolani was naked. She was "sitting on a rock . . . saturating her skin" with "fragrant cocoanut oil." In an effort to convey an image of the supposedly debauched royal lady to her listeners, Taylor deployed an unfortunate description, one laden with connotations not just about Kapiʻolani's gender but also about her race: Taylor compared Kapiʻolani to a "seal or a sea elephant."[32]

Yet, Taylor insisted, within a few short years after the missionaries' arrival, Kapiʻolani had been completely transformed, exhibiting both the refined manners and style indicative of a true Christian lady. To Taylor, the transformed Kapiʻolani appeared "unlike any other Hawaiian woman of her day."[33] Taylor took special note of the ease with which Kapiʻolani "adopted the style brought by the first missionary ladies," recalling that "on public occasions," the royal woman was consistently clad in a dress rather than the pāʻū or even the holokū (loose-fitting dress), favoring the Western-style clothing in "grave and quiet shades" rather than the "gayest colors" that the other royal women seemed to prefer. Kapiʻolani finished off her appearance with the proper accouterments: "her feet were always clad in stockings and shoes," and her hair was "becomingly arranged with side puffs, and a high tortoise shell comb."[34]

Taylor spared her audience no detail. Indeed, she took great pains to elaborate on nearly every aspect of Kapiʻolani's appearance. In her address, Taylor presented her audience with a portrait of a woman who had not simply taken up the pretty adornments of Western fashion but appeared to wear them in the intended fashion and for their intended purpose: as a display of feminine modesty and propriety. Though lacking a bonnet, Kapiʻolani adopted an alternate but approved mode of adorning and securing her hair—a small triumph for the missionaries, who battled throughout the islands to encourage women to cover their heads.[35] Moreover, Kapiʻolani not only consistently adorned herself in "tight fitting" Western-style dresses but also took up the somber shades the missionaries wore as a show of their piety and humility. Such was one detail among the many that Kapiʻolani got right. Taylor reassured her audience that missionary wives had helped to make Kapiʻolani over from head to toe, pointing out that she wore both shoes and stockings. Kapiʻolani's conversion was so complete, Taylor declared, that the royal woman became a "beloved Christian sister" to the mission wives. Kapiʻolani's transformation from the "dissolute" woman the missionaries found sunbathing on the beach in 1820 to the refined "Christian sister" Taylor recalled offered powerful testament of the ability of the mission to transform lives not just in Hawaiʻi but around the globe.[36]

Writers eagerly pointed out the deeper spiritual alteration facilitated by the acceptance of Western gender norms. Indeed, Kapiʻolani recommended herself as a "heroine" not simply for the transformation of her own character but for the manner in which she promised to reform her own people. Writers valorized Kapiʻolani for her role in challenging the powerful and wrathful goddess, Pele. Indeed, most writers—including nineteenth-century writer and champion of domesticity Sarah Josepha Hale—agreed that this constituted her most "heroic" deed.[37] Despite Keōpūolani's dramatic conversion just a few years prior, mission historians continued to fret about the "great amount of superstition remaining among the people" of Hawaiʻi. Moreover, missionaries had begun to acknowledge the limits of their influence on makaʻāinana. Rufus Anderson had to concede that the kinds of changes the missionaries sought in Hawaiʻi could only be undertaken "by some native of rank and character."[38] Kapiʻolani fulfilled just such requirements. Mission writers enshrined the story of her dramatic act in the mission literature; its details are repeated even in modern accounts of the event.[39]

In 1824 Kapiʻolani dramatically and publicly defied Pele at Kīlauea. Pele figured centrally in Hawaiian creation stories and, as the goddess of volcanoes, possessed the power to both create and destroy.[40] Missionaries who later recalled the event reported that Kapiʻolani traveled over 100 miles on foot to the volcano, intent on challenging her people's faith in the deity. The royal woman attracted a stream of curious followers along the way. To many of these Hawaiians, the missionaries insisted, Kapi'olani's journey seemed dangerous and "foolhardy." Impressed by Pele's destructive power, they reportedly begged her to desist.[41] Yet Kapi'olani, purportedly emboldened by her newly acquired Christian faith, seemed unafraid of Pele's wrath. Nearing the volcano, she is said to have declared: "Jehovah . . . is my God. . . . I fear not Pele."[42] Moreover, according to missionary accounts, she offered a challenge to her followers: "[S]hould I perish by [Pele's] anger, then you may fear her power. But if Jehovah save me when breaking through her *tabus*, then you must fear and serve Jehovah."[43] Kapi'olani "went to the center, descended into the brink of the lake of molten lava and there broke the tabu by eating the sacred berries which grew there."[44]

Viewing Pele as an example of native "superstition," American missionaries exalted Kapi'olani for her role in paving the way for the broader acceptance of Christianity. They praised her also for her exceptional character: she alone had braved the wrath of Pele, who might potentially visit earthquakes or worse upon the people of Hawai'i in order to express her displeasure. But Pele did not retaliate against Kapi'olani. Missionaries were happy to report that Kapi'olani's efforts on behalf of the mission were successful, claiming that the church was "enlarged by ninety converts" as a result of Kapi'olani's heroic feat.[45]

If Kapi'olani appeared as a dynamic heroine for the cause of Christianity, missionaries also understood her in a much more conventional way: as a tool of God's will. In describing Kapi'olani's daring exploit for the cause of Christianity, Rufus Anderson took pains to elaborate on her bravery and heroism while nevertheless restoring the real glory to God, as missionaries had done from their earliest days in Hawai'i. "The Lord," he wrote, "prepares instruments for his own work." Kapi'olani was "the honored instrument" in the "emergency" at Kīlauea. In his memoir, Anderson vigorously reminded his readers of the efficacy of the mission in promoting change in the islands, and he also prompted them to consider all people as potential converts. Even those who might otherwise be dismissed as too degraded, "intemperate," or "dissolute" to carry out God's work should not be overlooked as potential "instruments for change."[46]

Despite their successes, missionaries occasionally had to be reminded that all of God's subjects might potentially be redeemed and put to his service. They perhaps found the best exemplar of this principle in Ka'ahumanu. Reflecting on their first exchanges with Ka'ahumanu, the first company of missionaries often described her as "haughty," "imperious," and arrogant.[47]

Indeed, in the first critical years of the mission, missionaries and their wives reported that Ka'ahumanu appeared indifferent to the missionaries and their message. In those days, according to Sybil Mosley Bingham, the royal woman was so engaged in her own pursuits that it was a rare occasion when she "deigned to extend her little finger" to the missionaries; similarly, Ka'ahumanu appeared "utterly regardless of the life and happiness of her subjects." Yet, as mission wife Clarissa Chapman Armstrong later recalled, this "haughty, overbearing chiefess . . . became a meek and lowly woman" who availed herself to the mission.[48]

Missionary writers agreed that Ka'ahumanu's illness in the last days of 1821 marked a turning point in her transformation and improved her disposition toward the mission. During this time, Hiram Bingham wrote, "the hard and lofty-hearted Kaahumanu was laid low and brought to the borders of the grave." As the royal woman lay ill, Hiram and Sybil Bingham called upon her repeatedly. Though Hiram Bingham later stressed the beginnings of a bond between Ka'ahumanu and his wife, Sybil focused on other matters. It was during those visits, Sybil Mosley Bingham claimed, that Ka'ahumanu exhibited the first signs of her conversion. One day, as the royal woman listened to Hiram offer lessons in the Gospel, Sybil Mosley Bingham reported that Ka'ahumanu seemed transfixed, laying aside "all her affected airs." Moreover, she seemed "not only willing but desirous to hear something from the servants of the living GOD."[49] The very next day, Ka'ahumanu received the missionaries again. This time, she requested that the missionaries favor her with a prayer. Interpreting the request as a harbinger of things to come, Hiram Bingham happily obliged. Indeed, from that day forward, Bingham wrote, Ka'ahumanu exhibited "a marked difference in her demeanor toward the missionaries." The change became "more and more striking" over time until at last the missionaries were able "to acknowledge her as a disciple of the divine master."[50]

Though Hiram Bingham certainly recognized the power of prayer in this transformative event, he also—at least in retrospect—acknowledged the important role his wife had played in helping to bring Ka'ahumanu to the mission. During Ka'ahumanu's illness, as Hiram Bingham cared for the queen's soul, Sybil Bingham attended to her ailing body. Such was a fitting use of her talents in light of the mission board's official philosophy on women's role as supporters of the mission rather than as active participants in it. Yet Bingham insisted that the personal bond that formed between the two women as a result of Sybil Bingham's nursing care was a crucial element in Ka'ahumanu's reorientation toward the mission. While Hiram Bingham might have had a personal interest in elevating his wife's status within the mission, his writings nevertheless also offered powerful testament to the important space that mission wives occupied in the field. Mission wives like Sybil Bingham not only adhered to their prescribed roles but, in so doing, also provided active models of Christian womanhood—models that might be emulated by the very subjects of missionary reform.[51]

According to Hiram Bingham, the strategy worked. Though Ka'ahumanu was by no means a perfect pupil, Bingham claimed that as a result of his wife's attentions, the royal woman grew increasingly receptive to the missionary's teachings. In 1822 the Binghams called upon the queen to present her with a "little book containing the alphabet, a few lessons in reading and some hymns." They reportedly found Ka'ahumanu in her customary posture, engaged in her favorite pastime. The royal lady, Hiram Bingham recalled, was "on her mats, stretched at full length, with a group of portly dames like herself, engaged in a game of cards." The couple purportedly waited patiently until Ka'ahumanu finished her game. When the royal lady at last turned her attention to the missionary and his wife, Bingham recalled, they "gave her a little spelling book in her own language" and explained "how it could be made to talk to her." According to the account, the royal lady "listened, was deeply interested, pushed aside her cards, and was never known to resume them to the day of her death." The account held that Ka'ahumanu proved a quick study and, learning to read, "forsook her follies" to attend to school and worship services.[52]

The story emerged as a significant piece of missionary lore. Laura Fish Judd was like other mission writers in recounting the event as a critical step toward the successful conversion of the Hawaiian people.[53] The details are significant for the way that they link literacy to a larger kind of conversion or transformation. It is important, for example, that the missionaries encountered Ka'ahumanu in repose "on her mats," a posture the missionaries found sexually suggestive, immodest, and unfeminine. Moreover, the queen was engaged in a game of cards, a habit the missionaries believed only contributed to the perceived idleness and sloth of the Hawaiian people.[54]

In the story, however, Ka'ahumanu put down the cards and traded her idleness for the work of training her mind for literacy—and, presumably, preparing her heart for the Gospel. Literacy, in this account, was understood as profoundly transformative. As Judd later declared, once Ka'ahumanu realized the potential for reading, she gave up her cards forever. Additionally, Judd claimed that Ka'ahumanu demonstrated a natural aptitude for reading, reportedly mastering the art in a few short weeks. Judd's readers were invited to imagine a dramatic scene in which the royal woman cast aside her cards only to pick up the "little book" of spelling and hymns her missionary visitors provided to her, forever transforming her life. More important, according to the text, Ka'ahumanu requested more books for the "supply [of] her household," indicating her intention to use her influence to assist the missionaries in spreading Christianity in the islands.[55]

Yet Ka'ahumanu's intentions are not entirely clear. While it is true that Ka'ahumanu learned to both read and write and ultimately supported mission schools and the cause of literacy, it is not a foregone conclusion that she did so to help the missionaries proceed more easily with the project of Christianizing the islands. While literacy certainly facilitated the teaching of the Gospel, it could be put to other unrelated uses as well. Ka'ahumanu had enough interaction with foreign traders to know the purposes to which the written word could be put—including, among other things, making and reading contracts.[56] Moreover, written language facilitated communication not just with foreigners but also among and between Hawaiians. Written language also might have appeared as an appealing way to streamline communication between chiefs who resided on distant islands. In short, Hawaiians had many reasons—beyond simply learning the Gospel—to attend to the lessons the missionaries offered.[57]

Missionary literature seemed certain of the meaning of Ka'ahumanu's literacy, and the seemingly trivial meeting at which Ka'ahumanu accepted a small gift from her guests grew to become a significant moment. In the missionary telling, Ka'ahumanu's acceptance of literacy signaled the starting point of the royal woman's conversion. In laying down her cards and embracing the written word, Ka'ahumanu symbolically traded idleness for industry, ignorance for enlightenment, and savagery for civilization. True to the formula of the missionary conversion narrative, Ka'ahumanu's story was not simply one of personal transformation; rather, her newfound literacy seemed to signal her readiness to embrace Christianity for her own betterment and for the betterment of the Hawaiian people. Indeed, Hiram Bingham recalled that just a short time later, Ka'ahumanu traveled through the islands initiating a search for any remaining symbols of the old religion. The "idols" located by her party, Bingham reported, were destroyed. "On the 4th of June," Bingham recalled, Ka'ahumanu "sent for Kamehameha's image of Kālaipāhoa, the so-called poison deity, and caused it to be publicly burned with nine other images."[58] Ka'ahumanu's fervor—her "war with idolatry"—grew. "On the 26th of the same month, one hundred and two idols, collected from different parts of Hawai'i,

[handwritten: — perhaps Ka'ahumanu had other motives for literacy]

[handwritten: — Literacy = Civilization, readiness for Christianity]

where they had been hidden . . . were, by her authority, committed to the flames."[59]

If the missionaries had hoped to see the idols destroyed—even if only as a symbolic gesture of Hawaiians' break with their "false" gods—they could not do it themselves. In order for the gesture to have any merit, it would have to be undertaken by a native Hawaiian. Before his death, Ōpūkahaʻia had promised to reveal that Hawaiian idols, made of wood, were worthless. According to the missionary literature, Ōpūkahaʻia vowed to "go home, put 'em in a fire, burn 'em up."[60] Just a few short years later, Kaʻahumanu accomplished what the missionaries' star pupil had been unable to achieve. That Kaʻahumanu was both Hawaiian and a woman of considerable power and influence certainly pleased the missionaries; her rejection of the "vain idols" indeed had some force. Bingham declared that her participation in this regard "seemed likely to make her a burning and shining light among her people."[61] It is more certain that her actions of that summer secured a place for Kaʻahumanu as a heroine to the missionaries.

Kaʻahumanu, in fact, became the missionaries' most fervent advocate in the 1820s and 1830s. While the king and some of his chiefs (Governor Boki in particular) continued to view the missionaries as having little practical use, showing scant interest in the Christianity the Americans had come to offer and instead looking to the English for protection and political alliance, Hawaiian women of rank repeatedly and clearly demonstrated their preference for the missionaries. Kaʻahumanu in particular frequently put her political clout behind the mission project. Her example is instructive, given her growing political and cultural authority in the period. Though Kaʻahumanu, like Liholiho, at first appeared uninterested in Christianity, over time and as her political authority grew, she became more closely allied with the missionaries.

As the missionaries struggled to establish Christianity in the islands, Hawaiʻi's ruling elite struggled with problems of their own. Throughout the decade, the islands continued to attract foreigners and to accrue debt to foreign traders. The sandalwood trade in particular caused crushing debt in the islands; as aliʻi attempted to make good on what they owed, they ordered more sandalwood cut down until they depleted the supply, throwing the islands' ecology out of balance.[62] Moreover, the political power that appeared to favor Hawaiians under Kamehameha's rule was quickly eroded in the 1820s, sending the island's rulers scrambling to create protective alliances.[63] In 1823 Liholiho embarked on just such an expedition to England. He and his party had barely departed when Kaʻahumanu offered a public declaration of her alignment with the missionaries. Ka'ahumanu urged widespread compliance with missionary moral codes by ordering Honolulu's residents to observe the Sabbath.[64] Ka'ahumanu prohibited residents of the bustling port town from working and traveling on the missionaries' day of rest. When Liholiho died in 1824, Ka'ahumanu effectively assumed political power over the islands.[65]

In the years immediately following Liholiho's death, Ka'ahumanu became a staunch advocate of the missionary schools and churches and continued her efforts to translate Protestant morality into law. In 1825 she participated in a restructuring of Hawaiian legal codes, creating new ones closely resembling the Bible's Ten Commandments.[66] During her reign, she allied herself with American missionaries by strenuously protesting the presence of French Catholics in the islands, going so far as to expel them.[67] In short, Ka'ahumanu exercised her authority on behalf of the missionaries—a pattern that endured throughout the remainder of her life.[68]

By the time of Ka'ahumanu's death in 1832, the missionaries regarded her as a genuine Christian, a true friend of the mission, and a powerful ally. From the missionary perspective, Ka'ahumanu had helped dismantle the kapu system and assisted in promoting literacy and Christianity in the Hawaiian Islands. Using her profound influence, she created a new code of laws that the missionaries recognized as favorable to their aims. The missionaries thus regarded Ka'ahumanu as a powerful symbol of the efficacy of a mission education and the potential of the Hawaiian people for change.

While the stories that missionaries told about the "heroines of Hawai'i" focused in a narrative way on the changed character of the royal women and seemed to emphasize Hawaiian women's political and cultural influence, they ultimately served not to acknowledge the status of Hawai'i's queens but to reassert the supremacy of Western racial and gender ideologies. Keōpūolani, Kapi'olani, and Ka'ahumanu, that is, became known and beloved to missionaries for the manner in which they seemed to enact and embody the profound effects of successful Christian conversion. These Hawaiian women were significant to the missionary project of reform not just for their religious conversion but also for the extent to which they might appear to readers and onlookers as "remade" women, recognizable to Christian readers and mission donors for their seeming adoption and acceptance of Western gender roles. The adjudged success of the mission, indeed, seemed to hinge on producing gendered and racially recognizable converts.

During the period that American missions operated in the Hawaiian Islands and for an extended period afterward, the missionaries publicized their endeavors and declared them a success. They were, of course, interested in gaining the continued support of a donating Christian public at home. Stories of success, they knew, generated more revenue than tales of failure and struggle. Additionally, the ABCFM had enjoined missionaries at the outset of their journey—and at various intervals during their tenure in the islands—to be cautious in what they wrote about the islands. In 1834 the board wrote at least two times to the mission at Hawai'i reminding them of the necessity for discretion. The ABCFM had earlier been embarrassed by one of its missionaries at another station and was careful to avoid such problems in the future. In a letter to the missionaries, the board stressed that "missionaries should be very careful what they write in their private letters to this country. And they should never trust to the discretion of friends as to the publishing . . . [I]f they communicate anything that is not proper, or not expedient to be published, *in all cases* SAY expressly that it is not to be published."[69] Certainly, the ABCFM was interested in assuring the diplomacy of the project, but it was also undoubtedly concerned about projecting an image of the mission as being part of a successful endeavor to spread Christianity through the region. Converts, in short, made for positive publicity. No shit!

Despite the literature, Hawaiian women of high rank were not always the easy converts the missionaries proclaimed them to be. Reading between the lines of the missionaries' own literature on the mission project, in fact, one can see an alternate interpretation emerge that suggests that Hawaiian women of rank regarded themselves as agents in their interactions with their American missionary guests. Missionaries consistently portrayed Ka'ahumanu, Keōpūolani, and Kapi'olani as Christian converts, for example, describing them as "nursing mothers" to the mission. Mission writers like Mercy Whitney reported with some glee that the royal women also declared themselves to be "mothers" to the missionaries, who they referred to as "pet children."[70] Mercy Partridge Whitney noted as much in her diary, observing that during the missionaries' first summer, the queen had referred to her guests as "good American Children."[71] This trend was not confined to the early period of the mission; Laura Fish Judd wrote that Ka'ahumanu appeared to take great interest in the new band of missionaries. Judd recalled that the royal woman treated the new missionaries "like pet children, examined our eyes and hair, felt our arms, criticized our dress."[72] Clearly, Ka'ahumanu felt free to scrutinize her guests, touching and critiquing their bodies and attire. A short time later, Judd wrote about a similar scene. Though Judd described Ka'ahumanu in culturally unflattering terms, the

*** Alternate interp: regarded selves as agents

mission wife's reflections unintentionally tell us about Ka'ahumanu's perspective on her guests. "As she is an amazon in size," Judd wrote, "she could dandle any one of us in her lap, as she would a little child, *which she often takes the liberty of doing*."[73] Missionary accounts of such encounters unwittingly suggest that Hawaiian women of rank may have initially understood the missionaries as amusing and childlike and possibly not to be taken seriously.[74] Such an ordering of their relationship stood sharply at odds with the descriptions of enlightened, beneficent tutor and ignorant pupil that filled the diaries and published memoirs of the missionaries.

This is not to suggest, of course, that the missionaries fabricated the conversion of Hawaiian women of rank. It is in fact likely that just as the royal women accepted gifts of clothing and hats, they also accepted the offering of literacy and the Gospel, though perhaps not for the precise reasons that the missionaries believed. Still, Hawaiian islanders' acceptance of the missionaries' reforms seems at first perplexing: why would a people so recently freed from the restraints of traditional religious law willingly commit themselves to a new set of equally restrictive rules and customs? What need had they for corsets and spelling books? For the New Testament? For Christ?

Hawaiians, of course, had little actual need for the things that the missionaries offered, though some of the material items appeared appealing and desirable. They liked the hats and dresses, the corsets and fine jackets, and had asked for them explicitly. But to suggest that the Hawaiians were merely distracted by the trinkets of their American guests is misleading and overlooks the shrewdness of high-ranking Hawaiians—women in particular. It is critical to situate their actions in their particular historical context.

Reading through missionary writings, which provides an opportunity to interpret an author's underlying assumptions even as he or she emphasizes the righteousness and success of the mission, it is possible to ascribe a set of motivations to Hawaiians that may have remained undetected by the missionaries. It is possible, for example, that the Hawaiians participated in the lessons offered to them by their missionary guests not because they were particularly or exclusively interested in Christianity but because they were growing aware of Hawai'i's increasingly precarious political position within the nineteenth-century Pacific world.

Even before the missionaries arrived in Hawai'i, explorers and traders from around the globe visited the islands on a nearly constant basis. For the British and the Russians in the late eighteenth and early nineteenth century, Hawai'i offered an important strategic base. Increasingly over the nineteenth century, sandalwood and fur traders took a similar view of the

- Saw missionaries @ first as amusing, childlike

- Aware of Hawaii's precarious position w/in the Pacific world

Islands: Hawai'i was a good place to winter and an excellent post for conducting trade. For those with religious rather than economic aims, once the kapu system was overthrown in 1819, the islands appeared ripe for the adoption of a new religion. The American missionaries were not the only ones to perceive this void; French Catholics, in particular, seemed eager to fill the perceived empty space left behind by the dismantled kapus and sent their own missionaries to collect converts in the nineteenth century. Mormons came, too, though somewhat later. Moreover, the islands had been fraught with internal conflict as continual skirmishes between island chiefs marred the peace but also compromised their political unity. Ka'ahumanu achieved success in generating some political alliances, but she, too, was often in conflict with her chiefs. It is within this context that historians must interpret Ka'ahumanu's public alignment with American missionaries.

Though mission writers viewed Hawai'i's high-ranking women as important symbols of their successful conversion efforts, the native women were also shrewd political actors. Over the course of the nineteenth century, Hawai'i's high-ranking women emulated Kamehameha's strategy for dealing with foreign visitors, strategically adopting those Western ideas and cultural forms that seemed most useful in counteracting negative Western perceptions of the civility of Hawaiians.[75] Moreover, far from capitulating to the Westerners in their midst, ali'i deployed a kind of strategic accommodation as a means by which to articulate Hawai'i's political legitimacy to a foreign audience. They did so with the goal of preserving Hawaiian sovereignty. Similarly, Ka'ahumanu may have understood her alliance with the missionaries as a means by which to provide the Hawaiian people with the skills to negotiate successfully with the foreigners they would surely continue to encounter.[76] Ka'ahumanu, in other words, acted strategically and deliberately in ways that she perceived to be beneficial to the Hawaiian people within the context of growing Hawaiian political uncertainty. Hawaiian women of rank emerge from the story of the missionary period not as victims of the project but as political and cultural agents who used their considerable capital to shape the future of Hawai'i. In writing the official mission history, however, missionaries left little room for the complicated figures represented by Hawai'i's royal women.

Shrewd political actors; strategic
accomodation to articulate Hawaiian
political legitimacy

—Help people regotrate w/m
world

Conclusion

Nearly one year into the Hawaiian mission, Hiram Bingham and Asa Thurston called on King Liholiho. The purpose of their visit was to obtain his permission to build a permanent mission house in Honolulu. They began the conversation diplomatically. The missionaries thanked the king for his ongoing hospitality and then, judging his mood, explained that some "good friends in America had been so kind as to send . . . a house frame." The missionaries sought the king's "approbation to set it up." Liholiho's response was not what the missionaries had hoped for; indeed, "he gave a decided negative." Liholiho stood on historical precedent and explained that his father, King Kamehameha, had forbidden foreigners from building in the islands. Undissuaded, the missionaries tried another tack: they "appealed to his compassion," explaining that the mission wives were "accustomed to having good floors to live on." The missionaries worried that if their wives "were obliged to sit, and work, and sleep on the damp ground they might be sick and die." On this basis, Bingham and Thurston renewed their request. According to the missionaries, the king relented. He would allow the missionaries to erect the New England–style structure, but he added an important caveat. "[W]hen you go away," the king purportedly insisted, "take everything with you."[1]

Of course, the missionaries did not "go away," as Liholiho anticipated. The mission house they built in 1821 with Liholiho's qualified permission still stands on present-day King Street in downtown Honolulu. Just across the verdant mission yard and a narrow winding street stands Kawaiahaʻo Church, where Kaʻahumanu was baptized in 1825. While the mission house looks much the same as it did in the 1820s, the original thatched church has been rebuilt and remodeled on several occasions. In the late 1830s and early 1840s, the church was reconstructed using massive slabs of coral mined from the Pacific Ocean through Hawaiian labor. Despite its indigenous materials, the church was designed to resemble a New England–style church. Hiram Bingham's design features a massive steeple, visible—at least in mid-nineteenth-century Honolulu—from miles away.

The original mission house (at left) and thatched church as they appeared in 1820. (From Hiram Bingham, Residence of Twenty-One Years in the Sandwich Islands [1847]; courtesy Mission Houses Museum Library)

In 1864 Rufus Anderson called the church the "most conspicuous edifice in Honolulu."[2] The buildings reflect American missionaries' dual purposes of bringing both Christianity and "civilization" to Hawai'i. By building permanent structures, the missionaries endeavored not just to provide a "model" of the twin pillars of New England culture for Hawaiians to emulate but also to establish them in Hawai'i on a more permanent basis.

The missionaries' official tenure in the islands spanned just over thirty years. In all, the American Board of Commissioners for Foreign Missions sent twelve companies of missionaries to Hawai'i. During that time, the missionaries fanned out over the Hawaiian Islands, establishing mission stations as well as schools and churches not just on O'ahu but on neighboring islands as well. The ABCFM sent its last company of missionaries to the Hawaiian Islands in 1848. They declared the islands "Christianized" in 1853 and began to withdraw support for the missions they had established there.[3] By many measures, the mission could be considered a success for the cause of Christianity. Hawaiians swelled the roster of missionary churches, with over one-quarter of the islands' population claiming membership by the end of the missionaries' term there. Missionaries also helped to create an increasingly literate Hawaiian population.[4] Moreover, the missionaries credited themselves with beginning the process of cultural conversion by clothing, educating, and "reforming" the habits of Hawaiian people to become not only Christianized but "civilized" as well.

By 1853, "Christianized" -
Success story, also spread literacy

Kawaiaha'o Church (also called the Stone Church) in Honolulu. (Courtesy Mission Houses Museum Library)

Mission histories and memoirs—some of them published while the mission was still in effect—celebrated these alterations as victories. If they believed that God had led them to the Hawaiian Islands, they continued to attest to the belief that his will had prevailed.

And yet, the story of contact in the Hawaiian Islands is much more complex than the official mission literature suggests. The Hawaiian Islands presented a unique and sometimes challenging site for successful missionizing on several different fronts. From the outset of the mission, the Hawaiians with whom the missionaries had contact appear not as passive victims of Western intentions but as agents in their relationships with foreigners from around the globe. The nearly constant influx of foreigners to the islands affected American missionaries' efforts to convert Hawaiians. American missionaries represented just one group among many who visited the islands in the nineteenth century. For some ali'i seeking to form economic or political relations with foreigners, the missionaries appeared to be of little practical value. These ali'i felt little obligation to accept the missionaries or adapt to their plans. The islands' queens and other women of rank, in particular, had much to say about whether and how they interacted with missionary women

— Agents in relationships w/ foreigners
— One group among many

and played a profound role in shaping those interactions. Women of high rank had proven adept at negotiating with American missionaries and their wives, demonstrating their considerable cultural and political power.

When Hawaiian women of rank accepted missionary gifts, for example, they insisted on using them in the manner they saw fit, initially refusing to participate in the missionary project of reform. In the process, they reminded the missionaries of their tenuous position in the islands. Hawaiians could accept gifts of clothing, wearing Western fashions consistently in public, or they could choose (as they so often did) to wear them sporadically or in combinations jarring to the Western eye. They could adopt Christian ideals of family government, including monogamy, or they could persist in their older customs. They might adopt ideals of industry, sobriety, and modesty—or not—all without censure. Similarly, Hawaiians could accept the tenets of Christianity and practice them perfectly, they could blend them with remnants of the old religion, or they could refuse them altogether.

Hawaiians, of course, did accept some of what the missionaries had to offer. Many participated in the system of education and instruction offered by the missionaries, becoming proficient in English. High-ranking Hawaiian women reformed their marital and family arrangements and began dressing like Western "ladies"—at least in public. At the same time, the transformation was far from complete. Missionary wives experienced frustrating and uneven results when they tried to force Hawaiians to replicate American habits and institutions. Moreover, the missionaries could not compel Hawaiians to adopt missionary manners and customs and eschew those they had acquired in their relationships with the myriad other foreign visitors to the islands. Hawaiian culture, in fact, proved both remarkably resilient and adaptive.[5] It might best be said that the missionaries participated—vigorously—in an ongoing *process* of Westernizing the Hawaiian Islands.

Mission women's diaries reflect what we now understand about the Hawaiian Islands and about other "conquered" regions as well. "Conversion" is rarely complete, and even partial transformation comes slowly. The missionary wives, largely responsible for diplomatic relations with Hawaiians, described a world of interaction, exchange, and compromise. Conversion, these women understood, was a slow and partial process at best. Missionary wives realized what their husbands never readily admitted to, at least in print. They were guests of the Hawaiians, there at the good grace of the islands' ali'i. They knew that they could not demand compliance in matters of either faith or culture. In the early years of the nineteenth century,

Hawaiians remained free to pick and choose among the missionaries' wares, both material and ideological.

The geographic reality of Hawai'i surely shaped the mission in other ways as well. While the Hawaiian Islands' location at the crossroads of Pacific travel, trade, and exploration must have made them an exciting place to live in the nineteenth century, it nonetheless served to isolate missionaries from ideologically like-minded people and prevented them from enjoying uncontested influence in the islands. There were enough challengers from outside Hawai'i to keep American missionaries busy, but there were certainly obstacles to overcome from within as well. Yet less has been written about the reality of missionaries' dispersal throughout the islands. We know little about how different local leadership on each island shaped the missionaries' efforts to spread Christianity in the uniform way they intended.[6] In order to more fully understand the processes at work and to further recenter Hawaiians in the narrative of early-to-mid-nineteenth-century Hawai'i, it will be critical to gain a deeper sense of how ali'i on each island engaged differently with missionaries and other foreign guests relative to their individual political and diplomatic aims.

Further research exploring the distinct relationships ali'i cultivated with the islands' foreign guests will further clarify both the ongoing struggle for political authority in the islands and the diversity of opinion among ali'i regarding the benefit of foreign political, diplomatic, and trade relations. While Ka'ahumanu's continued support of the American missionaries created a necessary precondition for American colonization of the Hawaiian Islands, her authority did not go uncontested. Future research exploring internal political challenges will underscore the importance of the relationships between Hawai'i's high-ranking women and American missionary wives.

If missionaries were unprepared to compete for Hawaiians' attentions, the unfamiliar gender hierarchy they encountered in Hawai'i compelled them to reconsider their initial strategies for conversion and suggested new roles for women throughout the foreign-mission movement. Missionary wives acted as diplomats, alternately recognizing the official limitations placed upon them by the mission board and seizing opportunities when and where they presented themselves. In their relationships with Hawaiian women of rank, mission women built strong alliances with some of the most powerful figures in the Hawaiian Islands. Gaining the confidence and favor of the politically and culturally important women of rank, mission wives simultaneously advanced the cause of the mission and enhanced

Future directions

— Had to rethink strategy

✷✷ Women/wives as diplomats

their own roles within it. Their clever diplomacy extended not only to their interactions with the Hawaiian people but also to members of their own culture. In both their private and published writings, mission wives celebrated the newfound significance of their work without ever appearing to violate the terms of their proscribed gender role. Steeping themselves in what appeared to be a central concern of the mission—particularly the private and intimate domains of family, the home, and social interaction—mission wives found themselves locked with Hawai'i's high-ranking women at the very center of the Hawaiian-missionary drama. Mission writers who championed mission wives' part in the success of the Hawaiian mission helped to suggest a new and more expansive role for women in the foreign-mission movement. Missionary wives' active engagement in the mission, spurred by Hawai'i's women of rank, thus prompted an important shift in American women's reform activity.

While mission women's work in Hawai'i created new opportunities for women's participation in the foreign-mission movement, it also generated fresh possibilities for mission wives already in Hawai'i. Many missionaries and their wives, in fact, remained in the Hawaiian Islands once the mission officially disbanded. In their earliest writings, the missionaries had stressed the sacrifice that characterized their work. They had removed themselves from their homes and families and transplanted themselves among a people they could only describe as "heathen." While they elevated their cause, most anticipated that their labors were temporary and that they would return home once their mission was completed. They did not envision that they would live out their lives among a people they initially regarded as entirely foreign. Some of the earliest missionaries, in fact, had sent their own children back to the United States to live with family members rather than raise them among the "heathen," who, missionaries believed, might negatively impact the children's moral and intellectual development.[7]

In light of these misgivings, the decision by missionaries to remain in Hawai'i requires some explanation. American missionaries stayed, in part, because they had forged advantageous relationships during their stay in the islands. Their relationships with the queens and other women of rank had for many years allowed the missionaries to enjoy near-religious exclusivity in the islands. The missionaries pursued this advantage to the fullest, currying political favor as well. In the late 1840s, the Māhele—a process by which private landownership supplanted the tenancy system—allowed Hawaiians and foreigners alike to purchase land.[8] The arrangement favored missionaries who could (and did) broker extremely profitable deals on the land. The axiom that missionaries "came to do good and stayed to do well" seems undeniable in consideration of the massive acquisition of land near the close of the mission.[9] The effects of the missionary "land grab" in Hawai'i are still felt today.

And yet it is not clear that land ownership alone offered adequate motivation for the missionaries or their wives to stay. This seems particularly true for missionary wives who remained in the islands after their husbands had died, leaving them widows in a land they had once considered foreign. Mercy Partridge Whitney, who came to Hawai'i as a young bride in 1820, was among those who remained. Her husband, Samuel, died in 1845. Mercy lived in Hawai'i for nearly thirty years thereafter. She died in 1872 in Kaua'i.[10] At the mission's start, many mission wives expressed genuine distress upon leaving their families in the mainland. The close of the mission must have appeared to many as an opportunity for a long-overdue reunion back home. It is curious, then, that so many missionary wives opted to stay after fulfilling their obligation to God and to the Hawaiian people they had come to serve. During their years in the islands, mission wives had formed and sustained strong relationships with one another. Calling one another "sister," some women created bonds that endured over the span of the mission. Moreover, mission wives forged long-lasting relationships with Hawai'i's high-ranking women. These relationships undoubtedly proved critical to understanding mission wives' desire to stay. Yet other possibilities remain. The same women who agreed to participate in the mission as "help meets" and "angels of mercy" might have grown accustomed to the new place they occupied in the Hawaiian Islands mission and felt loathe to give it up. If mission wives were changed as a result of their labor for the mission, it remains for researchers to uncover how those changes shaped their choices not just during the mission but after and beyond it.

Finally, in their diaries and memoirs, missionary wives described a world that looked increasingly less like "heathen ground," as they had initially described it upon their arrival, and more like home.[11] As future research will likely show, the increasing foreign presence in Hawai'i over the eighteenth and nineteenth centuries reshaped not just its cultural landscape but its physical landscape as well. Otto Von Kotzebue observed the process already under way in the late eighteenth century when he remarked on the buildings constructed "after the European fashion." Combined with tropical flora and fauna, Kotzebue observed that "this place" had taken on "the mixed appearance of an European and Owhyee village."[12] The missionary house and church, then, were part of a larger, gradual environmental transformation in Hawai'i. While the Māhele incontrovertibly hastened the transformation, the process whereby the islands exhibited an increasingly "mixed appearance" was already well under way in the early years of the nineteenth century.

Historians will want to better understand not only the way in which changes in Hawai'i's built environment might have acted as inducements for foreigners to remain in the islands but also how changes to the islands' built environment fit into ali'i's plans for political diplomacy. Such inquiry will enhance historians' understanding of the way in which ali'i' engaged in the long process of strategic accommodation in their relationship to foreigners. Ali'i, as I have argued, adopted Western-style clothing as a means to enhance their individual status while conveying their civility to foreign visitors and establishing important, politically diplomatic relationships. High-ranking Hawaiians might have recognized a similar opportunity to incorporate European and American architectural styles into their built environment. Like clothing, the European- and American-style structures erected in eighteenth- and nineteenth-century Hawai'i acted as immediately ascertainable symbols of civilization. Foreign visitors, in fact, made consistent and regular observations about the state of Hawaiian culture based on their reflections on the physical and material manifestations of "civilization" they found in the islands. Additional scholarship in this area will only deepen our understanding of Hawaiians' increasingly sophisticated grasp of the symbolic language of things over this period and will demonstrate the adaptive strategies that ali'i employed to resist colonization.

If Liholiho hoped the missionaries would someday "go away," taking their frame structures, their religion, and their culture with them, some ali'i proved much more amenable to the missionaries and their plans. When Liholiho departed the islands in 1823 for a diplomatic mission to England, in fact, Ka'ahumanu continued her own diplomatic efforts. The royal woman's adoption of Christianity, forged in her relation to missionary wives, reshaped Hawai'i's cultural and political terrain in profound and long-lasting ways. By mobilizing her own political authority in ways that benefited the missionary aims, however, Ka'ahumanu also sought to secure Hawai'i's political future. Similarly, while the enduring presence of the church and the more-modest mission house might be read as incontrovertible evidence of missionaries' pervasive—and permanent—influence in the islands, an alternate interpretation may be that these buildings signal Hawaiians' ongoing strategic engagement with foreigners in their homeland.

Notes

ABBREVIATIONS

HHS Hawaiian Historical Society, Honolulu, Hawai'i
HL Houghton Library, Harvard University, Cambridge, Mass.
HMCS Hawaiian Mission Children's Society Library, Honolulu, Hawai'i
KHS Kauai Historical Society, Lihue, Hawai'i
YDL Yale Divinity Library, New Haven, Conn.

INTRODUCTION

1. For more on the Pacific—and Atlantic—travels of Hawaiian and other Pacific Islanders, see Thomas, *Islanders*. See also Okihiro, *Island World*, 138–42. For more on Humehume's Pacific and Atlantic travels, see Warne, *Humehume of Kaua'i*, and Stauder, "George, Prince of Hawaii."

2. Samuel and Nancy Ruggles, journal, July 25, 1820, Journals Collection, HMCS.

3. For discussion of these issues, see the introduction to Silva's *Aloha Betrayed*; and Trask, *From a Native Daughter*. See Osorio, "Living in Archives and Dreams"; Kamakau, *Ruling Chiefs of Hawaii*; Malo, *Hawaiian Antiquities*; 'I'i, *Fragments of Hawaiian History*.

4. Sahlins, *How "Natives" Think*, 14; Linnekin, *Sacred Queens and Women of Consequence*; Dening, *The Death of William Gooch*; Kame'eleihiwa, *Native Land and Foreign Desires*. See also White, *The Middle Ground*, and Richter, *Facing East from Indian Country*.

5. See Richter, *Facing East from Indian Country*; Taylor, *American Colonies*; and Igler, "Trading Places: The View of Colonial American History from the Pacific." See also Weiner, *Inalienable Possessions*.

6. For two foundational works on the labor of American missionary wives in Hawai'i, see Zwiep, *Pilgrim Path*, and Grimshaw, *Paths of Duty*. For more on Hawaiian women's status in the nineteenth century, see Linnekin's *Sacred Queens and Women of Consequence*. On the colonization of the islands, see Silva, *Aloha Betrayed*; Kame'eleihiwa, *Native Land and Foreign Desires*; Trask, *From a Native Daughter*; and Merry, *Colonizing Hawai'i*.

7. Stoler, "Tense and Tender Ties." See also the introduction to Ballantyne and Burton, *Bodies in Contact*.

8. For elaboration on Hawai'i in this period, see Silva, *Aloha Betrayed*; Buck, *Paradise Remade*; and Valeri, *Kingship and Sacrifice*.

9. On the Second Great Awakening, see Hatch, *The Democratization of American Christianity*; LeBeau, *Religion in America to 1865*; Howe, *What Hath God Wrought*, 186–95; Reynolds, *Waking Giant*, 126–35; and Wagner, "Mission and Motivation."

For a discussion of the gendered dimensions of the reform impulse, see Kaplan, "Manifest Domesticity"; Kent, *Converting Women*.

10. For a discussion of *kapu* laws, see Merry, *Colonizing Hawai'i*; Kame'eleihiwa, *Native Land and Foreign Desires*; and Young, "The Hawaiians"; For elaboration on the overthrow of the *kapu* laws, see Daws, *Shoal of Time*, 55–58.

11. For a discussion of the Sandalwood trade, see Wagner-Wright, *Ships, Furs, and Sandalwood*; and Silva, *Aloha Betrayed*. On the effects of Western contact, see Buck, *Paradise Remade*; Stannard, *Before the Horror*; and Banner, *Possessing the Pacific*. On competing influences in the islands, see Kashay, "Native, Foreigner, Missionary, Priest"; Kashay, "Competing Imperialisms and Hawaiian Authority"; and Birkett, "Hawai'i in 1819."

12. A portion of this research appears in an article published in 2010. See Thigpen, "You Have Been Very Thoughtful Today." Mauss, *The Gift*. See also Komter, *Social Solidarity and the Gift*, and Berking, *Sociology of Giving*. For elaborations on the way historians might use gift giving and exchange, see the introduction to Appaduari, *The Social Life of Things*; Davis, *The Gift in Sixteenth-Century France*; and Gutiérrez, *When Jesus Came, the Corn Mothers Went Away*. On gifts in a Hawaiian cultural context, see Weiner, *Inalienable Possessions*, and Linnekin, *Children of the Land*. See also Kirch, *On the Road of the Winds*.

13. For an elaboration on political strategies employed by nineteenth-century ali'i, see Sahlins, "Hawai'i in the Early Nineteenth Century." See also Kirch and Sahlins, *Anahulu*; Kashay, "From *Kapus* to Christianity"; Silva, *Aloha Betrayed*; Merry, *Colonizing Hawai'i*; and Grimshaw, "New England Missionary Wives, Hawaiian Women, and the 'Cult of True Womanhood.'"

CHAPTER 1

1. Kotzebue, *A Voyage of Discovery*, 300–302. See also "Letter of Kamehameha II to Alexander I, 1820," 831. Kamehameha referred both to Captain James Cook, the British explorer who was killed by Hawaiians during his second visit to the islands in 1779, and to the Russian attempt to occupy the island of Kaua'i in 1815. See Mills, *Hawai'i's Russian Adventure*, 26–28; Pierce, *Russia's Hawaiian Adventure*, 17–18; Kuykendall and Day, *Hawaii*, 35–37; and Daws, *Shoal of Time*, 51–53.

2. Judd's *Voyages to Hawaii before 1860* provides an excellent starting point for identifying foreign visitors to the islands. See also Daws, *Shoal of Time*, 44–49; Oliver, *The Pacific Islands*, 73–80; Thomas, *Islanders*, 1–4; Okihiro, *Island World*, 138–42; and Miller, "Ka'iana, the Once Famous 'Prince of Kaua'i,'" 1–22.

3. Silva, *Aloha Betrayed*, 26, See also Buck, *Paradise Remade*, 17–18, 61–62; Merry, *Colonizing Hawai'i*, 43–44; Kent, *Hawaii*, 20; and Holt, *Monarchy in Hawaii*, 9–10.

4. Kame'eleihiwa argued that even Stannard's "reasoned, careful" calculations underestimated Hawaiian population decline in the years between Cook's arrival in 1778 and the count conducted by American missionaries in 1823. Kame'eleihiwa, *Native Land and Foreign Desires*, 81, 20. See also Stannard, *Before the Horror*, 24–27; and Crosby, "Hawaiian Depopulation as a Model for the Amerindian Experience,"

175–202. For an overview of the major debates around pre- and postcontact population figures for the Hawaiian Islands, see Kirch, "Like Shoals of Fish," 53–54.

5. Okihiro, *Island World*, especially page 147. See also Campbell, *A History of the Pacific Islands*, 46–47; and Rifkin, "Debt and the Transnationalization of Hawai'i." For an earlier interpretation, see Kent, *Hawaii*.

6. Noenoe K. Silva has convincingly argued that Hawaiians "often took the tools of the colonizers and made use of them to secure their own national sovereignty and well-being." *Aloha Betrayed*, 15–16.

7. Daws, *Shoal of Time*, 55. See also Wong and Rayson, *Hawaii's Royal History*, 67.

8. Silva, *Aloha Betrayed*, 18. Buck, *Paradise Remade*, 12–14.

9. Kuykendall and Day, *Hawaii*, 37. See also Valeri, *Kingship and Sacrifice*, xviii.

10. Vancouver, *Voyage of Discovery to the North Pacific Ocean and Round the World*, 5.

11. Thomas, *The Extraordinary Voyages of Captain James Cook*, 268. Anthropologists and historians have engaged in an extended and vigorous debate over whether or not Hawaiians in the eighteenth century received Cook as the returning god Lono. It is not my purpose to engage the specifics of this fascinating debate here. Rather, the concerns raised in these discussions remind historians of the importance of attending to cultural structures in an effort to apprehend and interpret the activities of our historical subjects accurately. Where Marshall Sahlins rightly insisted that scholars ground historical interpretation in the "culture-specific qualities" that may have motivated our subjects, Gananath Obeyesekere urged historians to examine rigorously the secondary sources upon which we have long relied to reveal and explore "the distorted lens through which Westerners see Hawaiians." Borofsky, "Cook, Lono, Obeyesekere, and Sahlins," 256–57. See also Sahlins, *How "Natives" Think*, 14; Sahlins, and *Islands of History*; and Obeyesekere, *The Apotheosis of Captain Cook*.

12. The ship was accompanied by another, the *Chatham*, commanded by Lieutenant William Broughton.

13. Vancouver, *A Voyage of Discovery to the North Pacific Ocean and Round the World 1791–1795*, 18.

14. For additional sources on the lasting legacy of Vancouver's voyages, see Fisher and Johnston, *From Maps to Metaphors*. See also Dolin, *Fur, Fortune, and Empire*, 152, 154; and Thomas, *Islanders*, 127.

15. Daws, *Shoal of Time*, 38. See also Speakerman and Hackler, *Vancouver in Hawai'i*, 32 and 42. In March 1792 Vancouver attempted to ascertain the leadership of Hawai'i. To Vancouver, initial conflicting reports revealed "how very difficult it is . . . to obtain matter of fact from these people." Vancouver, *A Voyage of Discovery*, 1:158.

16. Kuykendall and Day, *Hawaii*, 23. Daws, *Shoal of Time*, 30.

17. Merry, *Colonizing Hawai'i*, 53; Kame'elehiwa, *Native Land and Foreign Desires*, 47.

18. Kame'elehiwa, *Native Land and Foreign Desires*, 41–43.

19. Ellis, *An Authentic Narrative of a Voyage Performed by Captain Cook and Captain Clerke*, 105. Silva, *Aloha Betrayed*, 21. Ralph Kuykendall hints at the violence that transpired in his account in *The Hawaiian Kingdom*, 1:19.

20. Kamakau, *Ruling Chiefs of Hawaii*, 103. Ellis, *An Authentic Narrative*, 2:121; Daws, *Shoal of Time*, 29.

21. Keme'elehiwa, *Native Land*, 47.

22. Kamakau, *Ruling Chiefs of Hawaii*, 107. See also Fornander, *An Account of the Polynesian Race*, 2:299.

23. Daws provides an excellent narrative account of Kamehameha's assent. See *Shoal of Time*, especially pages 29–53. See also Silva, *Aloha Betrayed*, 18. Day, *History Makers of Hawaii*. See also Kuykendall, *A History of Hawaii*, 1:62–79.

24. Kamehameha's rivals for power were Keoua and Keawema'uhili, Kīwala'ō's half brother and uncle, respectively.

25. Warne, *Humehume of Kaua'i*, 3.

26. Malo, *Hawaiian Antiquities*, 160–61. See also Kamakau, *Ruling Chiefs*, 154–55.

27. Kamakau, *Ka Po'e Kahiko*, 15.

28. Vancouver, *Voyage of Discovery*, 1:158.

29. Ibid., 1:161–62.

30. Some of the islands' foreign population—like the Englishman John Young and Don Francisco de Paula Marin, a Spaniard—ultimately acted like "advisors" and interpreters to the king. Vancouver, *Voyage of Discovery*, 2:122. See also Gast and Conrad, *Don Francisco de Paula Marin*; and Daws, *Shoal of Time*, 42.

31. Vancouver, *Voyage of Discovery*, 2:809.

32. Ibid., 2:123–24, 127.

33. Ibid., 2:127.

34. Ibid.

35. Ibid., 2:129.

36. Ibid., 2:130.

37. Ibid., 2:126–30.

38. Silverman, *Kaahumanu*, 16–17.

39. Vancouver, *Voyage of Discovery*, 1:145.

40. Ibid., 3:10.

41. Kame'eleihiwa, *Native Land and Foreign Desires*, 29–31. See also Sahlins's chapter titled "The Historiography of the Makahiki" in *How "Natives" Think*. See also Kamakau, *Ka Po'e Kahiko*, 19–21, and *Ruling Chiefs*, 181. Beckwith, *Hawaiian Mythology*, 33–36. Vancouver, *Voyage of Discovery*, 3:5–6.

42. Vancouver, *Voyage of Discovery*, 3:5–6.

43. Ibid., 3:30.

44. Ibid., 3:31–32; Fornander, *An Account of the Polynesian Race*, 2:341.

45. Vancouver, *Voyage of Discovery*, 3:54.

46. Ibid., 3:29.

47. Ibid.

48. Ibid., 3:32.

49. Ibid., 3:51–52. Kuykendall, *The Hawaiian Kingdom*, 1:41–42.

50. Kuykendall, *The Hawaiian Kingdom*, 1:44.

51. Kamakau, *Ruling Chiefs of Hawaii*, 168–73. 'Ī'ī, *Fragments of Hawaiian History*, 15. See also Daws, *Shoal of Time*, 39–40; and Kuykendall and Day, *Hawaii*, 27.

52. Fornander, *An Account of the Polynesian Race*, 2:348.

53. Linnekin, "New Political Orders," 189.

54. Broughton, *Voyage of Discovery to the North Pacific Ocean*, 38.

55. Ibid., 39.

56. Speakerman and Hackler, *Vancouver in Hawaii*.

57. Malo, *Hawaiian Antiquities*, 76. See also Buck, *Arts and Crafts of Hawaii*, 231–48.

58. Buck, *Arts and Crafts of Hawaii*, 231.

59. Malo writes that "the feathers of the *mamo* bird were more choice than those of the *o-o* because of their superior magnificence when woven into cloaks." Malo, *Hawaiian Antiquities*, 76.

60. Kirch, *How Chiefs Became Kings*, 42–45. Kaeppler, "Hawaiian Art and Society," 118. Weiner, *Inalienable Possessions*, 84–85. Linnekin, *Sacred Queens and Women of Consequence*, 48. See also Kaeppler, "Hawaiian Art and Society," 105–31.

61. Arthur, *Religion, Dress, and the Body*, 3. See also Roach-Higgins's and Eicher's essay, "Dress and Identity," in *Religion, Dress, and the Body*, 11–14.

62. For a brief sketch of Western fashion in Hawai'i, see Arthur, "Fossilized Fashion in Hawai'i," 15–28.

63. Silva, *Aloha Betrayed*, 15–16.

64. For more on the peaceful transfer of power of Kaua'i, see Kamakau, *Ruling Chiefs*, 194–97; Daws, *Shoal of Time*, 43; and Kuykendall, *The Hawaiian Kingdom*, 1:49–51.

65. Kamakau, *Ruling Chiefs of Hawaii*, 195.

66. Ibid.

67. 'Ī'ī, *Fragments of Hawaiian History*, 16.

68. Kamakau, *Ruling Chiefs of Hawaii*, 196.

69. For some of the varying interpretations of Kaumuali'i's cession of Kaua'i and Ni'ihau, see 'Ī'ī, *Fragments of Hawaii History*, 16; Kamakau, *Ruling Chiefs of Hawaii*, 196–97; Daws, *Shoal of Time*; 43–44; and Silva, *Aloha Betrayed*, 24.

70. Mills, *Hawai'i's Russian Adventure*, 20–25, 111–18. See also Pierce, *Russia's Hawaiian Adventure*, 7–16, 63–65, 72–73. Kuykendall, *The Hawaiian Kingdom*, 1:58–59.

71. Kotzebue, *Voyage of Discovery*, 1:305, 299.

72. Ibid., 1:302, 300.

73. Ibid., 1:314, 315.

74. Ibid., 1:315.

75. These negotiations, as well as the description of the king's attire, are confirmed by Hawaiian mo'olelo. See the Kona Historical Society's "Na Mo'olelo o Kona" collection at http://www.konahistorical.org/index.php/oral_history/. See also Choris, *Voyage Pittoresque Autour de Monde*, 3.

76. Choris, *Voyage Pittoresque Autour de Monde*, 3.

77. Liebersohn, "Images of Monarchy," 48; Forbes, *Encounters with Paradise*, 57–58.

78. Liebersohn, "Images of Monarchy," 52.

79. Ibid., 44–64.

80. Kotzebue, *Voyage of Discovery*, 1: 300, 316.

81. Kamakau, *Ruling Chiefs*, 210.

82. Arago, *Narrative of a Voyage Round the World*, 81, 79.

CHAPTER 2

1. See Grimshaw, *Paths of Duty*, 1–23, and Zwiep, *Pilgrim Path*, 23–27.

2. The "Hawaiian helpers" were known to the missionaries as Thomas Hopu, William Kanui, and John Honolii. George "Tamoree"—the son of Kaumauali'i, Kaua'i's former king—was also on board. See *Missionary Album*, 7. See also Warne, "The Story behind the Headstone."

3. *Panoplist and Missionary Herald*, vol. 15, 528.

4. "Letter from Sybil Moseley Bingham to Jeremiah Evarts," October 23, 1819, Letters and Papers of the Board, HL. See also "Diary of Mercy Partridge Whitney," December 31, 1819, Journals Collection, HMCS. See Nancy and Samuel Ruggles's "Journal from Boston, USA, to the Sandwich Isles," November 6, 1819, Journals Collection, HMCS.

5. On the Second Great Awakening, see Hatch, *The Democratization of American Christianity*, 17–18; Howe, *What Hath God Wrought*, 186–95; LeBeau, *Religion in America to 1865*, 91; and Wagner, "Mission and Motivation," 62–70.

6. For more on gender and authority in the Second Great Awakening, see Juster, *Disorderly Women*, 145–79.

7. The scholarly literature on "mission" and "empire" overlaps in instructive ways. For more on the gendered nature of empire, see Levine's edited collection *Gender and Empire*. Particularly useful is Catherine Hall's essay "Of Gender and Empire," 46–76. See also Kaplan, *The Anarchy of Empire in the Making of U.S. Culture*; Midgley, *Gender and Imperialism*; Clancy-Smith and Gouda, *Domesticating the Empire*; Tyrell, *Woman's World, Woman's Empire*; Hill, *The World Their Household*; and Hunter, *The Gospel of Gentility*.

8. Of the first company of missionaries, all but two of the American members— the Loomises—came from Connecticut or Massachusetts. All were born in the 1780s or 1790s. See American Board of Commissioners for Foreign Missions, "Missionaries: Birthplace, Residence, Dates of Sailing," HL.

9. See "Letter of Certification for Mercy Partridge from Heman Humphrey" in Letters and Papers of the Board, HL. See Hatch, *The Democratization of American Christianity*, 17–18, and Hutchison, *Errand to the World*, 51–52.

10. "Letter from Mercy Partridge to Josiah Brewer," February 4, 1819, and August 30, 1819, HMCS. "Letter from Sybil Bingham to Jeremiah Evarts," October 23, 1819, Letters and Papers of the Board, HL. *Paths of Duty*, 13; and Zwiep, *Pilgrim Path*, 27.

11. Reynolds, *Waking Giant*, 131. See also Howe, *What Hath God Wrought*, 187–88.

12. See Gallaudet, *An Address, Delivered at a Meeting for Prayers, with Reference to the Sandwich Islands Mission*, 7. See also Wagner, "Mission and Motivation," 65.

13. Wagner, "Mission and Motivation," 65–66. See also Wagner-Wright, *The Structure of the Missionary Call to the Sandwich Islands*.

14. Butler, Wacker, and Balmer, *Religion in American Life*, 183–84.

15. Bingham, *A Residence*, 81.

16. See Hatch, *The Democratization of American Christianity*, 5, 9–11. For a discussion of women's place within the awakening, see also Howe, *What Hath God Wrought*, 190–91.

17. Braude, "Women's History Is American Religious History," 99. For more on women's emergent role, see Cott, *The Bonds of Womanhood*. See also Welter, *Dimity Convictions*, 83–102; and Ryan, *Cradle of the Middle Class*, 12–13, 83–89.

18. For more on the intersection of race and gender ideology, particularly in the colonial context, see Brown, *Good Wives, Nasty Wenches, and Anxious Patriarchs*; McClintock, *Imperial Leather*; Ryan, *Mysteries of Sex*, 103–24; and Singh, *Gender, Religion, and "Heathen Lands."* See also Morgan, *Laboring Women*, 12–49.

19. See Hall, "Of Gender and Empire," 46–47.

20. Maffly-Kipp, "Eastward Ho!," 127.

21. Dwight, *Memoirs of Henry Obookiah*. Obookiah's story had already been established in *The Narrative of Five Youths*. The story was also retold in the annual reports of the mission in 1816, 1817, and 1819. See *ABCFM Annual Reports, 1810–1820*, 136, 166, 247. See also Anderson, *History of the Sandwich Islands Mission*, 11. Thurston, *The Missionary's Daughter*, 22–24.

22. Anderson, *History of the Sandwich Islands Mission*, 11.

23. Dwight, *Memoirs of Henry Obookiah*, 14, 17.

24. "Minutes of the First Annual Meeting" in *ABCFM Annual Reports, 1810–1820*, 10. Maffly-Kipp, "Eastward Ho!," 127.

25. Dwight, *Memoirs of Henry Obookiah*, 17–18. Tracy, *History of American Missions*, 29–30.

26. The meetings, which culminated in the formation of the ABCFM, are detailed in American Board of Commissioners for Foreign Missions, "Minutes of the First Annual Meeting," *ABCFM Annual Reports, 1810–1820*, 9–10.

27. Phillips, *Protestant America and the Pagan World*, 46.

28. American Board of Commissioners for Foreign Missions Treasury Department, "Donations from November 17, 1811–September 25, 1818," HL; "Minutes of the First Annual Meeting," 13.

29. For a full discussion of the ABCFM's formation and organization, see Phillips, *Protestant America*; Harris, *Nothing but Christ*; and Putney, *Missionaries in Hawai'i*, 18–19.

30. For a discussion of the mission's increasingly global outlook, see Okihiro's *Island World*, 89–92; Burlin, *Imperial Maine and Hawai'i*, 8–17; Cumings, *Dominion from Sea to Sea*, 75–77; Kent, *Hawaii*, 26–29; Hutchinson, *Errand to the World*, 51–53; and Kashay, "Agents of Imperialism."

31. "Minutes of the First Annual Meeting," 13.

32. *ABCFM Annual Reports, 1810–1820*, 10–11. See also Anderson, *Memorial Volume of the First Fifty Years of the American Board of Commissioners for Foreign Missions*, 226–41.

33. For more on the India mission, see Tracy, "History of the American Board of Commissioners for Foreign Missions," 35–40; Anderson, *History of the Missions of the American Board of Commissioners for Foreign Missions in India*, 1–22. See also Cayton, "Canonizing Harriet Newell," 73–76; and Maxfield, "The 'Reflex Influence' of Missions," 73–77. Phillips, *Protestant America and the Pagan World*, 32–36.

34. Hall and Newell, *The Conversion of the World*, 55, 5, 11.

35. Dwight, *Memoirs of Henry Obookiah*, 14.

36. Ibid., xv. See also Lyons, "Memoirs of Henry Obookiah," 36–37. For scholarly discussion of Ōūkahaʻia, see Okihiro, *Island World*, 76–78; and Daws, *Shoal of Time*, 61–62.

37. "Letter from Chauncey Goodrich to the Reverend Samuel Worcester, August 17, 1819," HL.

38. "Letter from Samuel Whitney to Samuel Worcester, August 23, 1819," HL. See also "Letter from Reverend Wheeler to Reverend Elias Cornelius, April 15, 1817," HL. Wheeler described Samuel Ruggles, another potential missionary, as "suitable" for the work though "not very advanced in his literary pursuits" and in "feeble health."

39. See American Board of Commissioners for Foreign Missions, "Missionaries: Colleges and Degrees," HL. See also Hatch, *Democratization*, 17; Butler, Wacker, and Balmer, *Religion in American Life*, 185–86; and Reynolds, *Waking Giant*, 131–32.

40. "Letter from Chauncey Goodrich to Rev. Samuel Worcester, August 17, 1819," Letters and Papers of the Board, HL.

41. "Letter from Chauncey Goodrich to Rev. Samuel Worcester, August 17, 1819," HL.

42. Ibid.

43. For more on the social and educational status of the missionaries, see Grimshaw, *Paths of Duty*, 7.

44. See "Missionaries: Colleges and Degrees," HL. See also *Missionary Album*.

45. Kashay, "O That My Mouth Might Be Opened," 42, 43.

46. American Board of Commissioners for Foreign Missions, "Instructions of the Prudential Committee of the American Board of Commissioners for Foreign Missions to the Sandwich Islands"; Bingham, *A Residence*, 62.

47. The board was so insistent on sending a physician with their missionaries that the first company was almost delayed in their departure as they scrambled to find someone to fill the spot. Of the ten separate companies deployed to the islands, six deployed with a physician. Only the fourth, six, seventh, and ninth companies did not bring physicians with them. See "Memorandum for Conversation with Reverend William Ellis, April 1825" in Valuable Documents, HL. See Wagner-Wright, "When Unity Is Torn Asunder," 40. See also *Missionary Album*.

48. Thomas and Lucia Ruggles Holman were stationed near the king's residence at Kailua. The arrangements were made at the king's insistence. See Hiram Bingham, *A Residence*, 91. Kuykendall, *The Hawaiian Kingdom*, 1:103.

49. Hall and Newell, *Conversion of the World*, 8. Emphasis in original.

50. Bingham, *A Residence*, 62.

51. Ellis, *Memoir of Mrs. Mary Mercy Ellis, Wife of Rev. William Ellis*, vii. Grimshaw, *Paths of Duty*, 6. See Sturma, *South Sea Maidens*, 4; D'Emilio and Freedman, *Intimate Matters*, 87.

52. For more on women's emergent role as moral guardians, see Pascoe, *Relations of Rescue*. See also Jacobs, *Engendered Encounters*, 24–55; and Kahn, "From Redeemers to Partners," 141–63.

53. The Chamberlains had been married nearly thirteen years when the *Thaddeus* departed. They brought their five offspring, who ranged in age from one to twelve years, with them.

54. Grimshaw, *Paths of Duty*, 12–13.

55. Mercy Partridge, "Letter to Josiah Brewer," August 30, 1819, HMCS. See also Grimshaw, *Paths of Duty*, 13.

56. For a full discussion of the marital arrangements of Lucy Goodale and Asa Thurston, see Thurston, *Life and Times of Mrs. Lucy G. Thurston*, 3. See also Grimshaw, *Paths of Duty*, 1–3, and Zwiep, *Pilgrim Path*, 18–19.

57. "Letter from Hiram Bingham to Jeremiah Evarts, August 21, 1819," Letters and Papers of the Board, vol. XVI, HL. See also Restarick, "Sybil Bingham, as a Youthful Bride, Came to Islands in Brig *Thaddeaus*," 1–2.

58. Cott, *Bonds of Womanhood*, 3–5.

59. Grimshaw, *Paths of Duty*, 5–7.

60. "Instructions of the Prudential Committee of the American Board of Commissioners for Foreign Missions to the Sandwich Islands Mission," 18–20, YDL.

61. Ibid., 30–31. See also Ellis, *Memoir of Mrs. Mary Mercy Ellis*, xi–xii.

62. See "Instructions of the Prudential Committee of the American Board of Commissioners for Foreign Missions to the Sandwich Islands Mission"; and Humphrey, *The Promised Land*, xii, xiv. See also Gallaudet, *An Address, Delivered at a Meeting for Prayers, with Reference to the Sandwich Islands Mission*, 12; and Bilhartz, "Sex and the Second Great Awakening," 136–88.

63. Welter, *Dimity Convictions*, 22. For a full discussion of the critical distinctions being made in the nineteenth century between the "natural" differences between men and women, see Rotundo, *American Manhood*, 22–25. See also Kimmel, *Manhood in America*, 53–54, and Kimmel, *The History of Men*, 37.

64. Humphrey, *The Promised Land*, 25; Humphrey, *Memorial Sketches*, 43.

65. Gallaudet, *An Address, Delivered at a Meeting for Prayers, with Reference to the Sandwich Islands Mission*, 12.

CHAPTER 3

1. Samuel and Nancy Ruggles, journal, November 8, 1819, Journals Collection, HMCS. See also Sybil Moseley Bingham, journal, November 9, 1819, Journals Collection, HMCS.

2. Sybil Moseley Bingham, journal, January 6, 1820, Journals Collection, HMCS.

3. Sybil Moseley Bingham, journal, January 26, 1820, Journals Collection, HMCS. See also Samuel and Nancy Ruggles, journal, January 26, 1820, Journals Collection, HMCS.

4. Sybil Moseley Bingham, journal, March 30, 1820, Journals Collection, HMCS. See also Bingham, *A Residence*, 69–70; Anderson, *History of the Sandwich Islands Mission*, 18, 19; and Tracy, et al. *History of American Missions to the Heathen*, 91–92.

5. Anderson, *History of the Sandwich Islands Mission*, 20. See also Daws, *Shoal of Time*, 63–64.

6. See Thomas, *Islanders*, 77–80; Skwiot, "Migration and the Politics of Sovereignty, Settlement, and Belonging in Hawai'i," 440–41; Oliver, *The Pacific Islands*, 73–86.

7. Kamakau, *Ruling Chiefs of Hawaii*, 220. See also Kame'eleihiwa, *Native Land and Foreign Desires*, 69–74; Kirch and Sahlins, *Anahulu*, 118–19; Kuykendall, *The Hawaiian Kingdom*, 1:64–65.

8. For more on *kapu* laws, see Kirch, *How Chiefs Became Kings*, 29; Merry, *Colonizing Hawai'i*, 52; Kashay, "Native, Foreigner, Missionary, Priest," 5; Howe, *Where the Waves Fall*, 163–68; Kuykendall, *The Hawaiian Kingdom*, 1:8.

9. For more on food restrictions, see Malo, *Hawaiian Antiquities*, 29.

10. Kame'eleihiwa, *Native Land and Foreign Desires*, 75; Kuykendall, *The Hawaiian Kingdom*, 1:65–69.

11. Kamakau, *Ruling Chiefs*, 224–25. See also Dibble, *A History of the Sandwich Islands*, 125–28; 'I'ī, *Fragments of Hawaiian History*, 157; Kame'eleihiwa, *Native Land and Foreign Desires*, 74–79; Kashay, "From *Kapus* to Christianity," 68; Osorio, *Dismembering Lāhui*, 10–11. For more on the order ending 'aikapu, see Gast and Conrad, *Don Francisco de Paula Marin*, 75, 234. See also Malo, *Hawaiian Antiquities*, 29.

12. Kashay, "From *Kapus* to Christianity," 2–3. Linnekin, *Sacred Queens*, 14; and Ralston, "Changes in the Lives of Ordinary Women in Early Post-Contact Hawaii," 48.

13. Bingham, *A Residence*, 81. See also Sybil Moseley Bingham, journal, March 31, 1820, Journals Collection, HMCS. Goodale, *The Missionary's Daughter*, 14.

14. Bingham, *A Residence*, 70.

15. Sybil Moseley Bingham, journal, April 11, 1820, Journals Collection, HMCS.

16. Bingham, *A Residence*, 90. For more on Rives, see 'I'ī, *Fragments of Hawaiian History*, 86–87. See also "Letter of Kamehameha II to Alexander I, 1820," 832.

17. Bingham, *A Residence*, 89. See also Tracy, *History of the American Missions*, 92; and Anderson, *History of the Sandwich Islands Mission*, 18–20. Grimshaw, *Paths of Duty*, 27–30. Zwiep, *Pilgrim Path*, 69–73.

18. Bingham, *A Residence*, 89.

19. *Panoplist and Missionary Herald*, 119. See also Gulick, *Pilgrims of Hawaii*, 79; and Anderson, *History of the Sandwich Islands Mission*, 23.

20. *Panoplist and Missionary Herald*, vol. 17, 120.

21. Bingham, *A Residence*, 90.

22. Ibid. For official mission accounts on the first days in Hawai'i, see Tracy, *History of American Missions*, 92–93; and Anderson, *Missions of the American Board*, 18–20. For a Hawaiian source on the initial negotiations with missionaries, see Kamakau, *Ruling Chiefs*, 246–48. See also Grimshaw, *Paths of Duty*, 26–30; Zwiep, *Pilgrim Path*, 69–73; and Kuykendall, *The Hawaiian Kingdom*, 1:102–3.

23. Sybil Moseley Bingham, journal, April 11, 1820, Journals Collection, HMCS.

24. Bingham, *A Residence*, 90. See also Anderson, *Missions of the American Board*, 20.

25. Sybil Moseley Bingham, journal, April 11, 1820, Journals Collection, HMCS. See also Gulick, *Pilgrims of Hawaii*, 79.

26. Gulick, *Pilgrims of Hawaii*, 79. The Whitneys and the Ruggles departed from O'ahu on May 2 for Kaua'i. George Kaumuali'i accompanied them. The missionaries later gained permission to establish a mission on the island.

27. Mercy Partridge Whitney, journal, April 11, 1820, Journals Collection, HMCS. See also Sybil Moseley Bingham, journal, April 11, 1820, Journals Collection, HMCS. See Wagner-Wright, "When Unity Is Torn Asunder," 45.

28. Dwight, *Memoirs of Henry Obookiah*.

29. Bingham, *A Residence*, 89–91.

30. Jocelyn Linnekin offers insight into the unfamiliar gender roles that missionaries encountered in Hawaiʻi. See Linnekin, "New Political Orders," 201.

31. For more on the acquisition of English-language names and the "accumulation of Western identity," see Friedman, *Cultural Identity and Global Process*, 114.

32. Sybil Moseley Bingham, journal, June 20, 1820, Journals Collection, HMCS.

33. Arago, *Narrative of a Voyage Round the World*, 104. Kuykendall, *The Hawaiian Kingdom*, 1:65; Campbell, *A History of the Pacific Islands*, 77–78.

34. Freycinet, *Hawaiʻi in 1819*, 22–23. For more on Jean Rives, see Arago, *Narrative of a Voyage*, 2:96–97.

35. Freycinet, *Hawaiʻi in 1819*, 23. See also Arago, *Narrative of a Voyage*, 115.

36. Freycinet, *Hawaiʻi in 1819*, 23.

37. Ibid., 24, 28. See also Bassett, *Realms and Islands*, 158–59; Piano, "Kalanimōkū," 13–14; Dunmore, *Visions and Realities*, 158–59.

38. Freycinet, *Hawaiʻi in 1819*, 24, 28. Bassett, *Realms and Islands*, 158–59.

39. Arago, *Narrative of a Voyage Round the World*, 108.

40. Ibid., 106–9. Dibble, *History of the Sandwich Islands Mission*, 316, 317. See also Kuykendall, *The Hawaiian Kingdom*, 1:71, 72.

41. ʻĪʻī, *Fragments of Hawaiian History*, 141–43; Kamakau, *Ruling Chiefs*, 325–26.

42. For more on Kamehameha's control over the sandalwood trade and the transformation that took place after his death, see Kameʻeleihiwa, *Native Land and Foreign Desires*, 73; Denoon, "Land, Labour, and Independent Development," 157–58; Johnson, *The United States and the Pacific*, 34, 35 and 84; and Wagner-Wright, *Ships, Furs, and Sandalwood*.

43. Freycinet, *Hawaiʻi in 1819*, 28. Arago, *Narrative of a Voyage Round the World*, 110–11. Basset, *Realms and Islands*, 159.

44. Freycinet, *Hawaiʻi in 1819*, 34, 35. Arago, *Narrative of a Voyage*, 124.

45. Kamakau, *Ruling Chiefs*, 326.

46. Linnekin, "New Political Orders," 194. Thurston, *The Missionary's Daughter*, 14–15. Zwiep, *Pilgrim Path*, 98.

47. Gulick, *Pilgrims of Hawaii*, 80–81.

48. Bingham, *A Residence*, 94

49. Ibid., 95. Zwiep, *Pilgrim Path*, 77.

50. Tracy, *History of American Missions*, 93. Bingham, *A Residence*, 95–95. Linnekin, "New Political Orders," 194.

51. Tracy, *History of American Missions*, 93; *A Narrative of Five Youth from the Sandwich Islands*. Okihiro, *Island World*, 74–75. See also Zwiep, *Pilgrim Path*, 77.

52. Bingham and Thurston, "History of the Defection of Dr. Thomas Holman," HL. See also Wagner-Wright, "When Unity Is Torn Asunder," especially pages 47–52; and Zwiep, *Pilgrim Path*, 87–92, 147–49; Tracy, *History of American Missions*,

93. See also Andrew, *Rebuilding the Christian Commonwealth*, 112–13; Smith, *Yankees in Paradise*, 33–34, 48–79.

53. Lucy Goodale Thurston, letter, August 31, 1820, HMCS.

54. Anderson, *History of the Sandwich Islands Mission*, 20. See also Kamakau, *Ruling Chiefs*, 250; Kuykendall, *The Hawaiian Kingdom*, 1:71–72. Bingham, *A Residence*, 132.

55. Bingham, *A Residence*, 132; Sybil Moseley Bingham, journal, introduction to transcribed copy, 3, HMCS.

56. Robert Crichton Wyllie, "Address to the House of Representatives of the Hawaiian Kingdom," HHS; Kamakau, *Ruling Chiefs*, 250; Gast and Conrad, *Don Francisco de Paula Marin*, 247, 249, 250; Anderson, *History of the Sandwich Islands Mission*, 27; Daws, *Shoal of Time*, 68. See Kuykendall, *The Hawaiian Kingdom*, 1:248–49.

57. Thurston, *The Missionary's Daughter*, 12.

58. Marin kept copious notes about the king's movements. See "The Marin Journal" in Gast and Conrad, *Don Francisco de Paula Marin*, especially for the year 1821. See also Bingham, *A Residence*, 145; and Daws, *Shoal of Time*, 64–65.

59. Bingham, *A Residence*, 132–33. See also Tracy, *History of the American Board*, 103.

60. Bingham, *A Residence*, 134.

61. Anderson, *Missions of the American Board*, 21–22. Philips, *Protestant America and the Pagan World*, 241. Such perceptions endured; see Harris, *Nothing but Christ*, 105–11.

62. See Gast and Conrad, *Don Francisco de Paula Marin*, 246–54. See also Judd, *Voyages to Hawaii before 1860*.

63. Sybil Moseley Bingham, journal, June 21, 1821, Journals Collection, HMCS. See also December 14, 1821. Zwiep, *Pilgrim Path*, 77.

CHAPTER 4

1. Samuel and Nancy Ruggles, journal, April 5, 1820, Journals Collection, HMCS.

2. Samuel and Nancy Ruggles, "Journal from Boston, U.S.A. to the Sandwich Isles," April 2, 1820, Journals Collection, HMCS.

3. Thurston, *Life and Times of Mrs. Lucy G. Thurston*, article XV.

4. Samuel and Nancy Ruggles, journal, April 2, 1820, Journals Collection, HMCS.

5. For a discussion on gifts as a form of communication, see Rothschild, *Colonial Encounters in a Native American Landscape*, 14.

6. Komter, *Social Solidarity and the Gift*.

7. For some of the vast literature on gift giving and exchange, see Mauss, *The Gift*; Berking, *Sociology of Giving*; Godelier, *Enigma of the Gift*; Wyschogrod, Goux, and Boynton, *The Enigma of Gift and Sacrifice*. For historical applications, see Appadurai, *The Social Life of Things*, and Davis, *The Gift in Sixteenth-Century France*.

8. See Ann Laura Stoler, "Tense and Tender Ties." See also the introduction to Ballantyne and Burton, *Bodies in Contact*.

9. Berking, *The Sociology of Giving*, 3. See also Komter, *Social Solidarity and the Gift*, 30–35.

10. Samuel and Nancy Ruggles, journal, April 5, 1820, Journals Collection, HMCS.

11. Elisha Loomis's journal, dated March 31, 1820, as referenced in Gulick, *Pilgrims of Hawaii*, 74.

12. Hiram Bingham, *A Residence*, 62. For more on the perception of gifts as "tribute," see Gutiérrez, *When Jesus Came, the Corn Mothers Went Away*, 52.

13. Mercy Partridge Whitney, diary, April 6, 1820, HMCS. This perception is similar to Captain Cook's interpretation of his treatment by Hawaiians nearly half a century earlier. Daws, *Shoal of Time*, 5, 2. See also Kuykendall and Day, *Hawaii*, 13.

14. Samuel and Nancy Ruggles, journal, April 5 and 10, 1820, Journals Collection, HMCS.

15. Mercy Whitney, diary, May 31, 1820, Journals Collection, HMCS.

16. See Samuel and Nancy Ruggles, journal, July 25, 1820, HMCS. Where the missionaries offered gratitude to the king, they nevertheless attributed his behavior to the exercise of God's will. Sarah Joiner Lyman expressed like sentiments in 1834, noting that "the Lord opens the hearts of the people" to satisfy missionary needs. See Martin, *Sarah Joiner Lyman of Hawaii*, 72.

17. Whitney, diary, April 5 and July 7, 1820, Journals Collection, HMCS. On Kaua'i, where the situation was somewhat different, Kaumuali'i provided the Ruggles with housing and a taro patch. These gifts might be interpreted as repayment for the return of his son—known alternately by his American name, George, and his Hawaiian one, Humehume—who had accompanied the missionaries to the islands aboard the *Thaddeus*. Ruggles, July 25, 1820, HMCS. For accounts of Humehume's travels, see Warne, *Humehume of Kaua'i*; Okihiro, *Island World*, 80–82; and Stauder, "George, Prince of Hawaii."

18. Kuykendall and Day, *Hawaii*, 30; Daws, *Shoal of Time*, 44–55.

19. Kame'eleihiwa, *Native Land and Foreign Desires*, 10.

20. Noenoe K. Silva, *Aloha Betrayed*, 40, 39. Silva insists that such exchanges, "if not excessive . . . [were] not usually resented by the maka'āinana." Before the introduction of a cash economy, Hawaiian society might be understood as "stratified but interdependent." See also Kame'eleihiwa, *Native Lands*, 11; Holt, *Monarchy in Hawaii*, 3–5; Young, *Rethinking the Native Hawaiian Past*, 37–39.

21. For more on mana, see Kirch, *How Chiefs Became Kings*, 38, 41; Shore, "Mana and Tapu," 137–43; Malo, *Hawaiian Antiquities*, 135; and Buck, *Paradise Remade*, 35.

22. Godelier, *The Enigma of the Gift*, 12.

23. For a fuller discussion of exchange as a means by which to cancel debt, see Wyschogrod, Goux, and Boynton, *The Enigma of Gift and Sacrifice*.

24. "Instructions from the Prudential Committee of the American Board of Commissioners for Foreign Missions," in Humphrey, *The Promised Land*, ii–iii. See also Gallaudet, *An Address*; and Miller, "Domesticity Abroad," 68–69.

25. Laura Fish Judd, for example, described "spending the day" with Queen Ka'ahumanu "at her rustic country-seat." She and young mission assistant Elizabeth Ward spent the day engaged in sewing. Judd, *Honolulu*, 32–33.

26. Humphrey, *The Promised Land*, 25. See also Gallaudet, *An Address*, 12.

27. For more on "intimate frontiers," particularly with regard to the domestic, see Stoler, "Tense and Tender Ties," 4.

28. For more on women's importance to the mission, see Sanchez, "Go after the Women," 284.

29. Gallaudet, *An Address*.

30. Missionaries, nevertheless, continued to ponder the role of Christian women in the mission. See Mercy Whitney's 1837 essay, "What Are Some of the Peculiar Qualifications Important for a Missionaries [sic] Wife?," Missionary Letters, HMCS. See also Coan, "The Appropriate Duties of Christian Females in Public and Social Worship," 3–5.

31. Bingham, *A Residence*, 148, 149. See also Sybil Moseley Bingham, journal, December 15–18, 182[2] (undated pages), HMCS.

32. See Zwiep, *Pilgrim Path*, 176; Silverman, *Kaahumanu*, 78. For mission literature on the "changed relationship between Ka'ahumanu and the mission wives," see Bingham, *A Residence*, 148–49; Gulick, *Pilgrims of Hawaii*, 26; Judd, *Honolulu*, 13.

33. S. M. Bingham, journal, March 11, 182[2] (undated pages), HMCS.

34. Ibid.

35. Zwiep, *Pilgrim Path*, 144; Grimshaw, *Paths of Duty*, 156.

36. Grimshaw, "New England Missionary Wives, Hawaiian Women, and 'the Cult of True Womanhood,'" 19, 80. Missionaries condemned the habit of card playing. It not only presented a problem for successful conversion but also confirmed missionary beliefs about the supposed sloth and idleness of Hawaiians.

37. S. M. Bingham, journal, March 11, 182[2] (undated pages), HMCS.

38. Ibid., March 14, 182[2] (undated pages), HMCS. See also Anderson, *History of the Sandwich Islands Mission*, 32.

39. Grimshaw, *Paths of Duty*, 48. Kirch and Sahlins, *Anahulu*, 57. Keōpūolani and Kapi'olani joined Ka'ahumanu in her public support of the mission.

40. For more on Liholiho's motives for his travels, see Kame'eleihiwa, *Native Land and Foreign Desires*, 82–85; and Kuykendall, *The Hawaiian Kingdom*, 1:76–77. For the newly enacted laws and the political ramifications of Liholiho's death, see Daws, *Shoal of Time*, 72; and Merry, *Colonizing Hawai'i*, 40. See also Marshall Sahlins, *Anahulu*, 61.

41. Merry, *Colonizing Hawai'i*, 45.

42. Hays, *The Kingdom of Hawaii*, 73.

43. Gavan Daws has argued that Ka'ahumanu took this opportunity to "exercise her mana on behalf of Protestant morality," a pattern that endured throughout the remainder of her life. Daws, *Shoal of Time*, 83.

44. Sybil Moseley Bingham, transcribed journal, 1819–1820, 3, HMCS.

45. Laura Fish Judd, *Honolulu*, 12.

46. Ibid.

47. Ibid., 13. Given the dates, it is likely that the "Mrs. B" of Laura Fish Judd's description refers to Sybil Moseley Bingham. Both Sybil Moseley Bingham's diary and Hiram Bingham's memoir corroborate the extent of Bingham's engagement in such labor for Hawaiian royalty.

48. Grimshaw, "New England Missionary Wives," 84.

49. Bingham, *A Residence*, 109.

50. See Wagner, "Mission and Motivation," 19, 66–67; Gaustad and Schmidt, *The Religious History of America*, 140–41. See also Brown, *Good Wives*, 45. Brown argued that the construction of an "other" helped to "crystallize self-conscious articulations of one's own group identity," a process that also appears to have been at work in the islands. Sybil Moseley Bingham, journal, March 9, 1823, Journal Collections, HMCS; Clarissa Lyman Richards, journal, January 27, 1823, and May 1, 1823, Journal Collections, HMCS; Laura Fish Judd, journal, December 19, 1827, Journal Collection, HMCS.

51. Bingham, *A Residence*, 101.

52. Kent, *Hawaii*, 26, 101; S. M. Bingham, journal, March 14, 1822, HMCS.

53. Sybil Moseley Bingham, journal, October 4, 1822, Journals Collection, HMCS.

54. For more on the connection between the bonnet and Christian ideals of feminine modesty, see Johnston, *Missionary Writing and Empire, 1800–1860*, 147–48.

55. Sybil Moseley Bingham, journal, October 4, 1822, HMCS.

56. Ibid.; Zwiep, *Pilgrim Path*, xv.

57. S. M. Bingham, journal, October 4, 182[2] (undated pages), HMCS.

58. Judd, *Honolulu*, 40. Clarissa Lyman Richards, journal, April 23, 1823, Journals Collection, HMCS. S. M. Bingham, journal, March 31, 1820, Journals Collection, HMCS.

59. For more on missionaries' use of clothing as a tool for conversion, see Jacobs, "Three African American Women Missionaries in the Congo, 1887–1899," 330–31.

60. Grimshaw, "New England Missionary Wives," 78, 79.

61. Judd, *Honolulu*, 5.

62. Holman, *Journal of Lucia Ruggles Holman*, 17.

63. Grimshaw, "New England Missionary Wives," 85.

64. Campbell, *A Voyage Round the World*, 136. Mission journals, too, referenced the pā'ū. See Betsey Curtis Lyons, journal, September 19, 1832, Journals Collection, HMCS. See also Holman, *Journal of Lucia Ruggles Holman*, 17–19.

65. Weiner, *Inalienable Possessions*, 83–84, 175; Linnekin, *Sacred Queens and Women of Consequence*, 40–45; Buck, *Arts and Crafts of Hawaii*, 165–215; Kaeppler, *The Fabrics of Hawaii*, 7–15.

66. See the Betsey Curtis Lyons, journal, September 19, 1832, Journals Collection, HMCS.

67. Martin, *The Lymans of Hilo*, 57.

68. Judd, *Honolulu*, 9. Grimshaw, "New England Missionary Wives," 84–85.

69. Martin, *Sarah Joiner Lyman of Hawaii*, 73–75, 57.

70. Judd, *Honolulu*, 9.

71. Bingham, *A Residence*, 343. Bingham describes the "commodious house of worship" that was built "under the auspices of Ka'ahumanu and Kaukeaouli." For a discussion of some of the many iterations of the Kawaiaha'o Church, see Gowans, *Fruitful Fields*, 137–43. See also Damon, *The Stone Church at Kawaiahao*, 17–18; Buchanan, *Historic Places of Worship*, 140–42.

72. Judd, *Honolulu*, 33. See also Silverman, *Kaahumanu*, 135.

73. Judd, *Honolulu*, 33.

74. Ibid.

CHAPTER 5

1. Mercy Partridge Whitney, journal, December 5, 1825, HMCS. See also 'Ī'ī, *Fragments of Hawaiian History*, 275; and Anderson, *History of the Sandwich Islands Mission*, 60.

2. Bingham, *A Residence*, 215.

3. Mercy Partridge Whitney, journal, December 29, 1825, HMCS; Ruggles, journal, April 2, 1820, Journals Collection, HMCS. Thurston, *The Missionary's Daughter*, 27; Betsey Curtis Lyons, journal, June 4, 1832, Journals Collection, HMCS. For more on "mothers" as converts, see Sanchez, "Go after the Women"; and Murphy, "Native American and Metis Women as 'Public Mothers,'" 164–82.

4. Anderson, *Kapiolani, the Heroine of Hawaii*; Ellis, *Memoir of Mrs. Mary Mercy Ellis*; Richards, *Memoir of Keopuolani*; Thurston, *The Missionary's Daughter*; Taylor, "Kapiolani."

5. Chin, "Beneficent Imperialists"; Rothschild, *Colonial Encounters in a Native American Landscape*; Yohn, *A Contest of Faiths*; Singh, *Gender, Religion, and "Heathen Lands"*; Tyrell, *Woman's World, Woman's Empire*; Hunter, *The Gospel of Gentility*; Jacobs, *Engendered Encounters*; Taylor and Huber, *Gendered Missions*.

6. Grimshaw, "New England Missionary Wives, Hawaiian Women, and 'the Cult of True Womanhood"; Welter, "The Cult of True Womanhood, 1820–1860."

7. Howe, *Where the Waves Fall*; Miller, "Domesticity Abroad"; Ruiz, "Una Mujer sin Fronteras." Ruiz's "conjugated identities," which refers to "an invention or inflection of one's sense of self," is instructive in this context. Ruiz argues that conjugated identity represented a "self-reflexive, purposeful fluidity of individual subjectivities for political action." See also Silva, *Aloha Betrayed*, 15–16.

8. Silva, *Aloha Betrayed*, 32. For some of the historiographical literature on female conversion, see Greer, *Mohawk Saint*, and Shoemaker, "Kateri Tekakwitha's Tortuous Path to Sainthood," 55. See also Newman, "Fulfilling the Name," 232–56; Díaz, "Native American Women and Religion in the American Colonies"; Tilton, *Pocahontas*; and Townsend, *Pocahontas and the Powhatan Dilemma*. See also Richter, *Facing East from Indian Country*, 81; and Green, "The Pocahontas Perplex."

9. Richards, *Memoir of Keopuolani*, 31–39; Stewart, *Journal of a Residence*, 121, 161; Kamakau, *Ruling Chiefs of Hawaii*, 254; Sinclair, "The Sacred Wife of Kamehameha I, Keopuolani."

10. For more on Keōpūolani, see Kame'eleihiwa, *Native Land and Foreign Desires*, 142–45. See also Mookini, "Keopuolani"; and Sinclair, "The Sacred Wife of Kamehameha I, Keopuolani," 219–20.

11. Richards, *Memoir of Keopuolani*, 16. See Maurer, *How the Gospel Came to Hawaii*,

12. For more on Keōpūolani's authority, see Kame'eleihiwa, *Native Land and Foreign Desires*, 144; and Daws, *Shoal of Time*, 54–60.

12. It is critical to note that men also observed certain prohibitions under the *kapu* laws. For a discussion of the 'aikapu, see Kame'eleihiwa, "Nā Wāhine Kapu/

Divine Hawaiian Women," 7–8; Ralston, "Changes in the Lives of Ordinary Women in Early Post-Contact Hawaii," 51–53; and Young, *Rethinking the Native Hawaiian Past*, 75–76.

13. Richards, *Memoirs of Keopuolani*, 16. See also Gulick, *Pilgrims of Hawaii*.

14. Kashay, "From *Kapus* to Christianity," 19–25. See also Linnekin, *Sacred Queens and Women of Consequence*, 12.

15. For more on the *kapu* as oppressive to women, see Kuykendall, *The Hawaiian Kingdom*, 1:67; Peterson, *Notable Women of Hawaii*, 220; and Daws, *Shoal of Time*. For insight into the breaking of the *'aikapu*, see Silva, *Aloha Betrayed*, 29–30; Zwiep, *Pilgrim Path*; and Withington, *The Golden Cloak*. For explanation of the *'aikapu* as part of a larger system, see Kame'eleihiwa, *Native Land and Foreign Desires*, 33–36.

16. Silva, *Aloha Betrayed*, 29–30; Kame'eleihiwa, *Native Land and Foreign Desires*, 81–82.

17. Richards, *Memoirs of Keopuolani*, 19. On Ellis's role in Hawai'i, see Kuykendall, *The Hawaiian Kingdom*, 1:103. For more on Keōpūolani's teachers, see Kamakau, *Ruling Chiefs of Hawaii*, 254; and Kame'eleihiwa, *Native Land and Foreign Desires*, 143.

18. Richards, *Memoirs of Keopuolani*, 19. See also Bingham, *A Residence*, 183; Anderson, *History of the Sandwich Islands Mission*, 29. See also Kame'eleihiwa, *Native Land and Foreign Desires*, 143. Mookini, "Keopuolani, Sacred Wife, Queen Mother, 1778–1832," 19. See also Wagner, "Mission and Motivation." Western perceptions about the "problem" of polygamy were certainly not confined to American missionaries—nor were they limited to those who labored in Hawai'i. Jacques Arago complained about the practice on his visit in 1819. See *Narrative of a Voyage Round the World*, 94–95 and 144. For views on polygamy in the American West, see D'Emilio and Freedman, *Intimate Matters*, 87. As a strategy for conversion, marital reform emerged as a common practice. See Kipp, "Emancipating Each Other."

19. Bingham, *A Residence*, 169. See Grimshaw, *Paths of Duty*, 48, for more on missionaries' efforts to reform Hawaiians' sexual practices. For more on the perceptual relationship between gender and civilization, see Bederman, *Manliness and Civilization*; and Sturma, *South Sea Maidens*. For more on sexual regulation as a tool of imperialism, see Stoler, "Tense and Tender Ties"; Ballantyne and Burton, *Bodies in Contact*; and McClintock, *Imperial Leather*. See also Skwiot, "Geneaologies and Histories in Collision."

20. Mercy Whitney, journal, February 20, 1820, Journals Collection, HMCS; and Ellis, *Memoir of Mrs. Mary Mercy Ellis, Wife of Rev. William Ellis*. The perception persisted well into the nineteenth century. See Pitman, *Heroines of the Mission Field*; and Stewart, *Journal of a Residence in the Sandwich Islands*.

21. See Ralston, "Changes in the Lives of Ordinary Women in Early Post-Contact Hawaii," 54–55.

22. See Richards, *Memoir of Keopuolani*, 19; Stewart, *Journal of a Residence in the Sandwich Islands, during the Years 1823, 1824, and 1825*. See also Kame'eleihiwa, *Native Land and Foreign Desires*, 142.

23. Malo, *Hawaiian Antiquities*, 55. Ellis, *Journal of William Ellis*, 316.

24. Merry, *Colonizing Hawai'i*, 53.

25. Stewart, *Journal of a Residence*, 161.

26. Ibid., 132.

27. Richards, *Memoirs*, 31, 39. Ellis, *Memoir of Mrs. Mary Mercy Ellis, Wife of Rev. William Ellis*, 135. Peterson, *Notable Women of Hawaii*, 219–20. For more on the practice of baptizing ill and dying converts, see Greer, *Mohawk Saint*, 6, 57.

28. Anderson, *Kapiolani*.

29. Ibid., 1.

30. Ibid., 5

31. Taylor, "Kapiolani," 5.

32. Ibid., 4. For a discussion of the relationship between the perceptions of the body and racial identification, see Morgan, *Laboring Women*, especially chapter 1, "'Some Could Suckle over Their Shoulder,'" 12–49; and Brown, *Good Wives, Nasty Wenches, and Anxious Patriarchs*, 13–41.

33. Taylor, "Kapiolani," 5.

34. Ibid., 6. For the missionary's struggle with royal women over color, see Judd, *Honolulu*. For literature on the holokū (or "Mother Hubbard" dress), see Arthur, "Cultural Authentication Refined," 129–39.

35. Johnston, *Missionary Writing and Empire, 1800–1860*, 147–48.

36. Taylor, "Kapiolani," 5–6. Anderson, *Kapiolani*, 3. See also Brown's discussion of Pocahontas's similar transformation in *Good Wives and Nasty Wenches*, 42–45.

37. For more on Hale's influence, see Howe, *What Hath God Wrought*, 608–9; Ann Douglas, *The Feminization of American Culture*, 45–48, 56–57.

38. Anderson, *Kapiolani*, 5.

39. For a discussion of the multiple ways in which the event has been represented, see Merry, "Kapiolani at the Brink." Daws, *Shoal of Time*, 98.

40. For Hawaiian sources on Pele, see Kamakau, *Ruling Chiefs of Hawaii*, 185–86; and Malo, *Hawaiian Antiquities*, 116. See also Okihiro, *Island World*, 21–28, 213; Silva, *Aloha Betrayed*, 76–79; and Kuykendall, *The Hawaiian Kingdom*, 1:7.

41. Gulick, *Pilgrims of Hawaii*, 50.

42. Anderson, *Kapiolani*, 6.

43. Ibid.

44. Gulick, *Pilgrims of Hawaii*, 50. See also Anderson, *Kapiolani*, 6; and Ellis, *Memoir of Mrs. Mary Mercy Ellis*, 129. See also Kamakau, *Ruling Chiefs of Hawaii*, 382.

45. For more on narratives of native heroism, see Tilton, *Pocahontas*, 51.

46. Anderson, *Kapiolani*, 5, 22; Stewart, *Journal of a Residence*, 121; Thurston, *The Missionary's Daughter*, 38–39.

47. Bingham, *A Residence*, 148; Anderson, *History of the Sandwich Islands Mission*, 105, 108; Gulick, *Pilgrims of Hawaii*, 49; Judd, *Honolulu*, 7; Thurston, *The Missionary's Daughter*, 55. Thurston, *Life and Times of Mrs. Lucy G. Thurston*, 216; Betsey Curtis Lyons, journal, June 4, 1832, Journals Collection, HMCS; Clarissa Richards Lyman, journal, February 1824, Journals Collection, HMCS.

48. Judd, *Honolulu*, 7. Clarissa Chapman Armstrong, journal, May 6 [1889 or 1890?], Journals Collection, HMCS.

49. Bingham, *A Residence*, 148. Sybil Moseley Bingham, journal, December 16, 1821, Journals Collection, HMCS.

50. Bingham, *A Residence*, 149.

51. Ibid.

52. Judd, *Honolulu*, 13. Bingham, *A Residence*, 149.

53. Judd, *Honolulu*, 13. Bingham, *A Residence*, 162.

54. Judd, *Honolulu*, 13.

55. Ibid.

56. Axtell has made a similar argument in *Beyond 1492*, 118. See also Shoemaker, "Kateri Tekakwitha's Tortuous Path to Sainthood," 66.

57. Silva, *Aloha Betrayed*, 32.

58. Bingham, *A Residence*, 162.

59. Ibid. See also Anderson, *Missions of the American Board*, 23.

60. Dwight, *Memoirs of Henry Obookiah*, 16.

61. Bingham, *A Residence*, 162.

62. Howe, *Where the Waves Fall*, 160–61, 168–69. Silva, *Aloha Betrayed*, 26; Merry, *Colonizing Hawai'i*, 44;

63. Kuykendall, *The Hawaiian Kingdom*, 1:77.

64. Bingham, *A Residence*, 177–78; Anderson, *Missions of the American Board*, 46; Anderson, *History of the Sandwich Islands Mission*, 51; Kuykendall, *Hawaiian Kingdom*, 117; Daws, *Shoal of Time*, 72.

65. Merry, *Colonizing Hawai'i*, 48, 40. Kuykendall and Day, *Hawaii*, 50.

66. Kame'eleihiwa, *Native Land and Foreign Desires*, 154; Grimshaw, *Paths of Duty*, 48. Kirch and Sahlins, *Anahulu*, 57; Merry, *Colonizing Hawai'i*, 45

67. Bingham, *A Residence*, 341. Hiram Bingham, "Letter to the Secretary of the ABCFM," May 15, 1839, Sandwich Islands Mission Collection, HMCS; Richard Armstrong, "The French and the Sandwich Islands," Sandwich Islands Mission Collection, HMCS; Document of Expulsion to P. A. Brinsmade, Sandwich Islands Mission Collection, HMCS; King Kamehameha III, Letter to William IV, October 23, 1837, HMCS. Hays, *The Kingdom of Hawaii*, 73.

68. Daws, *Shoal of Time*, 83.

69. "General Letter to the Sandwich Islands Mission," 1834, 7, ABCFM Letters, HHS.

70. Mercy Partridge Whitney, journal, July 25, 1820, HMCS. See also July 30, 1820; July 6, 1821; and December 29, 1825; all in Journals Collection, HMCS.

71. Mercy Partridge Whitney, journal, July 25, 1820, Journals Collection, HMCS. It should be noted that the king followed suit, promising to be a "father" to the American missionaries. This, however, is an isolated reference. Hawai'i's high-ranking women seemed more disposed to describe their relationship with the missionaries in such decidedly maternal terms.

72. Judd, *Honolulu*, 6.

73. Ibid., 11.

74. Even relatively contemporary sources suggest the Hawaiian habit of referring to the missionaries as children; the *Missionary Album* notes that Samuel Ruggles was "so loved by Hawaiians that they called him 'Keiki' (child)," 168.

75. Silva, *Aloha Betrayed*, 9–10. Sahlins, "Hawai'i in the Early Nineteenth Century," 190. Howe, *Where the Waves Fall*, 172.

76. Grimshaw, "New England Missionary Wives," 96.

CONCLUSION

1. Gulick, *Pilgrims of Hawaii*, 87–88; Bingham, *A Residence*, 126. For more on Kamehameha's policy with regard to foreigners and land use, see Kameʻeleihiwa, *Native Land and Foreign Desires*, 59–60.

2. Rufus Anderson, *The Hawaiian Islands*, 118.

3. Mary Zwiep, *Pilgrim Path*, xvi. Smith, *Yankees in Paradise*, 315–22. For missionary schools, see Kuykendall, *The Hawaiian Kingdom*, 1:100–116.

4. Smith, *Yankees in Paradise*, 319.

5. Ibid., 321.

6. Harris, *Nothing but Christ*, 7.

7. For more on ongoing mission debates about child rearing, see Grimshaw, *Paths of Duty*, 129–37.

8. Noenoe K. Silva, *Aloha Betrayed*, 39–43; Osorio, *Dismembering Lāhui*, 44–73; Kameʻeleihiwa, *Native Land and Foreign Desires*, 302–6; Merry, *Colonizing Hawaiʻi*, 93–95; Grimshaw, *Paths of Duty*, 179–80; Dougherty, *To Steal a Kingdom*, 97–117.

9. Dougherty, *To Steal a Kingdom*, 107.

10. Dozens of missionary wives, in fact, lived out their lives in Hawaiʻi as widows. While some outlived their husbands by only a few years, others experienced a period of widowhood that extended twenty or thirty years. Their stay in the islands, then, was protracted and should be interpreted as deliberate.

11. Sybil Moseley Bingham, journal, July 13, 1820, Journals Collection, HMCS.

12. Kotzebue, *A Voyage of Discovery*.

Bibliography

ARCHIVAL SOURCES

Hawaiian Historical Society, Honolulu, Hawai'i
Atkinson, A. T. "Early Voyagers of the Pacific Ocean."
Wyllie, R. C. "Address to the House of Representatives of the Hawaiian Kingdom, on the Inefficiency of High Duties on Spirits, in Promoting Temperance, Morality and Revenue, and the Expediency of Lowering the Duties, in Conformity with the Strong Recommendation of the Chamber of Commerce of Honolulu." Hawaiian Historical Society, 1851.
———. "Answers to Questions Proposed by His Excellency, R. C. Wyllie, His Hawaiian Majesty's Minister of Foreign Relations and Addressed to All the Missionaries in the Hawaiian Islands, May 1846." Hawaiian Mission Children's Society, 1846.

Hawaiian Mission Children's Society Library, Honolulu, Hawai'i
American Board of Commissioners for Foreign Missions. "American Board of Commissioners for Foreign Missions: Constitution, Laws, and Regulations, 1835."
———. "Instructions to the Missionaries about to Embark for the Sandwich Islands and to the Rev. Messrs. William Goodell, & Isaac Bird, Attached to the Palestine Mission: Delivered by the Corresponding Secretary of the American Board of Commissioners for Foreign Missions."
———. "Letter of Agreement with ABCFM." Collection: Stockton, Betsey, Letters Sent 1824.
———. Prudential Committee. "Letter to the King of France." Collection: Ms.S. Honolulu: Hawaiian Mission Children's Society, 1840.
Armstrong, Clarissa Chapman. "Journal Fragments/Typescript." 1831–1838.
———. "Letter to J. M. Cooke." Collection: Missionary Letters. Honolulu, 1838.
———. "Letter to Ludentia." 1831.
———. "Letter to Mrs. [Sister Lyons?]." Collection: Missionary Letters. Wailuku, 1836.
———. "Letter to Sisters Mary and Jane." 1834.
———. "Reminiscences of a Missionary Chair." 1886.
Armstrong, Richard. "The French and the Sandwich Islands."
Baldwin, Charlotte. "Letter to Husband." Collection: Baldwin, Charlotte. 1854.
———. "Letter to Miss Sophronia Baldwin." Collection: Baldwin, Charlotte Fowler "Mrs. Dwight," 1833–1850. 1839.
———. "Letter to Mrs. Chapin." Collection: Baldwin, Charlotte Fowler "Mrs. Dwight," 1833–1850. 1833.

———. "Letter to Mrs. Gulick." Collection: Baldwin, Charlotte Fowler "Mrs. Dwight," 1833–1850. N.d.

———. "Letter to Sister Abigail." Collection: Baldwin, Charlotte Fowler "Mrs. Dwight," 1833–1850. 1831.

Baldwin, Charlotte F. (Mrs. D.). "Journal of Mrs. D. Baldwin."

Bingham, Hiram. "Letter to Sec. of the ABCFM about Catholics." Collection: Sandwich Islands Mission. May 15, 1838.

Bingham, Sybil. "Journal of Sybil Moseley Bingham." Typescript, 1820.

———. "Journal of Sybil Moseley Bingham (Transcribed) at HMCS." 1819–1820.

———. "Sybil Mosely Bingham to Family and Friends, October 23, 1819–April 2, 1847." Transcribed copy.

Bishop, Delia Stone. "Journal of a Trip around the Islands." Collection: Bishop, Delia Stone (Mrs. A.) Journal, 1829. 1829.

Bishop, E. E., Collection: Missionary Journals. 1819.

———. "Journal." Collection: Missionary Journals. Valley of Waimea, Island of Tauwai (Kauai), 1823.

Brown, Lydia. "Letter to Juliette M. Cooke." Collection: Missionary Letters. Wailuku, 1837.

———. "Letter to Mrs. Chamberlain." Collection: Missionary Letters. Wailuku, 1835.

Chamberlain, Maria Patton (Mrs. Levi). "Journal of Maria Chamberlain." Collection: Missionary Journal, 1825–1845.

Clark, Mary Kitteredge. "Letter to 'Precious Daughter.'" Collection: Clark, Mary K. (Mrs. Ephraim W.). 1853.

———. "Letter to Miss Confran." 1834.

———. "Letter to Miss Lucia Smith." Collection: Clark, Mary K. (Mrs. Ephraim W.). N.d.

———. "Letter to Mrs. Delia L. Bishop." Collection: Clark, Mary K. (Mrs. Ephraim W.). 1830.

———. "Letter to Mrs. Ruggles." Collection: Clark, Mary K. (Mrs. Ephraim W.). 1828.

———. "Letter to Sister Annie." Collection: Clark, Mary K. (Mrs. Ephraim W.). 1852.

———. "Letter to Sister Lyons." Collection: Clark, Mary K. (Mrs. Ephraim W.). 1854.

———. "Letter to Sister Ruggles." Collection: Clark, Mary K. (Mrs. Ephraim W.). 1829.

Coan, Titus. "The Appropriate Duties of Christian Females in Public and Social Worship." 1862.

Comb, Rebecca M. "Letter to Charlotte Fowler Baldwin." Collection: Baldwin, Charlotte Fowler "Mrs. Dwight," 1830–1832. 1832.

"Document of Expulsion, Letter Addressed to P. A. Brinsmade." Collection: Ms.S. Honolulu: Hawaiian Mission Children's Society, 1837.

Fowler, A., and Lydia. "Letter to Charlotte Fowler Baldwin." Collection: Baldwin, Charlotte Fowler "Mrs. Dwight," 1830–1832. 1832.

Judd, Laura Fish. "Journal of Voyage on 'Parthian,' Boston to Honolulu, [November 5?], 1827–March 31, 1828." Collection: Journals Collection, November 5[?], 1827–March 31, 1828.

———. "Letter from Laura Fish Judd to Mrs. Ruggles." Collection: Judd, Laura Fish (Mrs. Gerrit P.), Letters to Members of the Mission. Honolulu, July 1830.

———. "Letter to Daughter Laura." Collection: Judd, Laura Fish (Mrs. Gerrit P.), to Her Husband and Daughters, 1855–1859 (file #10). "Sweet Home," 1859.

———. "Letter to Daughter Laura." Collection: Judd, Laura Fish (Mrs. Gerrit P.), to Her Husband and Daughters, 1855–1859 (file #10). "Sweet Home," 1859.

———. "Letter to Daughter Laura." Collection: Judd, Laura Fish (Mrs. Gerrit P.), to Her Husband and Daughters, 1855–1859 (file #10).1858.

———. "Letter to Fanny Gulick." Collection: Judd, Laura Fish (Mrs. Gerrit P.), Letters to Members of the Mission, 1828–1848. Honolulu, 1831.

———. "Letter to Husband." Collection: Judd, Laura Fish (Mrs. Gerrit P.), to Her Husband and Daughters, 1855–1859 (folder 10). [Glenhola?], 1859.

———. "Letter to Mrs. Ruggles." Collection: Judd, Laura Fish (Mrs. Gerrit P.), Letters to Members of the Mission, 1828–1848. Honolulu, 1831.

———. "Letter to Mrs. Ruggles." Collection: Judd, Laura Fish (Mrs. Gerrit P.), Letters to Members of the Mission. Honolulu, 1830.

———. "Letter to Mrs. Ruggles." Collection: Judd, Laura Fish (Mrs. Gerrit P.), Letters to Members of the Mission. 1828.

———. "Letter to Mrs. Ruggles." Collection: Judd, Laura Fish (Mrs. Gerrit P.), Letters to Members of the Mission, 1828–1848. Honolulu, n.d.

Ka'ahumanu, Queen. "Letters to Missionaries." Collection: Missionary Letters. Honolulu, 1825–1832.

———. "Letter to Jeremiah Evarts." Honolulu: Hawaiian Mission Children's Society, 1828.

Kamehameha III. "Letter from the King of the Sandwich Islands to William IV. Historical Account of the Attempt to Force the Roman Catholic Religion into the Sandwich Islands." Honolulu: Hawaiian Mission Children's Society, 1837.

Knapp, Charlotte. "Letter to Lucy Wilcox." Collection: Missionary Letters. Waimea, 1838.

———. "Letter to Mrs. Lucy Wilcox." Collection: Missionary Letters. Waimea, 1837.

Liliu'okalani, Queen. "Excerpted Diaries of Queen Liliu'okalani (Transcribed by William Dewitt Alexander)." Collection: Missionary Journals, 1893–1894.

———. "Letter: Death of Mary Castle." Collection: Castle Family Papers. Honolulu, 1907.

Loomis, Bingham, and "Kalanimoku, by Bingham and Loomis." Collection: American Board of Commissioners for Foreign Missions–Hawaii Papers: Hawaiian Mission Children's Society, 1827–1830[?].

Moseley, Sybil. "Miss Moseley's Address to Her Scholars on Leaving Her School." 1814.

Partridge, Mercy. "Letter to Edward Partridge." January 1819.

———. "Letter to Her Parents." October 12, 1819.

———. "Letter to Josiah Brewer." February 4, 1819.

———. "Letter to Josiah Brewer." August 30, 1819.

Perrine, M. L. R. "Letter of Introduction (Charlotte Fowler to Dwight Baldwin)." 1830.

Richards, Clarissa Lyman. "Journal." Collection: Missionary Journals. 1824.

———. "Journal of Clarissa L. Richards." Collection: Missionary Journals. 1822.

Ruggles, Nancy Wells. "Letter to Family, Friends, L. Chamberlain, 1822–1833." Collection: Ruggles, Nancy Wells, Letters Sent 1822–1833.

Ruggles, Samuel, and Nancy Ruggles. "Copy of Journal from Boston, U.S.A. to the Sandwich Isles by Samuel and Nancy Ruggles on Board the Brig. Thaddeus, October 23, 1819–August 1820." Collection: Journals Collection. Honolulu, 1819–1820.

Smith, Abigail. "Letter to Mrs. L. G. Lyons." Collection: Missionary Letters.

Stockton, Betsey. "Journal Exerpts from Betsey Stockton, 1822–1824." Collection: Journals Collection, 1822–1824.

———. "Letter to Levi Chamberlain." Collection: Letters, 1824.

Thurston, Lucy Goodale. "Letter." 1820.

———. "Letter to Mr. Anderson." Collection: Thurston, Lucy Goodale Letters, 1832–1829. 1832.

———. "Letter to Mr. Goodell." Collection: Thurston, L., November 9, 1832–June 2, 1841. 1829.

———. "Letter to Rev. Mr. Wm. Goodell." Collection: Letters, 1832–1829. 1834.

Whitney, Mercy P. "Diary of Mercy Partridge Whitney." Collection: Missionary Journals, 1820–1834.

———. "Letter to Lucy Wilcox." Collection: Letters. Waimea, 1838.

———. "Report of the Maternal Association at Waimea Kauai." Collection: Missionary Letters. Waimea, Kauai, 1837.

———. "What Are Some of the Peculiar Qualifications Important for a Missionaries [sic] Wife?" Collection: Missionary Letters, 1837.

Houghton Library, Harvard University, Cambridge, Mass.

American Board of Commissioners for Foreign Missions. "A Brief Sketch of the Missionary Life of Mrs. Sybil Moseley Bingham." Cambridge, Mass.: Houghton Library, 1895.

———. "Memorandum from Conversation with Rev. Wm. Ellis, April 1825." Cambridge, Mass.: Houghton Library, 1825.

———. "Missionaries: Birthplace, Residence, Dates of Sailing."

———. "Missionaries: Colleges and Degrees."

———. Missionaries: Colleges or Seminaries Attended, 1812–1922."

———. "Mission Journal Pt. II."

———. "A Statement Respecting the Law of the Land and Giving the Names of the Kings of the Islands." 1829.

American Board of Commissioners for Foreign Missions Treasury Department. "Donations from November 17, 1811–September 25, 1818."

Bingham, Hiram. "Letter from Hiram Bingham to J. Evarts." 1823.

———. "Letter to Jeremiah Evarts." August 21, 1819.

———. "Memoranda Respecting Kanaimoku." N.d.

Bingham, Hiram, and Asa Thurston. "History of the Defection of Dr. Thomas Holman." 1821.

Bingham, Sybil Moseley. "Letter to Jeremiah Evarts." October 23, 1819.

Gillett, Timothy P. "Letter to Samuel Worscester." August 25, 1819.

Humphrey, Heman. "Letter of Certification of Mercy Partridge." October 3, 1819.

Tamoree, King. "Letter from King to Samuel Worscester." Collection: American Board of Commissioners for Foreign Missions, 2, Harvard, 1820 or 1821 (conflicting dates).

Wheeler, Rev. "Letter to Reverend Elias Cornelius." April 15, 1817.

Kauai Historical Society, Lihue, Hawaiʻi

Isenberg, Dora R., ed. "Laura Fish Judd: Arranged from Diaries by Dora R. Isenberg."

———. "Mr. and Mrs.Thurston: Arranged from Diaries by Dora R. Isenberg."

———. "W. H. Rice and Wife: Arranged from Diaries by Dora R. Isenberg."

Yale Divinity Library, New Haven, Conn.

American Board of Commissioners for Foreign Missions. "Instructions of the Prudential Committee of the American Board of Commissioners for Foreign Missions to the Sandwich Islands." Lahainaluna: Press of the Mission Seminary, 1838.

Anderson, Gerald H. "Bibliographic Record: Hiram Bingham."

———. "Bibliographic Record: Gerrit P. Judd."

———. "Bibliographic Record: Kaahumanu."

———. "Bibliographic Record: Marcus Whitman."

Dwight Family Papers. "System of Doctrines."

Evarts Family Papers. "Letter from Sybil Moseley Bingham to Jeremiah Evarts." March 23, 1825.

PUBLISHED PRIMARY SOURCES

Adler, Jacob, ed. *The Journal of Prince Alexander Liholiho.* Honolulu: University of Hawaii Press for the Hawaiian Historical Society, 1967.

Alexander, W. D. "The Proceedings of the Russians on Kauai. 1814–1816 [sic]." *Papers of the Hawaiian Historical Society* 6 (1894): 1–18.

———. "The Relations between the Hawaiian Islands and Spanish America in Early Times." *Papers of the Hawaiian Historical Society* 1 (1892).

American Board of Commissioners for Foreign Missions. *ABCFM Annual Reports, 1810–1820.* Boston: Crocker and Brewster, 1834.

Anderson, Gerald H. "Papers and Records Bibliographic Record." Yale Divinity Library.

Anderson, Rufus. *The Hawaiian Islands: Their Progress and Condition under Missionary Labors.* Boston: Gold and Lincoln, 1864.

———. *History of the Missions of the American Board of Commissioners for Foreign Missions in India.* Boston: Congregational Publishing Society, 1875.

————. *History of the Missions of the American Board of Commissioners for Foreign Missions to the Oriental Churches*. Boston: Congregational Publishing Society, 1873.

————. *History of the Sandwich Islands Mission*. London, UK: Hodder and Stoughton, 1872.

————. *Kapiolani, the Heroine of Hawaii; Or, A Triumph of Grace at the Sandwich Islands*. New York: Charles Scribner and Co., 1866.

————. *Memorial Volume of the First Fifty Years of the American Board of Commissioners for Foreign Missions*. Boston: American Board of Commissioners for Foreign Missions, 1861.

Annual Reports, Read before His Majesty, to the Hawaiian Legislature, May 12, 1851, with the King's Speech to the Legislature, May 6, 1851. Honolulu: Government Press, 1851.

Arago, Jacques. *Narrative of a Voyage Round the World, in the Uranie and Physicienne Corvettes, Commanded by Captain Freycinet, during the Years 1817, 1818, 1819, and 1820; on a Scientific Expedition Undertaken by Order of the French Government*. N.p.: Truettel and Würtz, Truettel, Jun and Richter, 1823.

Bingham, Hiram. *A Residence of Twenty-One Years in the Sandwich Islands*. Hartford, Conn.: Hezekiah Huntington, 1847.

Bird, Isabella L. *The Hawaiian Archipelago: Six Months among the Coral Reefs and Volcanoes of the Sandwich Islands*. 3rd ed. London, UK: John Murray Publishing, 1880.

Bradley, Harold Whitman. *The American Frontier in Hawaii: The Pioneers, 1789–1843*. Stanford, Calif.: Stanford University Press, 1942.

Brain, Belle M. *The Transformation of Hawaii: How American Missionaries Gave a Christian Nation to the World*. New York: Fleming H. Revell Company, 1898.

Broughton, William Robert. *A Voyage of Discovery to the North Pacific Ocean: In Which the Coast of Asia, from the Lat. of 35 North to the Lat. of 52 North, the Island on Insu (Commonly Known under the Name of the Land of Jesso) the North, South, and East Coasts of Japan, the Lieuchieux and the Adjacent Isles, as Well as the Coast of Corea, Have Been Examined and Surveyed*. London, UK: T. Cadell and W. Davies in the Strand, 1804.

Bullard, Anne T. *Wife for a Missionary*. Cincinnati: Truman and Smith, 1835.

Campbell, Archibald. *A Voyage Round the World, from 1806 to 1812, in Which Japan, Kamschatka, the Aleutian Islands, and the Sandwich Islands Were Visited*. New York: Broderick and Ritter, 1819.

Child, Mrs. D. L. *The History of the Condition of Women in Various Ages and Nations*. Boston: Otis, Broaders & Co., 1843.

Choris, Louis. *Voyage Pittoresque Autour de Monde: Avec des Portraits de Sauvages d' Amérique, d'Asie, d'Afrique, et des îles du Grand Océan; des Paysages, des vues Maritimes, et Plusieurs Objets d'Histoire Naturelle*. Paris: Impr. De Firming Didot, 1822.

Cleveland, Richard J. *A Narrative of Voyages and Commercial Enterprises*. New York: John Owen, 1842.

Corney, Peter. *Early Northern Pacific Voyages*. Honolulu: Thos. G. Thrum, 1896.

Cumming, C. F. Gordon. *Fire Fountains: The Kingdom of Hawaii, Its Volcanoes, and the History of Its Missions*. Edinburgh and London, UK: William Blackwood and Sons, 1888.

Dibble, Sheldon. *A History of the Sandwich Islands*. Lahainaluna: Press of the Mission Seminary, 1843.

Dwight, Edwin W. *Memoirs of Henry Obookiah*. Honolulu: Woman's Board of Missions for the Pacific Islands, 1990.

———. *Memoirs of Henry Obookiah, a Native of Owhyhee, and a Member of the Foreign Mission School; Who Died at Cornwall, Conn., February 17, 1818, Aged 26 Years*. New Haven, Conn.: Office of the Religious Intelligencer, 1818.

Ellis, William. *An Authentic Narrative of a Voyage Performed by Captain Cook and Captain Clerke, in His Majesty's Ships Resolution and Discovery during the Years 1776, 1777, 1778, 1779 and 1780; in Search of a North-West Passage between the Continents of Asia and America. Including a Faithful Account of All Their Discoveries, and the Unfortunate Death of Captain Cook. Illustrated with a Chart and a Variety of Cuts*. London: G. Robinson, Pater-noster Row; J. Sewell, Cornhill; and J. Debrett, 1782.

———. *Journal of William Ellis, Narrative of a Tour of Hawaii, or Owhyhee: With Remarks on the History, Traditions, Manners, Customs, and Language of the Inhabitants of the Sandwich Islands*. Introduction by Thurston Twigg-Smith. Rutland, Vermont: Charles E. Tuttle Company, 1979.

———. *Memoir of Mrs. Mary Mercy Ellis, Wife of Rev. William Ellis, Missionary in the South Seas, and Foreign Secretary of the London Missionary Society*. Boston: Crocker and Brewster, 1836.

Forbes, Anna. *Insulinde: Experiences of a Naturalist's Wife in the Eastern Archipelago*. Edinburgh and London, UK: William Blackwood and Sons, 1887.

Franchère, Gabriel. *Narrative of a Voyage to the Northwest Coast of America in the Years 1811, 1812, 1813, and 1814*. Edited and translated by J. V. Huntington. New York: Redfield, 1854.

Freycinet, Louis Claude Desaulses de. *Hawai'i in 1819: A Narrative Account by Louis Claude De Saulses De Freycinet; Ella L. Wiswell, Translator; Notes and Comments by Marion Kelly*. Honolulu: Bernice Pauahi Bishop Museum, 1978.

Gallaudet, Thomas H. *An Address, Delivered at a Meeting for Prayers, with Reference to the Sandwich Mission, in the Brick Church in Hartfort, October 11, 1819*. Hartford: Lincoln Stone, Printers, 1819.

Garner, Stanton, ed. *The Captain's Best Mate: The Journal of Mary Chipman Lawrence on the Whaler Addison, 1856–1860*. Providence: Brown University Press, 1966.

Grimshaw, Beatrice. *In the Strange South Seas*. London, UK: Hutchinson, 1908.

Gulick, Rev., and Mrs. Orramel Hinckley. *The Pilgrims of Hawaii: Their Own Story of Their Pilgrimage from New England and Life Work in the Sandwich Islands, Now Known as Hawaii*. New York: Fleming H. Revell Company, 1918.

Hale, Sarah Josepha. *Woman's Record or Sketches of All Distinguished Women*. New York: Harper and Brothers Publishers, 1853.

Hall, Gordon, and Samuel Newell. *The Conversion of the World; Or, The Claims of Six Hundred Millions and the Ability and Duty of the Churches Respecting Them*. Andover, Mass.: Flagg and Gould, 1818.

Holman, Lucia Ruggles. *Journal of Lucia Ruggles Holman*. Honolulu: Bernice P. Bishop Museum, 1931.

Humphrey, Heman. *The Promised Land: A Sermon, Delivered at Goshen (Conn.) at the Ordination of the Rev. Messrs. Hiram Bingham and Asa Thurston, as Missionaries to the Sandwich Islands, September 29, 1819*. Boston: Samuel T. Armstrong, 1819.

Humphrey, Sophia Porter. *Memorial Sketches: Heman Humphrey*. Philadelphia: J. B. Lippincott and Co., 1869.

Hunnewell, James. "Honolulu in 1817 and 1818." *Hawaiian Historical Society* 8 (1909).

'Ī'ī, John Papa. *Fragments of Hawaiian History*. Honolulu: Bishop Museum Press, 1959.

Jarves, J. J. "Account of the Visit of the French Frigate L'artemise." *Hawaiian Spectator* 2, no. 3 (1839).

Judd, Laura Fish. *Honolulu: Sketches of Life, Social, Political, and Religious in the Hawaiian Islands 1828 to 1861*. New York: Anson D. F. Randolph and Company, 1880.

——. *Honolulu: Sketches of the Life, Social, Political, and Religious in the Hawaiian Islands from 1828 to 1861*. Honolulu: Judd Family, reprint ed., 2003.

Kamakau, Samuel Manaiakalani. *Ka Po'e Kahiko: The People of Old*. Honolulu: Bishop Museum Press, 1991.

——. *Ruling Chiefs of Hawaii*. Honolulu: Kamehameha Schools Press, 1961.

Kamehameha II. "Letter of Kamehameha II to Alexander I, 1820." *American Historical Review* 20, no. 4 (1915): 831–33.

Kotzebue, Otto von. *A Voyage of Discovery into the South Sea and Beering's Straits, for the Purpose of Exploring a North-East Passage, Undertaken in the Years 1815–1818, at the Expense of His Highness . . . Count Romanzoff, in the Ship Rurick, under the Command of the Lieutenant in the Russian Imperial Navy, Otto Von Kotzebue*. 3 Vols. London, UK: Longman, Hurst, Rees, Orme, and Brown, 1821.

Kraut, Mary H. *Hawaii and a Revolution: The Personal Experiences of a Newspaper Correspondent in the Sandwich Islands during the Crisis of 1893 and Subsequently*. London, UK: John Murray Publishing, 1898.

Lamb, W. Kaye [George Vancouver], ed. *A Voyage of Discovery to the North Pacific Ocean and Round the World, 1791–1795: with an Introduction and Appendices*. London, UK: Hakluyt Society, 1984.

Leland, Lillian. *Traveling Alone: A Woman's Journey around the World*. New York: The American News Company, 1890.

Malo, David. *Hawaiian Antiquities*. Honolulu: Bernice P. Bishop Museum, 1951.

Martin, Margaret Greer. *Sarah Joiner Lyman of Hawaii: Her Own Story*. Hilo: Lyman House Memorial Museum, 1970.

Maurer, O. E. *How the Gospel Came to Hawaii*. Honolulu: Central Union Church, 1945.

Montgomery, James, ed. *Journal of Voyages and Travels by the Rev. Daniel Tyerman and George Bennet, Esq., Deputed from the London Missionary Society, to Visit Their Various Stations in the South Sea Islands, China, India &C., between the Years 1821–1829*. London, UK: Frederick Westley and A. H. Davis, 1831.

Morgan, Dale, ed. *Honolulu: Sketches of Life in the Hawaiian Islands from 1828–1861*. Chicago: R. R. Donnelley and Sons Company, 1966.

A Narrative of Five Youth from the Sandwich Islands, Now Receiving an Education in This Country. New York: J. Seymour, 1816.

Panoplist and Missionary Herald. Vol. 14. Boston: Samuel T. Armstrong, 1818.

Panoplist and Missionary Herald. Vol. 15. Boston: Samuel T. Armstrong, 1819.

Panoplist and Missionary Herald. Vol 16. Boston: Crocker and Brewster, 1820.

Panoplist and Missionary Herald. Vol. 17. Boston: Samuel T. Armstrong, 1821.

Pilkington, Mrs. A Mirror for the Female Sex: Historical Beauties for Young Ladies Intended to Lead the Female Mind to the Practice of Moral Goodness. Hartford, Conn.: Hudson and Goodwin, 1799.

Pitman, Emma Raymond. Heroines of the Mission Field. New York: Andon D. F. Randolph & Company, 1880.

Portraits of American Protestant Missionaries to Hawaii. Honolulu: Hawaiian Mission Children's Society, 1901.

"Proclamation of Toleration." Hawaiian Mission Children's Society, 1839[?].

Reed-Danahay, Deborah E., ed. Auto/Ethnography. Oxford, UK: Berg Press, 1997.

Restarick, Bishop H. B. "Sybil Bingham, as a Youthful Bride, Came to Islands in Brig Thaddeaus ." Saturday, August 15, 1931.

Richards, William. Memoir of Keopuolani, Late Queen of the Sandwich Islands. Boston: Crocker and Brewster, 1825.

"Sketches of the Life, Labors, and Death of Rev. Samuel Whitney." The Friend (1846): 9–12.

Stewart, C. S. Journal of a Residence in the Sandwich Islands, during the Years 1823, 1824, and 1825. New York: John P. Haven, 1828.

Strong, William E. The Story of the American Board: An Account of the First Hundred Years of the American Board of Commissioners for Foreign Missions. Boston: Pilgrim Press, 1910.

Taylor, Mrs. Persis G. "Kapiolani: A Memorial Prepared by Mrs. Persis G. Taylor, and Read before the Woman's Board of Missions for the Pacific Islands, October 6, 1896." Honolulu, 1897.

Thurston, Lucy Goodale. Life and Times of Mrs. Lucy G. Thurston. Ann Arbor: S. C. Andrews, 1872.

———. Life and Times of Mrs. Lucy G. Thurston, Wife of Rev. Asa Thurston, Pioneer Missionary to the Sandwich Islands, Gathered from Letters and Journals Extending over a Period of More Than Fifty Years. Ann Arbor: S. C. Andrews, 1882.

———. The Missionary's Daughter: A Memoir of Lucy Goodale Thurston, of the Sandwich Islands. New York: American Tract Society, 1842.

Tracy, Joseph. "History of the American Board of Commissioners for Foreign Missions." In History of American Missions to the Present Time. Worcester, Mass.: Spooner and Howland, 1840.

Tracy, Joseph, and Solomon Peck, Enoch Mudge, William Cutter, Enoch Mack, eds. History Of American Missions to the Heathen, from their Commencement to the Present Time. Worcester: Spooner and Howland, 1840.

Trollope, Frances Milton. Domestic Manners of the Americans. Paris: Baudry's Foreign Library, 1832.

Tyerman, Daniel. Journal of Voyages and Travels by the Rev. Daniel Tyerman and George Bennet, Esq. London, UK: Frederick Westley and A. H. Davis, 1831.

Vancouver, George. Voyage of Discovery to the North Pacific Ocean and Round the World; in Which the Coast of North-West America Has Been Carefully Examined and Accurately Surveyed: Undertaken by His Majesty's Command, Principally with a View to Ascertain the

Existence of Any Navigable Communication between the North Pacific and North Atlantic Oceans, and Performed in the Years 1790, 1791, 1792, 1793, 1794, and 1795, in the Discovery Sloop of War, and Armed Tender Chatham, under the Command of Captain George Vancouver: In Three Volumes. London, UK: G. G. and J. Robinson, Paternoster-Row, and J. Edwards, Pall-Mall, 1798.

Westervelt, W. D. "The Passing of Kamehameha I." Paper presented at the Thirty-First Annual Report ot the Hawaiian Histoical Society for the Year 1822 with Papers Read at the Annual Meeting, January 25, 1923.

Whitney, Samuel. "Account of the Russians on Kauai." *Hawaiian Spectator* 1, no. 1 (1838).

Wight, Elizabeth Leslie [daughter to Judds]. *The Memoirs of Elizabeth Kinau Wilder.* Honolulu: Paradise of the Pacific Press, 1909.

SECONDARY SOURCES

Adelman, Jeremy, and Stephen Aron. "From Borderlands to Borders: Empires, Nation-States and the Peoples in between in North American History." *American Historical Review* 104, no. 3 (1999): 814–41.

Ahlstrom, Sydney E. *A Religious History of the American People.* 2nd ed. New Haven, Conn.: Yale University Press, 2004.

Allison, Robert J., ed. *The Interesting Narrative of the Life of Olaudah Equiano, Written by Himself.* Boston: Bedford Books, 1995.

Anderson, Karen. *Chain Her by One Foot: The Subjugation of Women in Seventeenth-Century New France.* New York: Routledge, 1991.

Andrew, John A. *Rebuilding the Christian Commonwealth: New England Congregationalists and Foreign Missions, 1800–1830.* Lexington: University Press of Kentucky, 1976.

Appadurai, Arjun, ed. *The Social Life of Things: Commodities in Cultural Perspective.* London, UK: Cambridge University Press, 1986.

Arthur, Linda. "Cultural Authentication Refined: The Case of the Holokū." *Clothing and Textiles Research Journal* 15, no. 3 (1997): 129–39.

———. "Fossilized Fashion in Hawai'i." *Paideusis: Journal of Interdisciplinary Cultural Studies* 1 (1998): 15–28.

———. *Religion, Dress, and the Body.* Oxford: Berg, 1999.

Arya, Anita Nahal. *Hawaii: An Ethnic Synthesis.* New Delhi: Allied Publishers, Limited, 1993.

Axtell, James. *After Columbus: Essays in the Ethnohistory of Colonial North America.* New York: Oxford University Press, 1988.

———. *Beyond 1492: Encounters in Colonial North America.* New York: Oxford University Press, 1992.

———. *Imagining the Other: First Encounters in North America.* Washington, D.C.: American Historical Association, 1991.

Bailey, Beth, and David Farber. *The First Strange Place: The Alchemy of Race and Sex in World War II Hawaii.* New York: Macmillan, Inc., 1992.

Ballantyne, Tony, and Antoinette Burton, eds. *Bodies in Contact: Rethinking Colonial Encounters in World History.* Durham, N.C.: Duke University Press, 2005.

———. *Moving Subjects: Gender, Mobility, and Intimacy in an Age of Global Empire*. Urbana: University of Illinois Press, 2009.

Banner, Stuart. *Possessing the Pacific: Land, Settlers, and Indigenous Peoples from Australia to Alaska*. Cambridge, Mass.: Harvard University Press, 2007.

Barr, Pat. *A Curious Life for a Lady*. London, UK: John Murray Publishers Limited, 1970.

Bassett, Marnie. *Realms and Islands: The World Voyage of Rose De Freycinet in the Corvette Uranie, 1817–1820*. London, UK: Oxford University Press, 1962.

Beckwith, Martha. *Hawaiian Mythology*. Honolulu: University of Hawaii Press, 1970.

———, ed. *Kepelino's Traditions of Hawaii*. Honolulu: Bishop Museum, 1932.

Bederman, Gail. *Manliness and Civilization: A Cultural History of Gender and Race in the United States, 1880–1917*. Chicago: University of Chicago Press, 1995.

———. "The Women Have Had Charge of the Church Work Long Enough: The Men and Religion Forward Movement of 1911–1912 and the Masculinization of Middle-Class Protestantism." *American Quarterly* 41, no. 3 (1989): 432–65.

Benedetto, Robert. *The Hawaii Journals of the New England Missionaries, 1813–1894*. Honolulu: Hawaiian Mission Children's Society, 1982.

Berking, Helmuth. *Sociology of Giving*. London, UK: Sage Publications, 1999.

Beyer, Carl Kalani. "Manual and Industrial Education for Hawaiians during the 19th Century." *Hawaiian Journal of History* 38 (2004): 1–34.

Bienstock, Gregory. *The Struggle for the Pacific*. Port Washington, N.Y.: Kennikat Press, 1970.

Bilhartz, Terry D. "Sex and the Second Great Awakening: The Feminization of American Religion Reconsidered." In *Belief and Behavior: Essays in the New Religious History*, edited by Philip R. VanderMeer and Robert P. Swierenga. New Brunswick, N.J.: Rutgers University Press, 1991.

———. *Urban Religion and the Second Great Awakening: Church and Society in Early National Baltimore*. Rutherford, N.J.: Fairleigh Dickinson University Press, 1986.

Birkett, Dea. *Spinsters Abroad: Victorian Lady Explorers*. Oxford: Basil Blackwell, 1989.

Birkett, Mary Ellen. "Hawai'i in 1819: An Account by Camille De Roquefeuil." *Hawaiian Journal of History* 34 (2000): 69–92.

Blackman, William Fremont. *The Making of Hawaii: A Study in Social Evolution*. London, UK: Macmillan & Co., Ltd, 1899.

Blanton, Casey. *Travel Writing: The Self and the World*. New York: Twayne Publishers, 1997.

Borofsky, Robert. "Cook, Lono, Obeyesekere, and Sahlins." *Current Anthropology* 9 (1997): 255–82.

———, ed. *Remembrance of Pacific Pasts: An Invitation to Remake History*. Honolulu: University of Hawaii Press, 2000.

Bowie, Fiona, Deborah Kirkwood, and Shirley Ardener, eds. *Women and Missions: Past and Present*. Providence: Berg Publishers, 1991.

Bown, Stephen. B. *Madness, Betrayal, and the Lash: The Epic Voyage of Captain George Vancouver*. Vancouver, B.C.: Douglas and McIntyre, 2008.

Bradley, Harold Whitman. *The American Frontier in Hawaii: The Pioneers, 1789–1843*. Stanford, Calif.: Stanford University Press, 1942.

Braude, Ann. "Women's History Is American Religious History." In *Retelling U.S. Religious History*, edited by Thomas A. Tweed. Berkeley: University of California Press, 1997.

Braund, K. E. H. "Guardians of Tradition and Handmaidens to Change: Women's Roles in Creek Economic and Social Life during the Eighteenth Century." *American Indian Quarterly* 14, no. 3 (1990): 239–58.

Brown, Kathleen. "The Anglo-Algonquian Gender Frontier." In *Negotiators of Change: Historical Perspectives on Native American Women*, edited by Nancy Shoemaker. London, UK: Routledge, 1995.

———. *Good Wives, Nasty Wenches, and Anxious Patriarchs: Gender, Race, and Power in Colonial Virginia*. Chapel Hill: University of North Carolina Press, 1996.

Brusco, Elizabeth, and Laura F. Klein, ed. *The Message in the Missionary: Local Interpretations of Religious Ideology and Missionary Personality*. Williamsburg, Va.: Department of Anthropology, College of William and Mary, 1994.

Buchanan, Paul D. *Historic Places of Worship: Stories of Fifty-One Extraordinary American Religious Sites since 1300*. Jefferson, N.C.: McFarland and Company, 1999.

Buck, Elizabeth. *Paradise Remade: The Politics of Culture and History in Hawaii*. Philadelphia: Temple University Press, 1993.

Buck, Peter [Te Rangi Hiroa]. *Arts and Crafts of Hawaii*. Honolulu: Bishop Museum Press, 1964.

Bunkers, Suzanne L., and Cynthia A. Huff, eds. *Inscribing the Daily: Critical Essays on Women's Diaries*. Amherst: University of Massachusetts Press, 1996.

Burlin, Paul. *Imperial Maine and Hawai'i: Interpretative Essays in the History of Nineteenth-Century American Expansion*. Lanham, Md.: Lexington Books, 2006.

Burridge, Kenelm. *Tangu Traditions: A Study of the Way of Life, Mythology, and Developing Experience of a New Guinea People*. Oxford, UK: Oxford University Press, 1969.

Busch, Briton C. "Whalemen, Missionaries, and the Practice of Christianity in the Nineteenth-Century Pacific." *Hawaiian Journal of History* 27 (1993): 91–118.

Butler, Jon, Grant Wacker, and Randall Balmer, ed. *Religion in American Life: A Short History*. New York: Oxford University Press, 2003.

Campbell, I. C. *A History of the Pacific Islands*. Berkeley: University of California Press, 1996.

Carpenter, Edmund Janes. *America in Hawaii: A History of United States Influence in the Hawaiian Islands*. London, UK: Sampson Low, Marston & Company, Ltd., 1899.

Carretta, Vincent. *Equiano, the African: Biography of a Self-Made Man*. Athens: University of Georgia Press, 2005.

Cater, W. F., ed. *Love among the Butterflies: The Travels and Adventures of a Victorian Lady*. London, UK: Collins, 1980.

Cayton, Mary Kupiec. "Canonizing Harriet Newell: Women, the Evangelical Press, and the Foreign Mission Movement in New England, 1800–1840." In *Competing Kingdoms: Women, Mission, Nation, and the American Protestant Empire, 1812–1960*, edited by Barbara Reeves-Ellingon, Kathryn Kish Sklar, and Connie A. Shemo. Durham, N.C.: Duke University Press, 2010.

Chapin, Helen Geracimos. *Shaping History: The Role of Newspapers in Hawai'i.* Honolulu: University of Hawai'i Press, 1996.

Chin, Carol C. "Beneficent Imperialists: American Women Missionaires in China at the Turn of the Twentieth Century." *Diplomatic History* 27, no. 3 (2003): 327–52.

Clancy-Smith, Julia, and Frances Gouda, eds. *Domesticating the Empire: Race, Gender, and Family Life in French and Dutch Colonialism.* Charlottesville and London, UK: University Press of Virginia, 1998.

College of William and Mary Department of Anthropology. *Women Missionaries and Cultural Change.* Williamsburg, Va.: College of William and Mary, 1987.

Corrigan, John. *Business of the Heart: Religion and Emotion in the Nineteenth Century.* Berkeley: University of California Press, 2002.

Cott, Nancy. *The Bonds of Womanhood: "Woman's Sphere" in New England, 1780–1835.* New Haven, Conn.: Yale University Press, 1977.

Crosby, A. W. "Hawaiian Depopulation as a Model for the Amerindian Experience." In *Epidemics and Ideas: Essays on the Historical Perception of Pestilence,* edited by Terence Ranger and Paul Slack. New York: Oxford University Press, 1992.

Cumings, Bruce. *Dominion from Sea to Sea: Pacific Ascendancy and American Power.* New Haven, Conn.: Yale University Press, 2009.

Cutter, Donald. "The Spanish in Hawaii: Gaytan to Marin." *Hawaiian Journal of History* 14 (1980): 26–15.

Damon, Ethel M. *The Stone Church at Kawaiahao.* Honolulu: Trustees of Kawaiahao, 1945.

Davidson, Cathy. *Revolution and the Word: The Rise of the Novel in America.* New York: Oxford University Press, 1986.

Davis, Natalie Zemon. *The Gift in Sixteenth-Century France.* Madison: University of Wisconsin Press, 2000.

Daws, Gavan. "Texts and Contexts: A First-Person Note." *Journal of Pacific History* 41, no. 2 (2006): 250–60.

———. *Shoal of Time.* Honolulu: University of Hawaii Press, 1968.

Day, A. Grove. *History Makers of Hawaii: A Biographical Dictionary.* Honolulu: Mutual Publishing of Honolulu, 1984.

Deloria, Philip J. "What Is the Middle Ground, Anyway?" *William and Mary Quarterly* 63, no. 1 (2006): 9–22.

D'Emilio, John, and Estelle B. Freedman. *Intimate Matters: A History of Sexuality in America.* Chicago: University of Chicago Press, 1997.

Dening, Greg. *The Death of William Gooch: A History's Anthropology.* Lanham, Md: University Press of America, 1988.

Denoon, Donald. "Land, Labour, and Independent Development." In *The Cambridge History of the Pacific Islanders,* edited by Donald Denoon with Stewart Firth, Jocelyn Linnekin, Malama Meleisea, and Karen Nero. Cambridge, UK: Cambridge University Press, 1997.

Denoon, Donald, with Stewart Firth, Jocelyn Linnekin, Malama Meleisea, and Karen Nero, eds. *The Cambridge History of the Pacific Islanders.* Cambridge, UK: Cambridge University Press, 1997.

Deutsch, Sarah. *No Separate Refuge: Culture, Class, and Gender on an Anglo-Hispanic Frontier in the American Southwest, 1880–1940*. New York: Oxford University Press, 1987.

———. *Women and the City: Gender, Space, and Power in Boston, 1870–1940*. New York: Oxford University Press, 2000.

Devens, Carol. *Countering Colonization: Native American Women and Great Lakes Missions, 1630–1900*. Berkeley: University of California Press, 1992.

Díaz, Mónica. "Native American Women and Religion in the American Colonies: Textual and Visual Traces of an Imagined Community." *Legacy: A Journal of American Women Writers* 28, no. 2 (2011): 205–31.

Dodge, Charlotte Peabody. *Hawaiian Mission Children's Society, 1852–1952*. Honolulu: Hawaiian Mission Children's Society, 1952.

Dolin, Jay. *Fur, Fortune, and Empire: The Epic History of the Fur Trade in America*. New York: W. W. Norton and Company, 2010.

Dougherty, Michael. *To Steal a Kingdom: Probing Hawaiian History*. Waimanalo: Island Style Press, 1992.

Douglas, Ann. *The Feminization of American Culture*. New York: Farrar, Straus and Giroux, 1977.

Dunmore, John. *Visions and Realities: France in the Pacific, 1695–1995*. Waikane, New Zealand: Heritage Press, 1997.

Dwight, Edwin W. *Memoirs of Henry Obookiah*. Honolulu: Woman's Board of Missions for the Pacific Islands, 1990.

Early, Lisa. "If We Win the Women: The Lives and Work of Female Missionaries at the Methodist Mission in the Solomon Islands, 1902–1942." University of Otago, 1998.

Edwards, Paul, ed. *Equaino's Travels: His Autobiography the Interesting Narrative of the Life of Olaudah Equiano or Gustavus Vassa the African*. New York: Frederick A. Praeger, 1967.

Ellis, Rev. William. *Memoir of Mrs. Mary Mercy Ellis, Wife of Rev. William Ellis, Missionary in the South Seas, and Foreign Secretary of the London Missionary Society*. Boston: Crocker and Brewster, 1836.

Equiano, Olaudah. *The Life of Olaudah Equiano*. 1837; New York: Negro Universities Press, 1969.

Ewins, Rod. *Staying Fijian: Vatulele Island Barkcloth and Social Identity*. Honolulu: University of Hawaiʻi Press, 2009.

Fahs, Alice. *The Imagined Civil War: Popular Literature of the North and South, 1861–1865*. Chapel Hill: University of North Carolina Press, 2001.

Fay, Mary Ann. "Women, Property, and Power in Eighteenth-Century Cairo." In *Bodies in Contact: Rethinking Colonial Encounters in World History*, edited by Tony Ballantyne and Antoinette Burton. Durham, N.C.: Duke University Press, 2005.

Fisher, Robin, and Hugh Johnston, eds. *From Maps to Metaphors: The Pacific World of George Vancouver*. Vancouver: UBC Press, 1993.

Flemming, Leslie A. *Women's Work for Women: Missionaries and Social Change in Asia*. Boulder, Colo.: Westview Press, 1989.

Forbes, David W. *Encounters with Paradise: Views of Hawaii and Its People, 1778–1941*. Honolulu: Honolulu Academy of the Arts, University of Hawaii Press, 1992.

Fornander, Abraham. *An Account of the Polynesian Race: Its Origins and Migrations, and the Ancient History of the Hawaiian People to the Times of Kamehameha I*. Rutland, Vt.: C. E. Tuttle Co., 1969.

Foster, Shirley. *Across New Worlds: Nineteenth-Century Women Travellers and Their Writings*. New York: Harvester Wheathsheaf, 1990.

Friedman, John. *Cultural Identity and Global Process*. London, UK: Sage Publications, 1994.

Fuchs, Lawrence. *Hawaii Pono: A Social History*. New York: Harcourt, 1984.

Garner, Stanton, ed. *The Captain's Best Mate: The Journal of Mary Chipman Lawrence on the Whaler Addison, 1856–1860*. Providence: Brown University Press, 1966.

Gast, Ross H., and Agnes C. Conrad. *Don Francisco de Paula Marin: A Biography*. Honolulu: University Press of Hawaii for the Hawaiian Historical Society, 1973.

Gaustad, Edwin S., and Leigh E. Schmidt. *The Religious History of America*. New York: HarperSanFrancisco, 2002.

Geertz, Clifford. *The Interpretation of Cultures*. New York: Basic Books, 1973.

Georgi-Findlay, Brigitte. *The Frontiers of Women's Writing: Women's Narratives and the Rhetoric of Westward Expansion*. Tucson: University of Arizona Press, 1996.

Gilroy, Amanda, ed. *Romantic Geographies: Discourses of Travel, 1775–1844*. Manchester, UK: Manchester University, 2000.

Ginzberg, Lori D. *Women and the Work of Benevolence: Morality, Politics, and Class in the Nineteenth-Century United States*. New Haven, Conn.: Yale University Press, 1990.

Godbeer, Richard. *Sexual Revolution in Early America*. Baltimore: Johns Hopkins University Press, 2002.

Godelier, Maurice. *The Enigma of the Gift*. Chicago: University of Chicago Press, 1999.

Goody, Esther N., ed. *From Craft to Industry: The Ethnography of Proto-Industrial Cloth Production*. New York: Cambridge University Press, 1982.

Gowans, Alan. *Fruitful Fields: American Missionary Churches in Hawaii*. Honolulu: Department of Land and Natural Resources, State Historic Preservatoin Division, 1993.

Gowen, Herbert H. *The Napoleon of the Pacific: Kamehameha the Great*. New York: Flemig H. Revell Company, 1919.

Green, Karina Kahananui. "Colonialism's Daughters: Eighteenth- and Nineteenth-Century Western Perceptions of Hawaiian Women." In *Pacific Diaspora: Island Peoples in the United States and across the Pacific*, edited by Paul Spickard, Janne L. Rondilla, and Bebbie Hoppolite. Honolulu: University of Hawai'i Press, 2002.

Green, Rayna. "The Pocahontas Perplex: The Image of Indian Women in American Culture." In *Unequal Sisters: A Multicultural Reader in U.S. Women's History*, edited by Ellen Carol DuBois and Vicki Ruiz. New York: Routledge, 1990.

Greer, Allan. *Mohawk Saint: Catherine Tekakwitha and the Jesuits*. New York: Oxford University Press, 2005.

Greer, Allan, and Jodi Bilinkoff, eds. *Colonial Saints: Discovering the Holy in the Americas*. New York: Routledge, 2003.

Greer, Richard. "Grog Shops and Hotels: Bending the Elbow in Old Honolulu." *Hawaiian Journal of History* 28 (1994): 35–67.

Grimshaw, Patricia. "'Christian Woman, Pious Wife, Faithful Mother, Devoted Missionary': Conflicts in Roles of American Missionary Women in Nineteenth-Century Hawaii." *Feminist Studies* 9, no. 3 (1983): 489–521.

———. "New England Missionary Wives, Hawaiian Women, and 'the Cult of True Womanhood.'" *Hawaiian Journal of History* 19 (1985): 71–100.

———. *Paths of Duty: American Missionary Wives in Nineteenth-Century Hawaii.* Honolulu: University of Hawaii Press, 1989.

Gunn Allen, Paula. *Pocahontas: Medicine Woman, Spy, Entrepreneur, Diplomat.* San Francisco: HarperSanFrancisco, 2003.

Gunson, Niel. *Messengers of Grace: Evangelical Missionaries in the South Seas, 1797–1860.* New York: Oxford University Press, 1978.

———. "Sacred Women Chiefs and Female 'Headmen' in Polynesian History." *Journal of Pacific History* 22, no. 3 (1987): 139–72.

Gutiérrez, Ramón A. "What's Love Got to Do with It?" *Journal of American History* 88, no. 3 (2001): 866–69.

———. *When Jesus Came, the Corn Mothers Went Away: Marriage, Sexuality, and Power in New Mexico, 1500–1846.* Stanford, Calif.: Stanford University Press, 1991.

Gutiérrez, Ramón A., and Elliott Young. "Transnationalizing Borderlands History." *Western Historical Quarterly* 41 (2010): 26–53.

Haas, Michael. *Multicultural Hawaii: The Fabric of a Multiethnic Society.* New York: Garland Publishing, 1998.

Hall, Catherine. "Of Gender and Empire: Reflections on the Nineteenth Century." In *Gender and Empire*, edited by Philippa Levine. Oxford: Oxford University Press, 2004.

Hall, David D. *Lived Religion in America: Toward a History of Practice.* Princeton, N.J.: Princeton University Press, 1997.

Halttunen, Karen. *Confidence Men and Painted Women: A Study of Middle-Class Culture in America, 1830–1870.* New Haven, Conn.: Yale University Press, 1982.

Hamalain, Leo, ed. *Ladies on the Loose: Women Travellers of the Eighteenth and Nineteenth Centuries.* New York: Dodd, Mead & Company, 1981.

Harper, Lila Marz. *Solitary Travelers: Nineteenth-Century Women's Travel Narratives and the Scientific Vocation.* Madison, N.J.: Fairleigh Dickinson University Press, 2001.

Harris, Paul William. *Nothing but Christ: Rufus Anderson and the Ideology of Protestant Foreign Missions.* New York: Oxford University Press, 1999.

Hartman, Mary S., and Lois Banner, eds. *Clio's Consciousness Raised: New Perspectives on the History of Women.* New York: Octagon Books, 1976.

Hatch, Nathan O. *The Democratization of American Christianity.* New Haven, Conn.: Yale University Press, 1989.

Havely, Cicely Palser. *This Grand Beyond: The Travels of Isabella Bird Bishop.* London, UK: Century Publishing, 1984.

Haycox, Stephen, James Barnett, and Caedmon Liburd. *Enlightenment and Exploration in the North Pacific, 1741–1805.* Seattle: University of Washington Press, 1997.

Hays, H. R. *The Kingdom of Hawaii*. Greenwich, Conn: New York Graphic Society, 1964.

Hernández, Kelly Lytle. "Borderlands and the Future History of the American West." *Western Historical Quarterly* 42 (2011): 325–30.

Hill, Patricia Ruth. *The World Their Household: The American Woman's Foreign Mission Movement and Cultural Transformation, 1870–1920*. Ann Arbor: University of Michigan Press, 1985.

Holt, John Dominis. *Monarchy in Hawaii*. Honolulu: Hogart Press, 1971.

Hooper, Anthony, and Judith Huntsman, eds. *Transformations of Polynesian Culture*. Auckland, New Zealand: Polynesian Society, 1985.

Howard, Alan, and Robert Borofsky, eds. *Developments in Polynesian Ethnology*. Honolulu: University of Hawaii Press, 1989.

Howe, Daniel Walker. *What Hath God Wrought: The Transformation of America, 1815–1848*. New York: Oxford University Press, 2007.

Howe, K. R. *Where the Waves Fall: A New South Sea Islands History from First Settlement to Colonial Rule*. Honolulu: University of Hawaii Press, 1984.

Huber, Mary Taylor, and Nancy C. Lutkehaus, eds. *Gendered Missions: Women and Men in Missionary Discourse and Practice*. Ann Arbor: University of Michigan Press, 1999.

Hunter, Jane. *The Gospel of Gentility: American Women Missionaries in Turn-of-the-Century China*. New Haven, Conn.: Yale University Press, 1984.

Hutchinson, William R. *Errand to the World: American Protestant Thought and Foreign Missions*. Chicago: University of Chicago Press, 1987.

Igler, David. "On Coral Reefs, Volcanoes, Gods, and Patriotic Geology; or, James Dwight Dana Assembles the Pacific Basin." *Pacific Historical Review* 79, no. 1 (2010): 23–49.

———. "Trading Places: The View of Colonial American History from the Pacific." *Huntington Frontiers* (Fall/Winter 2007): 17–21.

Ito, Karen L. *Lady Friends: Hawaiian Ways and Ties That Define*. Ithaca: Cornell University Press, 1999.

Ivory, Carol S. "Northwest Coast Uses of Polynesian Art." *American Indian Culture and Research Journal* 9, no. 4 (1985): 49–66.

Jacobs, Margaret D. *Engendered Encounters: Feminism and Pueblo Cultures, 1879–1934*. Lincoln and London, UK: University of Nebraska Press, 1999.

Jacobs, Sylvia. "Three African American Women Missionaries in the Congo, 1887–1899: The Confluence of Race, Culture, Identity, and Nationality." In *Competing Kingdoms: Women, Mission, Nation, and the American Protestant Empire, 1812–1960*, edited by Barbara Reeves-Ellington, Kathryn Kish Sklar, and Connie A. Shemo. Durham, N.C.: Duke University Press, 2010.

James, Janet Wilson. *Changing Ideas about Women in the United States, 1776–1825*. New York: Garland Publishing, 1981.

———, ed. *Women in American Religion*. Philadelphia: University of Pennsylvania Press, 1980.

Johnson, Donald D., with Gary Dean Best. *The United States in the Pacific: Private Interests and Public Policies, 1784–1899*. Westport, Conn.: Praeger, 1995.

Johnston, Anna. *Missionary Writing and Empire, 1800–1860.* Cambridge, UK: Cambridge University Press, 2003.

Jolly, Margaret. *Family and Gender in the Pacific: Domestic Contradictions and the Colonial Impact.* New York: Cambridge University Press, 1989.

Judd, Bernice. *Voyages to Hawaii before 1860: A Record, Based on Historical Narratives in the Libraries of the Hawaiian Mission Children's Society and the Hawaiian Historical Society, Extended to March 1860.* Enlarged and edited by Helen Yonge Lind. Honolulu: University Press of Hawaii for the Hawaiian Mission Children's Society, 1974.

Juster, Susan. *Disorderly Women: Sexual Politics and Evangelicalism in Revolutionary New England.* New York: Cornell University Press, 1996.

Kaeppler, Adrienne L. *The Fabrics of Hawaii (Bark Cloth).* Leigh-on-Sea: F. Lewis, 1975.

————. "Hawaiian Art and Society: Traditions and Transformations." In *Transformations of Polynesian Culture*, edited by Anthony Hooper and Judith Huntsman, 105–32. Aukland: The Polynesian Society, 1985.

Kahn, Susan Haskell. "From Redeemers to Partners: American Women Missionaries and the 'Woman Question' in India, 1919–1939." In *Competing Kingdoms: Women, Mission, Nation, and the American Protestant Empire, 1812–1960*, edited by Barbara Reeves-Ellingon, Kathryn Kish Sklar, and Connie A. Shemo. Durham, N.C.: Duke University Press, 2010.

Kameʻeleihiwa, Lilikala. *Native Land and Foreign Desires: Pehea Lā E Pono Ai? How Shall We Live in Harmony?* Honolulu: Bishop Museum Press, 1992.

————. "Nā Wāhine Kapu: Divine Hawaiian Women." Honolulu: ʻAi Pōhaku Press, 1999.

Kaplan, Amy. *The Anarchy of Empire in the Making of U.S. Culture.* Cambridge, Mass.: Harvard University Press, 2002.

————. "Manifest Domesticity." *American Literature* 70, no. 3 (1998): 581–606.

Kashay, Jennifer Fish. "Agents of Imperialism: Missionaries and Merchants in Early Nineteenth-Century Hawaii." *New England Quarterly* 80, no. 2 (2007): 280–98.

————. "Competing Imperialisms and Hawaiian Authority: The Cannoning of Lahaina, 1827." *Pacific Historical Review* 77 (2008): 369–90.

————. "From *Kapus* to Christianity: The Disestablishment of the Hawaiian Religion and the Chiefly Appropriation of Calvinist Christianity." *Western Historical Quarterly* 39 (2008): 17–39.

————. "Native, Foreigner, Missionary, Priest: Western Imperialism and Religious Conflict in Early Nineteenth-Century Hawaiʻi." *Cercles: Interdisciplinary Journal of Anglo-American Literature* 5 (2002): 3–10.

————. "'O That My Mouth Might Be Opened': Missionaries, Gender, and Language in Early Nineteenth-Century Hawaiʻi." *Hawaiian Journal of History* 36 (2002): 41–58.

Kasson, John F. *Rudeness and Civility: Manners in Nineteenth-Century America.* New York: Hill and Wang, 1990.

Keller, Rosemary Skinner, and Rosemary Radford Ruether, eds. *In Our Own Voices: Four Centuries of American Women's Religious Writing.* San Franscisco: HarperSanFrancisco, 1995.

Kent, Eliza F. *Converting Women: Gender and Protestant Christianity in Colonial South India*. Oxford, UK: Oxford University Press, 2004.

Kent, Noel J. *Hawaii: Islands under the Influence*. New York: Monthly Review Press, 1983.

Kerber, Linda. "Separate Spheres, Female Worlds, Woman's Place." *Journal of American History* 75, no. 2 (1988): 9–39.

Kidwell, Clara Sue. "Indian Women as Cultural Mediators." *Ethnohistory* 39, no. 2 (1992): 97–107.

Kimmel, Michael. *The History of Men: Essays in the History of American and British Masculinities*. Albany: State University of New York Press, 2005.

———. *Manhood in America: A Cultural History*. New York: Free Press, 1996.

Kipp, Rita Smith. "Emancipating Each Other: Dutch Colonial Missionaries' Encounter with Karo Women in Sumatra, 1900–1942." In *Domesticating the Empire: Race, Gender, and Family Life in French and Dutch Colonialism*, edited by Julia Clancy-Smith and Frances Gouda, 211–35. Charlottesville and London, UK: University Press of Virginia, 1998.

Kirch, Patrick. *The Archaeology of History*. Vol. 2 of *Anahulu: The Anthropology of History in the Kingdom of Hawaii*, edited by Patrick Kirch and Marshall Sahlins. Chicago: University of Chicago Press, 1992.

———. *How Chiefs Became Kings: Divine Kingship and the Rise of Archaic States*. Berkeley: University of California Press, 2010.

———. *Island Societies: Archaeological Approaches to Evolution and Transformation*. Cambridge: Cambridge University Press, 1986.

———. *On the Road of the Winds: An Archaeological History of the Pacific Islands before European Contact*. Berkeley: University of California Press, 2002.

Kirch, Patrick, and Jean Louis Rallu, eds. *The Growth and Collapse of Pacific Island Societies: Archaeological and Demographic Perspectives*. Honolulu: University of Hawai'i Press, 2008.

Kirch, Patrick, and Marshall Sahlins, eds. *Anahulu: The Anthropology of History in the Kingdom of Hawaii*. 2 vols. Chicago: University of Chicago Press, 1992.

Kolodny, Annette. *The Land before Her: Fantasy and Experience of the American Frontiers, 1630–1860*. Chapel Hill: University of North Carolina Press, 1984.

———. *The Lay of the Land: Metaphor as Experience and History in American Life and Letters*. Chapel Hill: University of North Carolina Press, 1975.

Komter, Aafke E. *Social Solidarity and the Gift*. Cambridge, UK: Cambridge University Press, 2005.

Kooijman, Simon. *Polynesian Barkcloth*. Princes Risborough, Aylesbury, Buckinghamshire, UK: Shire Publications, 1988.

Kroes, Rob. "American Empire and Cultural Imperialism: A View from the Recieving End." In *Rethinking American History in a Global Age*, edited by Thomas Bender. Berkeley: University of California Press, 2002.

Kuykendall, Ralph S. *The Hawaiian Kingdom*. Vol. 1, *Foundation and Transformation, 1778–1854*. Honolulu: University of Hawaii Press, 1938.

———. *A History of Hawaii*. New York: MacMillan Company, 1927.

Kuykendall, Ralph S., and A. Grove Day. *Hawaii: A History from Polynesian Kingdom to American Commonwealth*. New York: Prentice-Hall, 1948.

Lamb, Jonathan, Vanessa Smith, and Nicholas Thomas, eds. *Exploration and Exchange: A South Seas Anthology*. Chicago: University of Chicago Press, 2000.

Landsman, Gail H. "The'Other' as Political Symbol: Images of Indians in the Woman Suffrage Movement." *Ethnohistory* 39, no. 3 (1992): 247–78.

Lawrence, Karen R. *Penelope Voyages: Women and Travel in the British Literary Tradition.* Ithaca, N.Y.: Cornell University Press, 1994.

LeBeau, Bryan. *Religion in America to 1865*. New York: New York University Press, 2000.

Lebra, Joyce Chapman. *Shaping Hawai'i: The Voices of Women*. Honolulu: Goodale Publishing, 1991.

Levine, Philippa, ed. *Gender and Empire*. Oxford, UK: Oxford University Press, 2004.

Liebersohn, Harry. "Images of Monarchy: Kamehameha I and the Art of Louis Choris." In *Double Vision: Art History and Colonial Histories in the Pacific*, edited by Nicholas Thomas and Diane Losche. Cambridge: Cambridge University Press, 1999.

———. *The Traveler's World: Europe to the Pacific*. Cambridge, Mass.: Harvard University Press, 2006.

Liliuokalani. *Hawaii's Story by Hawaii's Queen*. Rutland, Vt., and Tokyo, Japan: Charles E. Tuttle Company, 1985.

Limerick, Patricia Nelson. "The Multicultural Islands." *American Historical Review* 97, no. 1 (1992): 121–25.

Linnekin, Jocelyn. "New Political Orders." In *The Cambridge History of Pacific Islanders*, edited by Donald Denoon with Stewart Firth, Jocelyn Linnekin, Malama Meleisea, and Karen Nero. Cambridge: Cambridge University Press, 1997.

———. "Mats and Money: Contending Exchange Paradigms in Colonial Samoa." *Anthropological Quarterly* 64, no. 1 (1991): 1–13.

———. *Sacred Queens and Women of Consequence: Rank, Gender, and Colonialism in the Hawaiian Islands*. Ann Arbor: University of Michigan Press, 1990.

Linnekin, Jocelyn, and Lin Poyer, eds. *Children of the Land: Exchange and Status in a Hawaiian Community*. New Brunswick, N.J.: Rutgers University Press, 1984.

———. *Cultural Identity and Ethnicity in the Pacific*. Honolulu: University of Hawaii Press, 1990.

Linton, Joan Pong. *The Romance of the New World: Gender and the Literary Formations of English Colonialism*. Cambridge, UK: Cambridge University Press, 1998.

Lyons, Jeffrey K. "Memoirs of Henry Obookiah: A Rhetorical History." *Journal of Hawaiian History* 38 (2004): 35–57.

Maffly-Kipp, Laurie F. "Eastward Ho! American Religions from the Perspective of the Pacific Rim." In *Retelling U.S. Religious History*, edited by Thomas A. Tweed. Berkeley: University of California Press, 1997.

Malley, Richard C. "On Shore in a Foreign Land: Mary Stark in the Kingdom of Hawaii." *Log of the Mystic Seaport* 37, no. 3 (1985): 79–92.

Mapp, Paul W. *The Elusive West and the Contest for Empire, 1713–1763*. Chapel Hill: University of North Carolina Press, 2011.

Marsden, George M. *Religion and American Culture*. New York: Harcourt Brace Jovanovich, 1990.

Martin, Margaret Greer, ed. *The Lymans of Hilo*. Hilo: Lyman House Memorial Library, 1979.

———. *Sarah Joiner Lyman of Hawaii: Her Own Story*. Hilo: Lyman House Memorial Museum, 1970.

Mason, Peter. *Infelicities: Representations of the Exotic*. Baltimore: Johns Hopkins University Press, 1998.

Mather, Helen. *One Summer in Hawaii*. New York: Cassell Publishing, 1891.

Mauss, Marcel. *The Gift: Forms and Functions of Exchange in Archaic Societies*. Translated by Ian Cunnison. London, UK: Cohen and West, 1970.

Maxfield, Charles A., III. "The 'Reflex Influence' of Missions: The Domestic Operations of the American Board of Commissioners for Foreign Missions, 1810–1850." New York: Union Theological Seminary, 1995.

McClintock, Anne. *Imperial Leather: Race, Gender, and Sexuality in the Colonial Contest*. New York: Routledge, 1995.

McCurry, Stephanie. *Masters of Small Worlds: Yeoman Households, Gender Relations, and the Political Culture of the Antebellum South Carolina Low Country*. New York: Oxford Unversity Press, 1995.

McDermott, John F., Wen-shing Tseng, and Thomas W. Maretzki, eds. *People and Cultures of Hawaii: A Psychocultural Profile*. Honolulu: John A. Burns School of Medicine and the University of Hawaii Press, 1980.

McLoughlin, William G. *Revivals, Awakenings, and Reform*. Chicago: University of Chicago Press, 1978.

Merry, Sally Engle. *Colonizing Hawai'i: The Cultural Power of Law*. Princeton, N.J.: Princeton University Press, 2000.

———. "'Kapiolani at the Brink': Dilemmas of Historical Ethnography in Nineteenth-Century Hawai'i." *American Ethnologist* 30 (2003): 44–60.

Midgley, Clare. *Gender and Imperialism*. New York: St. Martin's Press, 1998.

Miller, Char. "Domesticity Abroad: Work and Family in the Sandwich Island Mission, 1820–1840." In *Missions and Missionaries in the Pacific*, edited by Char Miller. New York: Edwin Mellen Press, 1985.

———. "The Making of a Missionary: Hiram Bingham's Odyssey." *Hawaiian Journal of History* 13 (1979): 36–45.

———. "The World Creeps In: Hiram Bingham III and the Decline in Missionary Fervor." *Hawaiian Journal of History* 15 (1981): 80–89.

Miller, David G. "Ka'iana, the Once Famous 'Prince of Kaua'i.'" *Hawaiian Journal of History* 22 (1988): 1–22.

Mills, Peter. *Hawai'i's Russian Adventure: A New Look at Old History*. Honolulu: University of Hawaii Press, 2002.

Mills, Sara. *Discourses of Difference: An Analysis of Women's Travel Writing and Colonialism*. London, UK: Routledge, 1993.

Missionary Album Sesquicentennial Edition, 1820–1970. Honolulu: Hawaiian Mission Children's Society, 1969.

Mookini, Esther T. "Keopuolani, Sacred Wife, Queen Mother, 1778–1823." *Hawaiian Journal of History* 32 (1998): 1–24.

Moorhead, Alan. *The Fatal Impact: An Account of the Invasion of the South Pacific, 1767–1840.* New York: Harper and Row, 1966.

Morgan, Dale L., ed. *Honolulu: Sketches of Life in the Hawaiian Islands from 1828–1861 by Laura Fish Judd.* Chicago: R. R. Donnelley and Sons Company, 1966.

Morgan, Jennifer. *Laboring Women: Reproduction and Gender in New World Slavery.* Philadelphia: University of Pennsylvania Press, 2004.

———. "Male Travelers, Female Bodies, and the Gendering of Racial Ideology, 1500–1770." In *Bodies in Contact: Rethinking Colonial Encounters in World History,* edited by Tony Ballantyne and Antoinette Burton. Durham, N.C.: Duke University Press, 2005.

Morgan, Philip D., and Sean Hawkins, eds. *Black Experience and the Empire.* Oxford, UK: Oxford University Press, 2004.

Morris, Mary, ed. *Maiden Voyages: Writings of Women Travellers.* New York: Vintage Books, 1993.

———. *Women Travellers.* London, UK: Virago Press, 1994.

Moss, Carolyn J., ed. *Kate Field: Selected Letters.* Carbondale: Southern Illinois University, 1996.

Mrantz, Maxine. *Women of Old Hawaii.* Honolulu: Aloha Graphics and Sales, 1975.

Murphy, Lucy Eldersveld. "Autonomy and the Economic Roles of Indian Women of the Fox-Wisconsin River Region, 1763–1832." In *Negotiators of Change: Historical Perspective on Native American Women,* edited by Nancy Shoemaker. New York: Routledge, 1995.

———. "Native American and Metis Women as 'Public Mothers' in the Nineteenth-Century Midwest." In *Bodies in Contact: Rethinking Colonial Encounters in World History,* edited by Tony Ballantyne and Antoinette Burton. Durham, N.C.: Duke University Press, 2005.

Neich, Roger, and Mick Pendergrast. *Pacific Tapa.* Honolulu: University of Hawaiʻi Press, 2004.

Nellist, George F., ed. *Women of Hawaii.* 2 vols. Honolulu: E. A. Langton-Boyle, 1938.

Newman, Andrew. "Fulfilling the Name: Catherine Tekakwitha and Marguerite Kanenstenhawi (Eunice Williams)." *Legacy: A Journal of American Women Writers* 28, no. 2 (2011): 232–56.

Obeyesekere, Gananath. *The Apotheosis of Captain Cook: European Mythmaking in the Pacific.* Princeton, N.J.: Princeton University Press, 1992.

Okihiro, Gary Y. *Island World: A History of Hawaiʻi and the United States.* Berkeley: University of California Press, 2008.

Oliver, Douglas L. *The Pacific Islands.* Cambridge, Mass.: Harvard University Press, 1951.

Osorio, Jonathan Kay Kamakawiwoʻole. *Dismembering Lāhui: A History of the Hawaiian Nation to 1887.* Honolulu: University of Hawaiʻi Press, 2002.

———. "Living in Archives and Dreams: The Histories of Kuykendall and Daws." In *Texts and Contexts: Reflections in Pacific Islands Historiography,* edited by Doug Munro and Brij V. Lal. Honolulu: University of Hawaiʻi Press, 2006.

Pascoe, Peggy. *Relations of Rescue: The Search for Female Moral Authority in the American West, 1874–1939.* New York: Oxford University Press, 1990.

Peterson, Barbara Bennett, ed. *Notable Women of Hawaii*. Honolulu: University of Hawaii Press, 1984.

Phillips, Clifton Jackson. *Protestant America and the Pagan World: The First Half Century of the American Board of Commissioners for Foreign Missions, 1810–1860*. Cambridge, Mass.: Harvard University Press, 1969.

Piano, Barbara Del. "Kalanimoku: Iron Cable of the Hawaiian Kingdom, 1769–1827." *Hawaiian Journal of History* 43 (2009): 1–28.

Pierce, Richard A. *Russia's Hawaiian Adventure, 1815–1817*. Kingston, Ontario: Limestone Press, 1976.

Pratt, Mary Louise. *Imperial Eyes: Travel Writing and Transculturation*. New York: Routledge, 1992.

Putney, Clifford. *Missionaries in Hawai'i: The Lives of Peter and Fanny Gulick, 1797–1883*: Amherst: University of Massachusetts Press, 2010.

Ralston, Caroline. "Changes in the Lives of Ordinary Women in Early Post-Contact Hawaii." In *Family and Gender in the Pacific: Domestic Contradictions and the Colonial Impact*, edited by Margaret Jolly. New York: Cambridge University Press, 1989.

———. "Hawaii 1778–1854: Some Aspects of Maka'ainana Response to Rapid Cultural Change." *Journal of Pacific History* 19, no. 1 (1984): 21–40.

Ram, Kalpana, and Margaret Jolly, eds. *Maternities and Modernities: Colonial and Post-Colonial Experiences in Asia and the Pacific*. Cambridge, UK, and New York: Cambridge University Press, 1998.

Reed-Danahay, Deborah E., ed. *Auto/Ethnography*. Oxford, UK: Berg Press, 1997.

Reeves-Ellington, Barbara, Kathryn Kish Sklar, and Connie A. Shemo, eds. *Competing Kingdoms: Women, Mission, Nation, and the American Protestant Empire, 1812–1960*. Durham, N.C.: Duke University Press, 2010.

Reynolds, David S. *Waking Giant: America in the Age of Jackson*. New York: HarperCollins, 2008.

Richardson, Alan, and Debbie Lee, eds. *Early Black British Writing: Olaudah Equiano, Mary Prince, and Others*. Edited by Alan Richardson. New Riverside Editions. Boston: Houghton Mifflin Company, 2004.

Richter, Daniel K. *Facing East from Indian Country: A Native History of Early America*. Cambridge, Mass.: Harvard University Press, 2001.

Rifkin, Mark. "Debt and the Transnationalization of Hawai'i." *American Quarterly* 60 no. 1 (2008): 43–66.

Roach-Higgins, Mary Ellen, Joanne Bubolz Eicher, and Kim K. P. Johnson, eds. *Dress and Identity*. New York: Fairchild Publications, 1995.

Robinson, Jane. *Wayward Women: A Guide to Women Travellers*: Oxford University Press, 1990.

Rosenberg, Emily S. "Gender." *Journal of American History* 77 no. 1 (1990): 116–24.

Rothman, Ellen K. *Hands and Hearts: A History of Courtship in America*. New York: Basic Books, 1984.

Rothman, Sheila M. *Woman's Proper Place: A History of Changing Ideals and Practices, 1870 to the Present*. New York: Basic Books, 1978.

Rothschild, Nan A. *Colonial Encounters in a Native American Landscape*. Washington, D.C., and London, UK: Smithsonian Books, 2003.

Rotundo, Anthony. *American Manhood: Transformations in Masculinity from the Revolution to the Modern Era*. New York: Basic Books, 1993.

Rowbotham, Judith. "'Soldiers of Christ'? Images of Female Missionaries in Late Nineteenth-Century Britain: Issues of Heroism and Martyrdom." *Gender and History* 12, no. 1 (2000): 82–106.

Rowson, Susanna. *Charlotte Temple and Lucy Temple*. New York: Penguin Books, 1991.

Ruether, Rosemary Radford, ed. *Gender, Ethnicity, and Religion: Views from the Other Side*. Minneapolis: Fortress Press, 2002.

Ruether, Rosemary Radford, and Rosemary Skinner Keller, eds. *Women and Religion in America*. Vols. 1–3. San Francisco: Harper and Row, 1981.

Ruiz, Vicki. "Dead Ends or Gold Mines? Using Missionary Records in Mexican American Women's History." In *Unequal Sisters: A Multicultural Reader in U.S. Women's History*, edited by Ellen Carol DuBois and Vicki Ruiz. New York: Routledge, 1990.

———. *From out of the Shadows: Mexican Women in Twentieth-Century America*. New York: Oxford University Press, 1998.

———. "Una Mujer Sin Fronteras: Luisa Moreno and Latina Labor Activism." *Pacific Historical Review* 73, no. 1 (2004): 1–20.

Russell, Mary. *The Blessings of a Good Thick Skirt: Women Travellers and Their World*. London, UK: Collins, 1986.

Ryan, Mary P. *Cradle of the Middle Class: The Family in Oneida County, New York, 1790–1865*. New York: Cambridge University Press, 1981.

———. *The Empire of the Mother: American Writing about Domesticity, 1830–1860*. New York: Haworth Press, 1982.

———. *Mysteries of Sex: Tracing Women and Men through American History*. Chapel Hill: University of North Carolina Press, 2006.

Sahlins, Marshall. "Hawai'i in the Early Nineteenth Century: The Kingdom and the Kingship." In *Remembrance of Pacific Pasts: An Invitation to Remake History*, edited by Robert Borofsky. Honolulu: University of Hawaii Press, 2000.

———. *Historical Ethnography*. Vol. 1 of *Anahulu: The Anthropology of History in the Kingdom of Hawaii*, edited by Patrick Kirch and Marshall Sahlins. Chicago: University of Chicago Press, 1992.

———. *Historical Metaphors and Mythical Realities: Structure in the Early History of the Sandwich Islands Kingdom*. Ann Arbor: University of Michigan Press, 1981.

———. *How "Natives" Think: About Captain Cook, for Example*. Chicago: University of Chicago Press, 1995.

———. *Islands of History*. Chicago: University of Chicago Press, 1985.

Salmond, Anne. *Aphrodite's Island: The European Discovery of Tahiti*. Berkeley: University of California Press, 2010.

Sanchez, George J. "'Go after the Women': Americanization and the Mexican Immigrant Woman, 1915–1929." In *Unequal Sisters: A Multicultural Reader in U.S. Women's History*, edited by Ellen Carol DuBois and Vicki Ruiz, 284–97. New York: Routledge, 1990.

Scarr, Deryck. *A History of the Pacific Islands: Passages through Tropical Time*. Richmond, Va.: Surry Curzon Press, 2001.

Schmitt, Robert C. "Some Firsts in Island Business and Government." *Hawaiian Journal of History* 14 (1980): 80–108.

Schudson, Michael. *Advertising, the Uneasy Persuasion: Its Dubious Impact on American Society.* New York: Basic Books, 1984.

Shershow, Scott Cutler. *The Work and the Gift.* Chicago: University of Chicago Press, 2005.

Shoemaker, Nancy. "Kateri Tekakwitha's Tortuous Path to Sainthood." In *Negotiators of Change: Historical Perspectives on Native American Women,* edited by Nancy Shoemaker. New York: Routledge, 1995.

——, ed. *Negotiators of Change: Historical Perspectives on Native American Women.* London, UK: Routledge, 1995.

Silva, Noenoe K. *Aloha Betrayed: Native Hawaiian Resistance to American Colonialism.* Durham, N.C.: Duke University Press, 2004.

Silverman, Jane L. *Kaahumanu: Molder of Change.* Honolulu: Friends of the Judiciary History Center of Hawaii, 1987.

——. "To Marry Again." *Hawaiian Journal of History* 17 (1983): 64–75.

Sinclair, Marjorie. "The Sacred Wife of Kamehameha I, Keopuolani." *Hawaiian Journal of History* 5 (1971): 3–23.

Singh, Maina Chawla. *Gender, Religion, and "Heathen Lands": American Missionary Women in South Asia (1860s–1940s).* New York: Garland Publishing, 2000.

Sklar, Katherine. *Catherine Beecher: A Study in American Domesticity.* New York: Norton, 1976.

——. "The Founding of Mount Holyoke College." In *Women of America: A History,* edited by Carol Berkin and Mary Beth Norton. Boston: Houghton-Mifflin, 1979.

Skwiot, Christine. "Migration and the Politics of Sovereignty, Settlement, and Belonging in Hawai'i." In *Connecting Seas and Connected Ocean Rims: Indian, Atlantic, and Pacific Oceans from the 1830s to the 1930s,* edited by Donna R. Gabaccia and Dirk Hoerder. Leiden and Boston: Brill, 2011.

Sleeper-Smith, Susan. "Women, Kin, and Catholicism: New Perspectives on the Fur Trade." *Ethnohistory* 47, no. 2 (2000): 423–52.

Smith, Bradford. *Yankees in Paradise: The New England Impact on Hawaii.* New York: J. B. Lipincott Company, 1956.

Smith, Harold F. *American Travellers Abroad: A Bibliography of Accounts Published before 1900.* Lanham, Md.: Scarecrow Press, 1999.

Speakerman, Cummins E., Jr., and Rhoda E. A. Hackler. "Vancouver in Hawai'i." *Hawaiian Journal of History* 23 (1989): 31–65.

Stannard, David E. *Before the Horror: The Population of Hawai'i on the Eve of Western Contact.* Honolulu: Social Science Research Institute, University of Hawaii, 1989.

Stauder, Catherine. "George, Prince of Hawaii." *Hawaiian Journal of History* 6 (1972): 28–44.

Stefoff, Rebecca. *Women of the World: Women Travelers and Explorers.* New York: Oxford University Press, 1992.

Stoddart, Anna M. *The Life of Isabella Bird (Mrs. Bishop).* London, UK: John Murray Publishers, 1906.

Stoler, Ann Laura, ed. *Haunted by Empire: Geographies of Intimacy in North American History*. Durham, N.C.: Duke University Press, 2006.

———. "Matters of Intimacy as Matters of State: A Response." *Journal of American History* 88, no. 3 (2001): 893–97.

———. "Tense and Tender Ties: The Politics of Comparison in North American History and (Post) Colonial Studies." *Journal of American History* 88, no. 3 (2001): 829–65.

Stonis, Michelle Ruth. "On Heathen Ground: The Double Bind of Women's Roles in the Sandwich Islands Mission, 1819–1863." M.A. thesis, California State University, Long Beach, 2005.

Strathern, Marilyn. *The Gender of the Gift: Problems with Women and Problems with Society in Melanesia*. Berkeley: University of California Press, 1988.

Sturma, Michael. *South Sea Maidens: Western Fantasy and Sexual Politics in the South Pacific*. Westport, Conn.: Greenwood Press, 2002.

Sykes, Karen. *Arguing with Anthropology: An Introduction to Critical Theories of the Gift*. New York: Routledge, 2005.

Tachihata, Cheiko, and Agnes Conrad. *The Written Record of Hawai'i's Women: An Annotated Guide to Sources of Information in Hawai'i*. Honolulu: Foundation for Hawaii Women's History, 2001.

Takaki, Ronald. *Raising Cane: The World of Plantation Hawaii (Asian American Experience)*. New York: Chelsea House Publishers, 1994.

Taylor, Alan. *American Colonies: The Settling of North America*. New York: Penguin, 2002.

Teng, Emma Jinhua. "An Island of Women: Gender in Qing Travel Writing about Taiwan." In *Bodies in Contact: Rethinking Colonial Encounters in World History*, edited by Tony Ballantyne and Antoinette Burton. Durham, N.C.: Duke University Press, 2005.

Thigpen, Jennifer. "'You Have Been Very Thoughtful Today': The Significance of Gratitude and Reciprocity in Missionary-Hawaiian Gift Exchange." *Pacific Historical Review* 79, no. 4 (2010): 545–72.

Thoen, Irma. *Strategic Affection? Gift Exchange in Seventeenth-Century Holland*. Amsterdam: Amsterdam University Press, 2007.

Thomas, Nicholas. *Entangled Objects: Exchange, Material Culture, and Colonialism in the Pacific*. Cambridge, Mass.: Harvard University Press, 1991.

———. *Islanders: The Pacific in the Age of Empire*. New Haven, Conn.: Yale University Press, 2010.

Tilton, Robert S. *Pocahontas: Evolution of an American Narrative*. Cambridge, UK: Cambridge University Press, 1994.

Townsend, Camilla. *Pocahontas and the Powhatan Dilemma*. New York: Hill and Wang, 2004.

Trask, Haunani-Kay. *From a Native Daughter: Colonialism and Sovereignty in Hawai'i*. Honolulu: University of Hawai'i Press, 1999.

Tweed, Thomas A., ed. *Retelling U.S. Religious History*. Berkeley: University of California Press, 1997.

Tyrell, Ian. *Woman's World, Woman's Empire*. Chapel Hill: University of North Carolina Press, 1991.

Ulrich, Laurel Thatcher. *Good Wives: Image and Reality in the Lives of Women in Northern New England, 1650–1750*. New York: Alfred A. Knopf, 1982.

Valeri, Valerio. *Kingship and Sacrifice: Ritual and Society in Ancient Hawaii*. Chicago: University of Chicago Press, 1985.

VanderMeer, Philip R., and Robert P. Swierenga, eds. *Belief and Behavior: Essays in the New Religious History*. New Brunswick, N.J.: Rutgers University Press, 1991.

Vevier, Charles. "American Contentalism: An Idea of Expansion, 1845–1910." *American Historical Review* 65, no. 2 (1960): 323–35.

Wagner, Sandra E. "Mission and Motivation: The Theology of the Early American Mission in Hawai'i." *Hawaiian Journal of History* 19 (1985): 62–70.

Wagner-Wright, Sandra, ed. *Ships, Furs, and Sandalwood: A Yankee Trader in Hawai'i, 1823–1825*. Honolulu: University of Hawai'i Press, 1999.

———. *The Structure of the Missionary Call to the Sandwich Islands, 1790–1830: Sojourners among Strangers*. San Francisco: Mellen Research University, 1990.

———. "When Unity Is Torn Asunder: The Distressing Case of Thomas and Lucia Holman." *Pacific Studies* 15, no. 2 (1992): 39–60.

Warne, Douglas, with the collaboration of Holly Kilinahe Coleman. *Humehume of Kaua'i: A Boy's Journey to America, an Ali'i's Return Home*. Honolulu: Kamehameha Pub, 2008.

———. "The Story behind the Headstone: The Life of Wiliam Kanui." *Hawaiian Journal of History* 43 (2009): 29–56.

Weiner, Annette. *Inalienable Possessions: The Paradox of Keeping-While-Giving*. Berkeley: University of California Press, 1992.

———. *Women of Value, Men of Renown: New Perspectives in Trobriand Exchange*. Austin: University of Texas Press, 1976.

Welter, Barbara. "The Cult of True Womanhood, 1820–1860." *American Quarterly* 18, no. 2 (1966): 151–74.

———. *Dimity Convictions: The American Woman in the Nineteenth Century*. Athens: Ohio University Press, 1976.

Wesley, Marilyn C. *Secret Journeys: The Trope of Women's Travel in American Literature*. New York: State University of New York Press, 1999.

Wexler, Laura. *Tender Violence: Domestic Visions in an Age of U.S. Imperialism*. Chapel Hill: University of North Carolina Press, 2000.

White, Richard. *The Middle Ground: Indians, Empires, and Republics in the Great Lakes Region, 1650–1815*. Cambridge, UK, and New York: Cambridge University Press, 1991.

Whitehead, John S. "Hawaii: The First and Last Far West?" *Western Historical Quarterly* 23, no. 2 (1992): 152–77.

———. "Noncontiguous Wests: Alaska and Hawai'i." In *Many Wests: Place, Culture, and Regional Identity*, edited by David M. Wrobel and Michael C. Steiner. Lawrence: University Press of Kansas, 1997.

Williams, Harold, ed. *One Whaling Family*. Boston: Houghton Mifflin Company, 1964.

Withington, Antoinette. *The Golden Cloak*. Honolulu: Honolulu Star-Bulletin, 1953.

Wong, Helen, and Ann Rayson. *Hawaii's Royal History*. Honolulu: Bess Press, 1987.

Wood, Houston. *Displacing Natives: The Rhetorical Production of Hawai'i.* Lanham: Rowman and Littlefield Publishers, Inc., 1999.

Wyschogrod, Edith, Jean-Joseph Goux, and Eric Boynton, eds. *The Enigma of Gift and Sacrifice.* New York: Fordham University Press, 2002.

Yohn, Susan. *A Contest of Faiths: Missionary Women and Pluralism in the American Southwest.* Ithaca, N.Y.: Cornell University Press, 1995.

Yoshihara, Mari. *Embracing the East: White Women and American Orientalism.* Oxford, UK: Oxford University Press, 2003.

Young, Kanalu G. Terry. *Rethinking the Native Hawaiian Past.* New York: Garland Publishing, 1998.

Yung, Judy. *Unbound Feet: A Social History of Chinese Women in San Francisco.* Berkeley: University of California Press, 1995.

Zikmund, Barbara Brown. "The Struggle for the Right to Preach." In *Women and Religion in America,* edited by Rosemary Radford Ruether and Rosemary Skinner Keller. San Francisco: Harper and Row, 1981.

Zwiep, Mary. *Pilgrim Path: The First Company of Women Missionaries to Hawaii.* Madison: University of Wisconsin Press, 1991.

Index

Page numbers in *italic* type indicate illustrations.